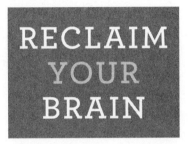

RECLAIM
YOUR
BRAIN

AVERY

an imprint of Penguin Random House

New York

RECLAIM YOUR BRAIN

How to
Calm Your Thoughts,
Heal Your Mind,
and Bring Your Life
Back Under Control

Joseph A. Annibali, M.D.

AVERY

an imprint of Penguin Random House LLC
375 Hudson Street
New York, New York 10014

Most Avery books are available at special quantity discounts for bulk purchase for sales
promotions, premiums, fund-raising, and educational needs. Special books or book
excerpts also can be created to fit specific needs. For details, write
SpecialMarkets@penguinrandomhouse.com.

Library of Congress Cataloging-in-Publication Data
Annibali, Joseph A.
Reclaim your brain : how to calm your thoughts, heal your mind, and bring your
life back under control / Joseph A. Annibali, M.D.
p.   cm.
Includes bibliographical references and index.
ISBN 978-1-59463-297-6
1. Calmness. 2. Brain. 3. Stress management. 4. Mindfulness
(Psychology). 5. Neuroplasticity. 6. Mental health. I. Title.
BF575.C35A43   2015   2015025742
158.1—dc23

Printed in the United States of America
1   3   5   7   9   10   8   6   4   2

BOOK DESIGN BY MAUNA EICHNER AND LEE FUKUI

Although the author and publisher have worked hard to ensure that all information in this
book is accurate at the time of publication and consistent with general psychiatric and
medical standards, neither the publisher nor the author is engaged in rendering professional
advice or services to the individual reader. The ideas, procedures, and suggestions contained
in this book are not intended as a substitute for consulting with your physician. Particular
situations may require a particular therapeutic approach not included in this book. For these
reasons and because human and mechanical errors sometimes occur, we recommend that
readers follow the advice of physicians directly involved in their care or the care of family
members. Neither the author nor the publisher shall be liable or responsible for any loss or
damage allegedly arising from any information or suggestion in this book.

For Dianne, Chris, and Elizabeth

Contents

Foreword

I first met Dr. Joseph Annibali at a five-day conference I was teaching on applying brain SPECT imaging, the brain-imaging tool we use at Amen Clinics. A highly trained psychiatrist and psychoanalyst who had already spent decades in clinical practice, Joe isn't one to rest on his laurels. He continually seeks out knowledge that will help his patients: people who are hurting, from all walks of life, who come to see him from far and wide. I was so impressed by his broad knowledge, kind heart, and open mind that I asked him to join our medical staff. Within a short time Joe became the chief psychiatrist in our Reston, Virginia, clinic, just outside of Washington, D.C., and is now a powerful leader and mentor among our staff of thirty medical professionals.

Our story at Amen Clinics began in 1991 when I ordered my first brain SPECT scans on patients with conditions like ADHD (attention deficit/hyperactivity disorder), severe aggression, and unresponsive anxiety and depression who had not improved with standard treatments. Over the years, with Joe's help, we have built the world's largest database of brain SPECT scans, now well over 115,000 scans on patients from 111 countries. These scans have significantly changed how we help our patients at Amen Clinics. We've learned that psychiatric illnesses are rarely single or simple disorders. Giving someone the diagnosis of depression is exactly like giving them the diagnosis of chest pain; the diagnosis does not tell you what the problem is and how serious it might be. Treatment needs to be tailored to the underlying problems in individual brains, not a cluster of symptoms. Significantly, with our approach our patients understand that their problems are medical rather than moral, which has increased their willingness to follow the treatment plans and decreased their stigma about having a psychiatric disorder.

The most important lesson we've learned from our treasure trove of scans, and the lesson that has kept Joe and me excited about this work each day, is that you are not stuck with the brain you have. As Joe discusses in this crucial book, if your brain is busy or racing out of control, if your brain is dysfunctional, you *can* reclaim it. In many thousands of cases, we have seen that you can improve brain function, even if you have been really bad to your brain. For example, Amen Clinics did the world's first and largest brain-imaging study on active and retired NFL players, where we saw high levels of brain injury. That was not a surprise. Your brain is soft, about the consistency of soft butter, and it is housed in a really hard skull with multiple sharp bony ridges, so it is easily damaged. All of the news about concussions in sports has been bad, with an increased incidence of depression, suicide, and dementia. But what really excited us with our NFL study was that on our program to help the players reclaim their brains, the same one Joe will outline in this book, 80 percent of our 170 players showed high levels of improvement, especially in their mood, memory, sleep, and brain function.

When Joe and I were in medical school in the late 1970s and early 1980s, we were taught that the brain doesn't heal. But now we know that is wrong. If you put the brain in a healing environment, often it can get better, much better, but it requires forethought and a great plan. And this healing is not just for football players. We have seen improvement in brain function for people with attention deficit/hyperactivity disorder (ADHD), anxiety, depression, obsessive-compulsive disorder (OCD), post-traumatic stress disorder (PTSD), Lyme disease, addictions, and even improvement in some people with Alzheimer's disease.

In this book, Joe shares many of the important lessons we have learned, while at the same time giving you his unique perspective on healing. I encouraged Joe to write this book because of his extensive experiences and perspective as a master psychiatrist who integrates the latest thinking about the mind with our work on looking at and optimizing the brain. **Reading this book will be like sitting on the psychiatrist's couch of the future.**

In recent years Joe has also become an expert on the effects on the brain of Lyme disease, in part because his own daughter has had it. Both Joe and I believe infectious diseases, like Lyme, will play a significant role in how psychiatrists will help people in the future, which you will learn about. Joe is also an expert on Irlen syndrome, a visual processing disorder, which can be associated with headaches, anxiety, learning challenges, and irritability.

One of the key ideas of this book is that you need first to heal (an injured brain if present) and balance the brain before other interventions can work well. Too often people see therapists to help their minds, when they first need to help their brains work better. Readers will learn a lot about what they can do to help themselves from the tools and approaches presented here. Most readers will not need to come for a SPECT scan to benefit from the information given in *Reclaim Your Brain*. The book is a great illustration of how much anyone can improve and heal when we pay attention to the mind and brain at the same time.

Reclaim Your Brain is your road map to a better brain and a better life. It is packed with useful information, powerful stories, and a completely new way of thinking that can help you feel better quickly as you heal and balance your busy brain, while at the same time teaching you how to protect the most important part of you (your brain) for many years to come. I am excited for you as you embark on reading and applying the principles in *Reclaim Your Brain*. They have changed my life and the lives of many others. With Dr. Annibali's expert guidance, I know they will help you change your life for the better.

Daniel G. Amen, M.D.
Author of *Change Your Brain, Change Your Life*
June 2015

Acknowledgments

This book would not exist without the encouragement, support, friendship, and advice given to me by Daniel Amen, M.D., to whom I am deeply grateful. I have profound admiration for Dr. Amen's trailblazing work, his clinical genius, and his courage. Thank you, Daniel.

I am also grateful to the Washington Psychoanalytic Institute, where I spent five stimulating years becoming a psychoanalyst and a number of years afterward as a faculty member. Freud may be dead, but many of his fundamental ideas live on, nourishing those like me who wish to understand other human beings most deeply.

Gary Moak, M.D., has been my devoted friend and sounding board for both personal and professional matters for more than forty years. I am grateful for our friendship, which started during our college days at Penn, and for his advice and encouragement about this project that started long before my book proposal ever saw the light of day. Gary reviewed many of the chapter drafts, giving useful feedback that helped enormously to improve areas where my writing and thinking were unclear.

Robert Licata, M.D., has been a colleague and dear friend for more than twenty-five years. Bob's pithy conceptualization of the relationship between the prefrontal cortex and the limbic system gave birth to a number of the ideas I explore in this book. He also graciously reviewed a number of chapter drafts.

For many years, Bob and I were members of a study group with our colleagues Dave Gebara, M.D., and Larry Spoont, M.D. In this study group we discussed a number of seminal books and papers and worked over many of the ideas that I explore in this book.

I am grateful to Madame Renelle Gannon, my French tutor of more than a decade, for far more than my reasonably proficient command of the French language. I am indebted to Madame Gannon for her encouragement and support, and for fascinating twice-weekly discussions about language, art, politics, history, philosophy, religion, and spirituality, always in French, *certainement.*

My sincere thanks are due to my agent, Celeste Fine, who remarkably obtained for me a book contract in no time flat, and her associate John Maas. This work would not have seen the light of day if my editor, Caroline Sutton, had not stuck with me through my early abortive attempts to learn how to write a book. I am grateful for her confidence in me and in the ideas I wanted to write about. Thank you as well to her associates Brittney Ross and Brianna Flaherty.

Whatever coherence and lucidity exist in this book are due in large part to Dedi Felman, writer and editor extraordinaire. She, too, was encouraging as she helped me wrestle my meandering ideas into a conceptual whole. During my moments of discouragement when I came face-to-face with how little I knew about writing a book that tells a clear story, Dedi told me to "trust the process," which I did. Thank you, Dedi.

In addition to Daniel Amen, M.D., many other individuals within Amen Clinics have given me help and support. Dr. Rob Johnson reviewed the chapter on addiction and gave helpful input on that chapter and on the spiritual themes I discuss in the conclusion. Sue Johnston, M.S.W., L.C.S.W., our clinic's mind-body therapist, reviewed the manuscript and gave helpful feedback.

I have been wonderfully blessed by the devotion of my wife and children. My wife, Dianne, has gifted me with her love and positivity, showing me how a loving relationship can heal a wounded soul. A beautiful heart can bring things into your life that all the money in the world couldn't obtain. For her love, encouragement, and support—both during the writing of this book and throughout our long relationship—I am eternally grateful. Dianne sacrificed in many ways so that I could have the time and energy to work on this book. My son, Chris, and my daughter, Elizabeth, have also been enormously supportive of me as I wrote this book. I have learned so much about life and love from them. It is a wonderful thing to see your children turn out wiser and smarter than you could ever be.

I have the most interesting job in the world. I get to talk to people about the things that matter to them most, as we work to find ways to manage their minds, balance their brains, and unleash their healing processes. I am grateful to the thousands of patients with whom I have had the privilege to work during my career of thirty-plus years. At times I've felt that I learned and benefited more from our relationships than they did. There are many patient stories in *Reclaim Your Brain*. In all cases, the patients I write about have been thoroughly disguised and/or melded into composites to protect their privacy.

As much as I appreciate the significant help and support I've received while writing this book, any misstatements and mistakes are my responsibility.

Joseph A. Annibali, M.D.
Chief Psychiatrist, Amen Clinics, Washington, D.C.
June 2015

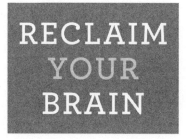

RECLAIM
YOUR
BRAIN

REINING IN THE BRAIN

Introduction

When I first met Emily, a magazine editor, she nervously picked her cuticles as her mobile phone inside her bag buzzed incessantly, alerting her to the umpteenth text message. Emily told me she had trouble concentrating. She described her brain as feeling like a "buzzing beehive" of random thoughts. Lately, she said, her claustrophobia was stifling her life.

Then there was Josh, a college student, who was skipping class and close to flunking out. He sat down in my office and we tried to talk. But it was hard to communicate; Josh was agitated, avoided eye contact, and tapped his feet incessantly. His mind, he said, was "like an out-of-control freight train," going so fast he couldn't stop it.

Corrine, an advertising executive, was also always on call. She juggled many accounts in her job. She felt a bit worried lately; she was mixing up details and forgetting crucial appointments. When I asked her how she felt when she tried to relax, she replied, "It's like I have three radio stations playing in my head at the same time." Yet she was confident she could take on even more and bigger projects.

Emily, Josh, Corrine, and others like them may have different conditions including stress, ADHD, anxiety, and depression. Yet, fundamentally, the experience they describe and wrestle with is the same—it's what I call a "busy brain." Some people with a busy brain describe their brain as being "in chaos"; others feel that their brain is on fire. In and of itself, a busy brain interferes with attention, concentration, focus, mood, and often much more. Busy brains leave us distracted, preoccupied, or quick-tempered.

A busy brain is more than just a description or a feeling. A busy brain literally is just that: It functions less effectively because of its own excessive activity. It can't do a good job selecting the best course to take because it can't shut off all the mental chatter urging other ways to go. Consequently, a busy brain may lose the ability to solve problems because it's going off on too many wrong or unproductive paths. In fact, I began my own exploration of busy brains when I noticed that individuals complaining of extra-busy brains had brain scans that revealed excessive activity in one particular area of the brain—the limbic system.

As the chief psychiatrist at Amen Clinics in Reston, Virginia, a board-certified practicing psychiatrist for thirty years, and a trained psychoanalyst, I have worked with thousands of people who report this common sensation—an overloaded, overstimulated, and keyed-up brain, regardless of whether they are ultimately diagnosed with ADHD, anxiety, depression, bipolar disorder, OCD, or even substance abuse or autism. Many people come to my office hoping to learn how to function better and to find peace.

In this book I want to share with you what I have shared with many of my patients. As we explore the root causes of a busy brain, you will gain a better understanding of what is going on in your brain and your body. Understanding the brain's physical functions will help you more effectively address problems as they arise. Crucially, you will learn strategies for calming your busy brain and managing your mind. Action plans feature steps that you can take immediately.

I begin by taking you on a journey of your brain and its activities. Importantly, the busy-brain feeling we experience typically correlates with actual "overactivity" in specific areas of the brain.

When you feel stuck, with your mind going around and around in a loop you can't seem to get out of, it may be because an area of your brain called the anterior cingulate is overactive, locked with its pedal to the metal. When you wrestle with anxiety, it may be because another area in your brain called the basal ganglia is overactive, revving in high gear. Negativity, anxiety, mood disorders: all of these can be illuminated by understanding how key brain areas function. Understanding what's literally happening in your busy brain is key to slowing it down, to taming the chaos.

A biological, neuroscientific approach illuminates a great deal about our brains. But this is not all we need to know. In order to reclaim your brain—and to best understand the self, the individual, the person, the soul—we need to look at both psychology and biology, mind and brain. Specifically, we must not overlook the power we now have to manage our minds.

Given what we now know, managing our mind is crucially important—and more effective than we ever suspected. Why? In a single word, *change*. What we now understand better than at any time previously is just how much and in how many ways the brain can be altered, and how the brain can transform itself for the better.

Many people think our brains are set in stone, but in fact our lifestyles and life circumstances *always* affect that three-pound organ in our head. Brain changes result from many causes, including developmental experiences, emotional traumas, substance abuse, physical brain trauma, infections, and many other things. Your brain can and does change because of stress—for example, we know that cells in the hippocampus die when an individual experiences prolonged stress—and therein lies the risk of more negative changes in a person's life when they don't listen soon enough to their too-busy brains. In fact, according to a comprehensive survey conducted by the National Institute of Mental Health, more than half of Americans are expected to develop a mental illness in their lifetimes. Calming your busy brain reduces the chance that things will get worse.

But if brain change can be for the worse, it can also be for the better. The great discovery of what we call self-directed neuroplasticity is that the brain is not fixed, but rather in constant flux, and that you can actually change your brain for the better. Circuits can be rewired; brain maps can be redrawn. New neural pathways can sprout to accommodate new functions or new environments. Whatever your experiences in childhood and beyond, it is possible to learn new ways of thinking, reacting, and behaving; new patterns can be established.

In *Reclaim Your Brain*, I show you how to rewrite your negative stories, how to slow down your busy brain with mindfulness techniques, how to create healthier relationships, and ultimately how to bring your brain and life back under control, all of which increase the likelihood for success and joy in life. We'll also explore how to manage conditions that contribute to a busy brain, such as anxiety, mood problems, ADHD, stuckness and OCD, addictions, and emotional traumas.

Though I am a psychiatrist and I believe wholeheartedly in the use of psychiatric medications where appropriate, my treatment doesn't begin or end with my prescription pad. Many times it is better to start with more natural and integrative interventions such as lifestyle changes, mindfulness exercises, neurofeedback, and nutritional supplements. I will discuss the many natural interventions that allow the reader to calm a busy brain without professional assistance or medication.

Throughout these chapters, I give many case examples, approaches, exercises, and suggestions to help you understand your brain function and find the best ways to calm and balance your brain. No one solution is right for everyone.

One important note: sometimes rebalancing our busy, overactive brain requires more than managing our troubled minds. It requires healing what's broken or damaged. It may seem obvious that healing the brain must take priority. But brain injuries are often missed or not avidly sought out in the first place. In the "Healing the Hurting Brain and Body" chapter at the end of the book, I describe various, often hidden, injuries to the brain and the body that can contribute to an overactive brain.

Many are quick to believe that their too-busy brains result from today's rapid-fire media culture, digital technology, and modern-world megadistractions. These ever-present distractions have a negative impact, no doubt. But an overactive brain is not strictly the result of our modern 24/7 device-driven culture. Hidden contributors to a busy brain can include genetics, vitamin deficiencies, dysfunctional thyroids, heavy metal toxicity, infections, and even physical brain trauma.

I assess patients by looking at the whole person: their life circumstances, medical histories, diets, habits, and brain activity. When necessary with some patients, I also use a brain-imaging technique called brain SPECT, described in Chapter 12, to detect imbalances in brain-circuit activity, brain injury, physical brain trauma, and other ways in which the brain can be damaged or malfunctioning without one being aware of it.

Please note that although you will hear a good amount about brain SPECT scans in *Reclaiming Your Brain*, you do not need a brain scan to make good use of this book. Josh, our student with a mind like a freight train; Emily, with her claustrophobia and inability to concentrate; and Corrine, our advertising executive who cannot relax, all profited from mind management techniques alone: managing negativity, learning simple mindfulness techniques, and rewriting the stories about themselves and the world that previously had so powerfully dominated their lives and relationships. The tools and approaches I present will be helpful for most people, regardless of whether you ever have a brain scan.

In this book, I offer solutions that will help you feel better, perform more productively, experience less stress, and be more fulfilled in life. With a calm mind, you can find clarity, strength, vision, and hope. You can reclaim your overloaded brain and bring your life back under control. Let's begin the journey.

→ 1 ←

Balancing the Brain

Many of us have at least some familiarity with the "busy brain" feeling of being overwhelmed. We all have days when instead of catching up, our task list seems to grow ever longer. A new work project lands on our desk even as we rush to complete the previous one. A young child or elderly parent falls sick, with the caretaking burden falling squarely on our shoulders. And then comes the last straw: the transmission on our old reliable car fails, incurring an expense we can't afford. With all that is on our plate, we feel revved up and in overdrive, perhaps on the brink of a panic attack. Thoughts go around and around, but instead of resting somewhere, they continue cycling: How will I catch up on the job? Take care of my children? Fix my car? Pay my bills?

What's literally going on in our body and brain when we experience these sensations of a busy brain? What does it mean for our brains to be "revved up," in overdrive, or, most crucially, unbalanced? A tour of the brain will help us begin to answer these questions.

The cerebral cortex, or the bulk of your brain, houses four lobes: the frontal lobe, the temporal lobe, the parietal lobe, and the occipital lobe. Located underneath your temples and behind your eyes on both sides of your brain, the **temporal lobe** is essential for speech, language, memory, and emotion; processing immediate events into recent and long-term memory; and storing and retrieving long-term memories. It is also involved in processing sounds and images. Traumatic brain injury often involves damage to the temporal lobe, leading to changes in memory, mood, and personality. The **occipital lobe** is in charge of visual processing. The occipital lobe is also affected by Irlen syndrome, which is a little-known but common visual processing difficulty that I'll discuss later. The **parietal lobe** is a general integration center that processes information from your different senses that is then passed to the front of the brain to use for decision making. It also controls bodily awareness and position sense, letting one part of your body know where it is in relation to the rest of the body and giving you an idea of where your body is located in space.

For the purposes of our discussion of balancing the brain, however, the **frontal lobe**, or the part located at the front of your brain, is absolutely crucial. The part of the frontal cortex closest to your eyes is called the **prefrontal cortex**, or **PFC**. This is the executive control center of your brain; think of it as the "governor" or the "CEO" of the brain. It manages your attention, concentration, short-term memory, organizational ability, impulse control, planning, judgment, learning, motivation, problem solving, and goal setting. Quite a list. A well-functioning PFC is crucial to your ability to rewrite the negative stories you tell yourself. Importantly, the PFC holds the limbic system in check, which helps the brain find and maintain its balance.

The **limbic system** is the seat of your emotions. Found in the center of your brain, beneath the cortex, it is a more "primitive" brain area compared to your organizational, learning, and impulse-controlling PFC. Major components of the limbic system include the anterior cingulate, the basal ganglia, the amygdala, and the thalamus. The **anterior cingulate** is your brain's gearshifter. When the anterior cingulate is too active, you become "stuck." Problems that involve the anterior cingulate include negative ruminations, obsessions, compulsions, and addictions. The **basal ganglia** sets the rate of your body's idle, much like a car engine. If it's running too high (and this can be the result of your genetics), you'll likely feel chronically anxious, worried, and keyed up. Excessively active basal ganglia are often accompanied by panic attacks and unhealthy avoidance of conflict. The **amygdala**, an almond-shaped area (*amygdala* means "almond" in Latin) is involved with basic survival issues. It is the equivalent of a primitive emergency alarm system. It quickly assesses threats and then triggers a fight-or-flight reaction. Problems arise when high levels of stress create "amygdala overactivation." Your executive function center, the PFC, can even be hijacked and shut down when the amygdala is in overdrive. The result? You'll be overwhelmed by anxiety, fear, or terror, and your brain won't be able to call on your PFC—the thinking part of your brain—to help you calm down. The problems we'll look at associated with the amygdala include post-traumatic stress disorder (PTSD) and other emotional traumas such as early childhood neglect and abuse. Finally, the **thalamus** is involved in appetite, sleep, bonding, and sexual desire; this part of your brain colors your emotions. Conditions that are related to a problematic thalamus include depression, bipolar disorder, and even premenstrual problems.

I've described the busy brain as an unbalanced brain. The balance referred to here is that between the prefrontal cortex (PFC) and the limbic system. When the brain is unbalanced, the evolutionarily more modern PFC is either too strong or too weak to counter the more primitive limbic system.

On the one hand, if there is too much guidance, too much control by the PFC, you have somebody who is ruled by his head and not enough by his feelings, passions, and urges. Think of Mr. Spock from *Star Trek*. He is in such mastery of his emotions that he sometimes fails to benefit from the insight others naturally derive from their passions or gut. When the PFC dominates, the brain is unhealthy and *unbalanced*.

On the other hand, if the limbic system is too strong and/or the

PFC is too weak, you have an individual who is ruled by her passions and urges and controlled too little by her head, by rationality. This would be an individual with overwhelming feelings and impulses but insufficient rationality to select goals and guide behavior. The Anti–Mr. Spock. Someone out of control, in extreme cases maybe even someone manic. Most—but not all—instances of a busy brain fit this second pattern, a PFC or governing system that is not strong enough to control the limbic system.

Critical imbalances between the limbic system and the prefrontal cortex adversely affect mental and emotional stability. Take Sierra, who cares for her mother who has worsening dementia; Sierra is overloaded between ministering to her mother, her duties at work, and the need to keep her own home running. When the April 15 deadline for filing her taxes rolls around, Sierra's already revved-up limbic system goes into overdrive as she rushes to complete her return. The stress of doing the tax return, an otherwise routine yearly chore, overwhelms the delicate balance between her prefrontal cortex and her limbic system. Her PFC is no longer holding back her limbic system. Her feelings and impulses start to overwhelm her. Sierra begins experiencing panic attacks.

Similarly, Thad, who has worked day and night for sixteen months preparing a major proposal for his company, finds himself becoming sleep-deprived, burned out, and depressed. With his stress response fully activated for sixteen months and his limbic system in sixth gear due to his work on the proposal that will make or break his career, the delicate balance that Thad's PFC has struck with his limbic system is thrown off and Thad can no longer ward off depression.

When the limbic system is too strong and/or the PFC too weak, the PFC is not strong enough to control the wild horses of the limbic system and the herd runs amok. How do we rein in the wild horses if the prefrontal cortex isn't doing its job properly? In the chapters that follow, I will discuss strategies for balancing an unbalanced brain. In essence, we can manage our minds. You may have heard that meditation has a positive impact on the brain, a finding supported by research and verified by brain scans. Similarly, in learning to rewrite the negative stories we tell ourselves, we can also have a positive impact on the brain: we can strengthen the control of the PFC over the wayward limbic areas, bringing the brain into better balance. Simultaneously, by learning new models of relationships, we may calm our hyperarousal and create new patterns of behavior.

But before we turn to the specifics of how we can exert more control over a runaway limbic system, there's another piece to the brain puzzle we must grasp. And that has to do with the necessity of *healing* a broken brain. For not all busy brains are equal. And if a brain has sustained significant injury, it must be treated and healed before we can effectively apply techniques of mind management.

Earlier in my psychiatric career, I was often stumped because I found that some patients markedly improved with treatment, whether via rewriting their stories, implementing mindfulness approaches, talk therapy, psychiatric medications, or other treatments, while other patients didn't get better at all, or they had a response to treatment opposite to what I expected. It wasn't supposed to be this way. After all, I was a well-trained psychiatrist and I really wanted to help my patients. But despite my professional knowledge and experience, and my sincere attempt to be of assistance, I wasn't always helping my patients as much as I'd hoped to. I wondered why this was so. I was prescribing the newest medications; I kept up with the advancements in the field. But few of the basic scientific discoveries had yet been translated into the field of psychiatry, and my own treatments continued at times to fall short. What I was missing became clearer when I met Bill, a patient who came to me for treatment shortly after I started working at Amen Clinics. Bill's case gave me the conviction that a brain must be healed and balanced before mind-management techniques can succeed.

Bill first came to see me after attempting suicide in his dorm room. A twenty-year-old Yale student, Bill was bright and had always been self-motivated, even as a kid. He taught himself to read and devoured science books. As a three-year-old, he seemed to know nearly as much about dinosaurs as professionals who had spent their lives studying them. Despite his intellectual gifts, Bill nonetheless experienced bouts of severe, extreme depression. And his overdose at Yale had nearly killed him.

While home on winter break from Yale, Bill "borrowed" his mother's Ambien without her knowledge. Back at school, he took a potentially lethal cocktail of Ambien, Effexor XR, and a fifth of whiskey. Bill left a suicide note underscoring the seriousness of his wish to die. Fortunately, Bill vomited the pills and whiskey, probably because he was not used to consuming that much liquor. That saved him from a likely fatal overdose. Unfortunately, Bill aspirated the vomit and developed aspiration pneumonia. It was touch and go for him in the ICU for several days.

Bill's roommate called 911 when he discovered Bill unconscious and covered with vomit. Bill was rushed to the hospital, which notified his shocked parents. They immediately drove to New Haven to be with him. Bill's mother said, "I worry that I've let my son down somehow. We've tried to do everything we could to help him, but we've failed." Understandably, Bill's mother felt guilty, as mothers tend to do. Once Bill was stabilized and discharged from the hospital, his family insisted that he take off a semester from Yale and get psychiatric help, which was when Bill came to see me.

I attempted to treat Bill with antidepressant medication, taught him techniques to rewrite his negative stories about himself and the world, and met with Bill for twice-weekly psychotherapy. Bill improved, but only moderately so. He smiled more and was able to laugh a bit, but he continued to feel down and depressed. Antidepressant medications—and we tried several with Bill—really never altered his fundamental negativity and his proneness for severe depressive dips. In psychotherapy, we explored his underlying rigid and unreasonable expectations of himself—in essence trying to help him rewrite his internal narrative, his story—but this was not sufficiently useful. Bill cooperated with treatment, but our treatment had not made enough progress to help Bill move toward being fully free of depression and able to return to Yale.

Because Bill had not made sufficient progress, I told him about brain SPECT scanning, a way to look at what the brain is doing, and asked him to consider it. I hoped that SPECT might reveal something about the root of Bill's problems that we were missing. Bill and his parents agreed, and Bill had his brain scanned a week later.

We were not disappointed. The SPECT results showed that Bill's brain was hurting in a way none of us had anticipated. He had significant damage to his left temporal lobe. Bill's brain wasn't just unbalanced; it was injured, even broken.

I knew that temporal lobe problems, especially on the left side, can contribute to or cause marked depression and negativity—and also rage at times, which fortunately Bill didn't have. Bill's SPECT findings showed me why antidepressants hadn't helped him; antidepressants don't fundamentally address brain injury, especially injury in the temporal lobes.

I carefully questioned Bill and his parents about whether he had a history of head injury. They had no specific recollections of head trauma, but they did tell me that Bill played soccer throughout high school. This was consistent with my experience with other patients; I've seen quite a few soccer players who had head injuries from playing that sport. Heading a hard soccer ball is not a good thing for the brain.

The evidence of physical brain injury reduced Bill's parents' guilt. They hadn't failed him. Bill's problems weren't the result of lack of adequate effort or love on their part or bad parenting; rather, there was a clear physical problem with Bill's brain. And Bill needed to reexamine the unhealthy negative stories he believed about himself, that he was weak and fundamentally flawed. This dramatic shift in understanding about the causes of one's difficulties is typical when brain SPECT reveals significant but previously unknown brain injury.

With this new information provided by SPECT, I put Bill on

Lamictal, a medication that targets temporal lobe problems. Lamictal was the answer to our prayers. Gradually, Bill improved. Eventually, after several months, he was close to 100 percent, with hardly any trace of depression. Bill continued Lamictal, returned to Yale the following semester, and ultimately graduated with honors. Following Yale, Bill attended and graduated from a top-notch law school and now works as a fourth-year associate for a large law firm. Without much exaggeration, SPECT imaging allowed me to save Bill's life; I am certain that, given the severity of his depression and suicidal urges, he would have ended up killing himself if we had not found successful treatment for him. Detecting and stabilizing his left temporal lobe was the key step in Bill's successful treatment. And it obviously impressed me that I was on the right track in looking at brain function, especially in individuals who did not respond previously to "treatment as usual."

As stressed here, hurting brains must be healed before we can proceed with managing the mind. But your brain isn't always broken, and none of this is meant to say that readers will need a SPECT scan. Further, due to neuroplasticity, mind management alone can result in important changes to the brain. Most readers will and can effectively employ the tools of mind management that follow.

With a better picture of the workings of the brain, let's get started with all that you can do by yourself to change and rebalance your overactive brain.

MANAGING
THE MIND

2

Conquering Negativity

When I first began to explore the busy-brain phenomenon, I quickly recognized another pattern in those who have it. Many of these individuals also struggled with excess negativity. It was as if not only were their brains caught in a loop, but that loop was almost uniformly negative. Remember Thad, who had been working sixteen months on a career make-it-or-break-it proposal? He was typically overwhelmed by his busy brain. The balance between his PFC and limbic system was thrown off. The wild horses had seized control. But even more striking, Thad was sinking into depression as his negative thoughts began to overtake his confidence. His busy brain was caught in a loop of feeling inadequate to the task, panic about the future, and general negativity.

There is an undeniable connection between the busy brain and the negative brain. Why, and what can be done about it? Gwen's story may provide some instructive lessons. Gwen, twenty-nine years old and single, consulted me for help with her relationships with men. To be more specific, she hadn't had a relationship with a man for six years. Gwen was well educated, stylishly dressed, attractive, outgoing, even playful; I couldn't understand what the problem was. Gwen said it was depressing not to be able to have relationships with men, but she was not depressed. Her health was good, she did not abuse drugs or alcohol, and she had never been physically or sexually abused. What was happening? Here was a woman who said that she wanted to find a life partner, marry, and have children. There was obviously a roadblock, but what was it?

Gwen wanted to meet with me weekly for psychotherapy to work on her relationship issues, which we did. Our discussions centered on her stories about different men becoming interested in her, their initial approaches, and reciprocated interest on Gwen's part, which were followed by Gwen's abruptly breaking off contact when things got too close. Whenever a relationship was close to becoming sexual, Gwen would end it. Gwen reported a number of satisfying college relationships that had included sexual intimacy. So why now the dismissals of otherwise viable partners?

As her pattern with men became clearer, I was able to point out to Gwen that she broke off the budding relationships for reasons that did not ring true. In one case, it was because the fellow couldn't attend her college reunion with her; he needed to be out of town for an important business trip. In another case, the guy didn't call her when he promised; it later became apparent that he'd lost his phone, but she terminated their relationship nonetheless.

Soon, Gwen felt safe enough with me to share that she had a secret that she'd never told anyone. She wasn't willing to tell me the secret, at least not yet. But she did say that the secret was so horrible, so disgusting, that she was sure that I would not want to continue seeing her if I knew it.

We continued meeting, reviewing her aborted attempts at forming relationships. The pattern became clearer and clearer. Gwen broke off each relationship just before it would have become sexual. And she continued to hint that her important secret had something to do with this. From time to time I commented that whatever the secret was, it seemed so important that it needed to see the light of day. Could we find a way to discuss it?

Finally, after six months, Gwen consented to tell me her secret. She first made me promise that I would not stop seeing her once I learned the secret. And she said that she would tell me the secret only if she turned her back on me, so she would not see what she imagined would be the disgust on my face when she told me her secret. I knew it was important to make it safe for Gwen to tell me her secret, so I agreed to her requests. And then she finally told me the secret.

What was it? What had such a powerful hold on Gwen that it derailed relationships and made her so strongly fear rejection from me? The answer: that she had herpes. Her last boyfriend, whom she'd met in college, had herpes and passed on the infection to Gwen.

Let's be clear: no one who gets herpes is going to rejoice about it. Once diagnosed, it is not uncommon to have an initial reaction of shame or feeling dirty. Many also are angry at the person who infected them. They may feel overwhelmed by the idea of having a lifetime of symptoms and the need to manage the disease over such a long time.

But few also react to the news quite as catastrophically as Gwen did. After an initial period of adjustment, most individuals infected with genital herpes learn to talk to existing and potential partners about it, to incorporate the new medication regimen into their daily routine, to avoid sex during periods of inflammation, and to generally move on with their lives. Genital herpes is more common than diabetes or asthma; about one in five Americans is infected. Most people, by necessity, learn to cope.

For Gwen, the problem was not the herpes itself; it was her thinking about it. Once diagnosed, Gwen believed that the herpes was so bad, so horrible, that nobody would want her. And as she held on to the secret, its impact on her only grew. As a result, that initial period of adjustment that most go through lasted six years for Gwen. During that time, she pushed away potential partners and could barely bring herself to tell me, the doctor she'd come to for help. Gwen was caught in an exceptionally bad case of negative thinking.

Why do some people seem to possess a natural optimism, while others spin downward in a negative spiral? What causes the brain to busy itself with negative thoughts rather than positive ones? Negative tendencies aren't all bad. They often reflect a realism that springs from experience. Whatever path we plot, obstacles may arise and mistakes can happen. On the upside, planning for the worst forces us to be prudent and to attend to the details. And details matter. Richard III said, "For want of a nail the shoe was lost . . . ," leading to the loss of his kingdom. Modern life is adorned with problems because someone neglected to take care of the little things. Perhaps you've been feeling too busy to take care of a toothache until it becomes an after-hours dental emergency. Or your friend was thinking a water spot on the ceiling isn't important until water floods through the roof during the next big storm. Or maybe you missed the first charge on your credit card bill made by someone who stole your account number. The caution and vigilance associated with negativity can serve as an effective preventive.

But excessive negativity can also be a self-fulfilling prophesy. There seems something true about sending out negative vibes and having the universe respond in kind. Plus, seeing only the negative can blind us to positive lessons to be learned from our experiences. Individuals who are stuck in negativity and feel that the world is against them often get locked in a vicious circle. Precisely because they feel powerless to combat what they see as the unfairness of life, they don't engage in the solid planning, persistence, and frank hard work that would allow them to attain realistic goals.

We may never really know all the factors that have contributed to our tendency to be negative. What's important to understand is that negativity is not unalterable. In fact, later I'm going to share with you approaches to counteract negativity that have worked for many people, including myself. It's also important to understand that negativity is not a defect. In fact, negativity is the default position of the human psyche, part of the brain's survival system, which is why it's so hard to eradicate.

Blame Our Wiring for
the Intransigence of Negativity

Why would our brains make us so negative? The reality is that the brain is hardwired for negativity. Studies of brain development and observations about early traumas support this.

First, let's look at brain development. We have two brain hemispheres—the right and the left. To simplify greatly, the right hemisphere deals more than the left with emotions and the gist of sensory experience and pattern recognition, while the left hemisphere deals with language, logic, and problem solving. Now it turns out that the right hemisphere is more negative than the left; the left hemisphere—to the extent that it does deal with emotions—is more positive than the right. Strokes in adults in the left hemisphere reduce positivity, and the individual often becomes depressed. Likewise, adult strokes in the right hemisphere reduce negativity, and the individual often becomes inappropriately happy or manic.

The left hemisphere orients itself toward positive emotions related to approach, exploration, and connection with others. The right hemisphere, as we have discussed, is oriented toward negative emotions related to withdrawal and self-protection. It is more closely related to the limbic system and to the rest of the body than is the left hemisphere.

Think of emotions as experiences that move us toward or away from something or someone. Emotions are the ways we experience and interpret the impact of our brain networks on our body states. The negative emotions we experience—think fight or flight—are more primitive and basic than our positive emotions. And negative emotions—grounded as they are in the right hemisphere and the primitive amygdala—can even override the more positive and logical left hemisphere when we are threatened. Situations of significant threat or danger can literally render us speechless—the left (verbal) hemisphere shuts down, and the right hemisphere and the amygdala dominate our experience.

The kicker is that in an ironic twist of fate, Mother Nature has seen fit to develop the negative right hemisphere before the more positive left hemisphere develops. Because in typical brain development the right hemisphere comes online first, infants and toddlers experience the world with a negative tinge and of course have no language or logic with which to understand or correct their early perceptions. Thus, a baseline, a foundation, of negativity is set early in life.

Later, the left hemisphere matures and we develop language and an ability to apply logic to otherwise emotionally driven situations. But the foundation of negativity has already been set in stone. Because so much of early emotional learning is guided by the right hemisphere, negative experiences early in life can have a detrimental and long-lasting impact on how we feel about ourselves, our personality structure, and how we tend to experience the world.

The development of our memory system also hardwires us for negativity. To again simplify greatly, we have implicit and explicit memory systems. *Implicit* corresponds to *nonverbal*. Think of riding a bicycle. We remember how to do it, but we cannot explain it in words. That's implicit. *Explicit* corresponds to *verbal*. We can remember the name of our fourth-grade teacher or the date we memorized for the attack on Pearl Harbor.

The implicit memory system is centered on the amygdala, which learns quickly and crudely about dangers but seems to hold on to them like a steel trap because it deals with threats to existence. The amygdala is for the most part not plastic; its memories are relatively fixed and rigid. The explicit memory system is based in the hippocampus, which is "plastic," or changeable, so we can learn new things and forget what is nonessential. The problem is that the explicit system, like the reasoning left hemisphere, takes longer to develop, leaving the infant once again prone to negatively tinged experiences of the world provided by the earlier-developing amygdala system.

The perceived dangers from early traumas, branded into the more primitive parts of the nervous system, including the amygdala, can last a lifetime. We all wish that love would triumph over fear, but neurobiologically speaking, that's a tall challenge. The infant and young toddler have only the amygdala memory system active in their brain. So they have the right hemisphere, which tends to interpret things negatively, and they have their only memory system being the amygdala. The amygdala's steel trap just won't let go of early traumas.

Later, as language skills begin to develop, young children begin to develop an effective explicit memory system centered on the hippocampus, in which memories can be modified and even forgotten. In fact, full development of the hippocampus likely occurs only in early adulthood. But until they are at least past the toddler stage, the only memory system children have is the amygdala system, which holds on to traumatic memories like the proverbial elephant— never forgetting.

Experiences early in life about relationships, trust, security, and love are under the control of the right hemisphere because the left is less functional at that point. We do not recall early traumas in words. That is to say, we do not recall them verbally, at least not in the familiar left hemisphere language-based way of remembering. But the impact of these traumas may be there nonetheless, in the nonverbal right hemisphere and amygdala, having a significant impact on us and affecting our functioning and relationships. We often thus repeat an early relationship pattern without being fully conscious that we've retained those feelings and patterns, a phenomenon that Freud described as *transference*. As Freud said, we repeat, rather than remember.

These issues have much to do with why psychotherapy can fail: nonverbal and preverbal issues are intrinsically more difficult to address than those that arise out of the more logical left hemisphere. It's difficult to interrupt deep-rooted right hemisphere patterns of behavior, especially patterns of which you've only recently become aware. Again, that the implicit memory system develops before the explicit memory system means that any kind of negative experiences early in life can have far-reaching and often unrecognized effects. A negative foundation is established, often without our conscious awareness.

A Busy Brain Is Most Often a Negative Brain

That we are hardwired for negativity goes a long way toward explaining why a busy brain is almost always a negative one. As the PFC loses control over the limbic system, the result is a flood of often negative thoughts and emotions. Let's look a bit more closely at what exactly is going on inside your busy brain.

Let's first take a big-picture view of how the brain works. Think of the brain as a modified reflex arc. With a simple reflex arc, we have an environmental stimulus (say, tapping on the kneecap tendon with a reflex hammer). The stimulus is relayed to the spinal cord and processed minimally, and then a nerve impulse is sent to the muscles of the leg to cause a jerk. This reflex arc is a simple mechanism to protect the organism from danger, with minimal processing of the stimulus. Now consider the brain as a more complicated reflex arc system to manage stimuli from the environment. We have stimuli that come into the brain, processing occurs, and then the brain orders a response. The pattern is STIMULI → PROCESSING → RESPONSE. Stimuli from the environment enter the brain. The brain has to process the stimuli and decide what, if anything, the organism should do. The brain "wants" to be calm (i.e., no pressure to decide or to act). But the brain becomes aroused, goes on alert, and springs into action when there is uncertainty, a threat, and also a potential reward (food, sex). When the brain is aroused, we eventually will be pressed to do something (run away or fight, gather the food, pursue our sexual object . . .). The pressure to do something is tension. It is unpleasant. This is the connection to negativity.

In a busy brain, the pressure and tension to do something are amplified, and thus the negativity is amplified. As mentioned earlier, in a busy brain, the limbic system and prefrontal cortex are out of balance. The prefrontal cortex potentially brakes the limbic system's pressure for us to feel an emotion or act on an urge, to take some action in response to environmental stimuli. It's like being in your car and pressing on the accelerator and brake pedal at the same time. The revving of the limbic system is the busy brain; we experience the excessive limbic activity as too-muchness and displeasure. If the prefrontal cortex is up to the task of managing and guiding the revving—the urges of the limbic system, the wild horses I mentioned earlier—we'll be in good shape. But if the prefrontal cortex is too weak, we're in trouble and the revving of the limbic system is too strong, resulting in an out-of-control busy brain.

This out-of-control brain is inherently a negative one. Think about the limbic system revving up: a busy brain often results from people being overloaded with stimuli, threats, demands, and so on. They have too much to process with insufficient guidance from the prefrontal cortex. They are overloaded, flooded. This is a dysphoric, unpleasant state, and negative almost by definition.

Being stuck in a negative loop is also how patients with a busy brain describe their emotional states. They complain about their busy brains and comment that they are usually focused on the negative. For example, Sarah, twenty-three, seeing me for ADHD, attacked herself for not being able to complete her term papers. Over and over, she'd say to herself, "I should be able to sit down and write those papers." And to top it off, Sarah then berated herself for attacking herself about her inability to do the term papers: "OK, I struggle to do the papers, but it is so stupid that I keep attacking myself over it. What a waste of time and energy. It's bad enough that I can't write the papers, but then I foolishly waste time and energy ruminating about it. I mean, there are worse things in the world. I'm not hurting anybody." People stuck in these negative loops continuously beat themselves up.

When we examine brain SPECT scans of individuals stuck in

these negative loops, the data tends to back up the individuals' self-reports. Busy brains as observed on brain SPECT correlate closely with reported subjective negativity. Also, a busy brain on SPECT often—but not always—includes overactivity of the anterior cingulate. An overactive cingulate usually makes one stuck on negative thoughts and feelings. Sarah had markedly overactive anterior cingulate activity that contributed to her stuckness and her tendency to get stuck on attacking herself for being stuck. The negative thoughts in her mind were like the mirrors in a scary fun house, bouncing off one another in troubling ways.

Why Is There More Dysfunctional/Negative Thinking Nowadays?

One interesting question raised by the prevalence of busy brains is whether there is more dysfunctional thinking now than previously, and if so why that might be case. If the busy-brain problem seems more widespread than ever, could that be connected to a modern plague of negativity? Evolution might hold some answers.

Let's go back to the model of the brain as a sophisticated reflex arc. The guiding principle of evolution vis-à-vis brain function seems to be to ensure survival and reproduction. Because of the ever-present threats to an organism's existence, the brain is biased to first interpret stimuli as negative. This negative bias optimizes chances for survival because behavior is based on the principle of "better safe than sorry." But the cost—in terms of negative thoughts and feelings—can be high. What increases our chances of survival may not be the same thing as what makes us happy.

Though we don't live in the jungle or the savannah anymore, the old evolutionarily determined patterns are still there, bred deep in our beings. But the threats to existence (lions, other hostile tribes) faced by our long-ago ancestors are minimal to nonexistent. Our modern lives are safer. So why would the modern-day world have more negative/dysfunctional thinking? Why would our brains feel even busier, as if the threats were multiplying rather than decreasing?

In part, we feel the pressure because the threats are still there. They've merely taken new forms. Threats come from credit card companies trying to manipulate us into signing up for high-interest-rate cards, hackers stealing our financial information, banking houses that are manipulating the stock market, potential employers who promise the moon and don't deliver when you take the job, and so on. In a sense, the modern world is akin to a magician—the threats are not obvious; we must always worry about what's up their sleeve. And we have to acknowledge that there continue to be real threats to safety and existence. Physical abuse, sexual assaults, and violence remain daily possibilities for many, especially females, the young, and those of us who are vulnerable to being preyed upon. Life can be difficult and dangerous.

Going back to the stimulus-response model of brain function, apart from these legitimate threats to health, safety, and even existence, consider that we are nowadays flooded with many more stimuli. Everyone is wedded to their iPhones, iPads, and iWhatevers. So many iStimuli. We have too much to process, most of it not essential for survival, not to mention successful, fulfilling relationships. We may never be able to get an accurate measure of the overall increase in dysfunctional thinking brought on by the iWorld. But it does seem clear that the information overload can contribute to the arousal of the primitive fight-or-flight mechanisms we have been discussing. And our brains can become so flooded, so overwhelmed, so scattered by the endless flood of information, that true cognitive impairment, or "digital dementia," can be the result.

We should not lose hope, however. As stated earlier, negativity, if not curable, is treatable. Let's look first at the common forms that negativity can take. As you begin to recognize the patterns of negative thinking, you'll be better prepared to address them and manage your negative thoughts.

What Is Negativity?

As those stuck in its viselike grip know well, a negative outlook encompasses gloominess, pessimism, a lack of hope. Negativity includes the way we view the world, the past, and the future. In our mental worlds we are critical or hostile toward ourselves or others. We judge rather than understand. Negativity is destructive; it would rather curse the darkness than light a candle. I might even go so far as to say that negativity is the opposite of love for oneself and others.

Here are some examples of negative thoughts: "I'm a total loser because I didn't make the basketball team." "Nobody will ever love me." "Everybody is against me." "I can't do anything." "If I apply to college, they'll never accept me." "If I ever got a flat, I could never change the tire." "She didn't want to go with me to the prom; I'll never get a date." "Bill is frowning; I bet it's because of what I said."

Negative thinking is typically a species of **black-and-white thinking**, in which the nuances, the shades of gray, are left out. Cognitive behavioral therapy (CBT) is a widely accepted treatment for anxiety, depression, and other issues. It focuses on changing unhealthy thinking patterns that contribute to our difficulties. Specialists in CBT define a number of different negative-thinking problems that they call *cognitive distortions*.

All-or-none thinking relates to defining yourself in extreme black-and-white categories and is related to perfectionism. Take the example of a student with a bad case of the flu who did poorly on her exam and then thought, "Now I'll never get into law school," ignoring her otherwise stellar academic record and forgetting the impact her severe flu had on her exam performance. Perfectionists often fear failure or making mistakes. As all-or-none thinkers, they hence try to avoid situations in which they might fail. Unfortunately, however, this also means they cut off meaningful opportunities to grow.

Another kind of negative thinking is the **mental filter**. This is where we focus on one small piece of the puzzle to the exclusion of all else. I have a large nose. If I focused constantly on my large nose, thinking I'm ugly because of it, I wouldn't see the rest of what others (my wife, at least!) say is reasonably good-looking. Mental filters can also turn otherwise positive experiences into negative ones. Corey held a dinner party that was by all accounts a smashing success. But he couldn't stop focusing on the fact that one of his colleagues had to leave early. Though his guest reassured Corey that it was because he had to be up early the next morning, Corey worried that the real reason was that the colleague had been offended by something said at the dinner. His colleague's early departure colored Corey's whole view of the evening. Despite the guests' protestations that they'd all had a great time, Corey's mental filter led him to see the party as an utter failure.

When we're trapped in a negative loop, we often **overgeneralize.** We think that if something happens once, it will happen again and again. A teenage boy who asked a female classmate to the prom was devastated when she declined. "I'll never get a date," he said. Once he overcame his overgeneralization and asked another girl, the next girl he asked actually gladly accepted.

Another kind of negative thinking is **disqualifying the positive,** or refusing to see or recognize the positive implications of what you've done. For example, the research proposal you slaved over for weeks was accepted immediately, yet you reject the evidence of the great work you did on the proposal and continue to see yourself as a loser who doesn't deserve his job.

Catastrophizing is imagining the worst, expecting disaster. You lose a document on your computer. "Oh no," you think. "That will make the project fail." You go immediately to the imagined catastrophe, rather than problem solving and realizing that your coworker likely has a copy of the document you lost.

We may also **jump to conclusions** or arrive at a negative conclusion not justified by the facts. Your boss fails to say hello to you and you conclude that your job is in jeopardy. What you don't realize is that your boss was distracted because her toddler was up all night with the flu. When you jump to conclusions, you are performing mind reading, but badly.

Labeling is the toxic application of labels to yourself. "I am a complete failure," you tell yourself. Complete? Really? No positive achievements? We can also destructively apply negative labels to others: "He never does any good work."

Emotional reasoning refers to concluding that your feelings are accurate descriptions of how things really are. How we feel about something may or may not reflect the actual situation. Feelings are just that—feelings. They are not necessarily a representation of reality. "I feel like this presentation didn't go well," I might say to a colleague, later to find out that my colleague—and our boss—thought the presentation was quite good.

Finally, there are the **Shoulds**. Later we'll see how destructive *should* and *shouldn't* can be. "I should be able to do this without any struggle." "He should not go on vacation; rather, he should stay home and study." "I shouldn't be gay." These statements generate internal pressure and create personal guilt and shame when we direct them at ourselves. When we direct them toward others, they make us judgmental and even toxic. Can we ever really know what we or others "should" do?

What can be done to combat rampant negativity? First, it's important to recognize that we all have an inner critic or judge inside our heads. It often feels like a stranger has invaded us, a stranger who judges others harshly and tortures or even hates us. Second, it's important to understand that the critical stranger actually is an invader. Because the negativity isn't you; it's your brain activity. And the two are not the same.

Let me reemphasize that—you are not just your brain, you are not just your thoughts. Why do I make this claim? Well, the whole is greater than the sum of the parts. The brain is a key part of who we are, yes. But we find that the *real* us is beyond our thoughts. This is why Buddhist and other meditative traditions claim that we find ourselves only beyond our thoughts, apart from our thoughts, in a state of mental peace, often in meditation or silence. Our heart beats, but we are not our heartbeat. Our brain thinks, but we are not our thoughts.

That's why, as we'll see shortly, you can learn to separate yourself from the rampant negativity in your brain. And in separating yourself from your poisonous negativity, you can calm your busy brain.

Managing Negativity

Managing negativity rebalances a brain that is out of balance or leaning toward the negative. The techniques to manage negativity strengthen the capacity of the PFC to offset the limbic system; they help to offset the negative default position of the brain. You are literally strengthening your PFC when you do these exercises. When you distract yourself and manage to get distance from your negative thoughts, and counteract the negative thoughts with more rational responses, you are enhancing your PFC's control over the limbic system. And a stronger PFC ultimately helps check the emotional turmoil we feel from an out-of-control limbic system. A stronger PFC not only reins in the horses, it helps prevent them from bolting in the first place.

How Do We Manage Negativity?

1. **Distance and Detach:** Remember, "You are not just your brain, you are not your thoughts." Thoughts arise automatically, just like the heart beats automatically and we breathe automatically. We don't control our thoughts. And yet they can control us if we let them. If we remind ourselves that our brain makes our negative thoughts, that we are not our brain, we gain much-needed distance from our negative thoughts. They happen; that's it. Don't fight them. But we can think about our thinking. We can put things into perspective: Our thoughts are not facts. With practice and experience, we can learn to more automatically

gain distance from our negative thoughts. Try observing the flow of negativity in your mind, the way you might sit on the bank of a stream and watch the water flow by. You might even view your negativity as a scientist would: "Oh, how interesting that there are self-critical thoughts occurring now." Another way to create distance and detachment is what I call the "Ronald Reagan Approach." In his presidential election debates with Walter Mondale, Mr. Reagan repeatedly and quite effectively said to Mr. Mondale: "There you go again." Tell yourself: "There's my brain being negative again."

2. **Distract Yourself:** Pour yourself into something productive and positive or at least seek out a change of gears. When we are preoccupied with something we enjoy (a crossword puzzle, a good book, a game of catch) or even just find something to absorb us (take a coffee break or talk to a colleague), it gives our system a chance to calm down and our thoughts a chance to refocus from negative to more neutral, if not positive. Another distraction technique is something I call "Sole Therapy": Focus on the bottom of your shoes as you walk. It moves your attention away from the negativity, distracting you.

3. **Remember Your Values:** Remind yourself what your values are. If you are ruminating over negative thoughts and decisions, refocusing on your core values will help reduce the negativity.

4. **Practice Gratitude:** Embrace an attitude of gratitude. Write down three things for which you are grateful. Studies show that simply writing down what you are grateful for can really change the brain and improve mood, moving you away from negativity.

5. **Shun the Shower of Shoulds:** Get out of the "Cold Shower of Shoulds." Among the torment of negative thinking that afflicts us often is a constant flood of "shoulds"—"I should do this . . . I should do that . . ." This cold shower of "shoulds" is nothing but destructive. Once we become more aware of our tendency to

stay too long in this destructive shower, we have a better chance of stepping out of this negative shower stall.

6. **Twist the Dial:** Imagine that there is a dial on the side of your head that you could use to turn down the negative thoughts. Imagine yourself turning down the negativity by twisting the dial.

7. **Have a Laugh:** Can you find the humor in what the negative critic is saying to you? Laughter can be the best medicine. Make fun of the negative thoughts. Laugh at them and yourself for believing them . . . but make sure that you do so gently.

8. **Power Up Your Problem Solving:** If the negative thoughts relate to a clear problem (e.g., a serious health issue), make a list of the steps you can take to deal with the situation. Break down the potential solution into small, achievable steps you can take to improve things.

9. **Find the Positive:** Try to find the positive in what seems to be a negative situation. Turning around a negative thought often shows us another side of the situation. A problem or crisis can even be an opportunity. Search for it.

10. **Breathe:** Take slow, deep breaths. This relaxes the body and the brain and reduces brain overactivity. We'll talk more about breathing in later chapters.

11. **Move:** Do something physical; exercise. Don't stay stuck and immobile, literally and metaphorically.

When Gwen, my patient with herpes, first revealed her secret, her reaction to telling me was striking. She told me some of the details. Then she wasn't able to discuss it for another several weeks. I gave her the time she needed to feel safe before we circled back. Eventually, we were able to begin to explore what it meant to her.

Gwen needed to overcome her persistent, terrifying negative

belief that she would be rejected immediately and permanently if she told any prospective partner about her herpes. First, I helped Gwen realize that her incredibly strong negative thoughts about herpes were just thoughts. They were not her, just her brain. Her brain made these thoughts just like her heart made heartbeats. When Gwen noticed the thoughts that "Any man will reject me if I tell him about my herpes," she learned to create distance by telling herself, "These are just my thoughts. They are not me. They are not true." Frankly, it took some doing to get her to accept this point of view, but she did eventually.

Reminding herself of her intrinsic values and of the good she brought to the lives of others, especially through her volunteer work tutoring immigrants in English, helped soften the strength of the negative blows Gwen delivered to herself in her psyche. Writing down things for which she was grateful also helped move Gwen away from her negativity. She wrote down things such as "I am grateful for my health," "I am grateful for my good job," and "I am grateful for my supportive friends."

Gwen embraced examining her "shower of shoulds." She imagined her negative comments, such as "I shouldn't have herpes" and "I should accept that I'll be single my whole life," coming out of the shower nozzle. This helped Gwen to imagine herself stepping out of this cold shower of shoulds, getting away from these comments and wiping them off with a towel.

Focusing on her breathing also helped Gwen distract herself from her negative thoughts. At first, she thought my idea of imagining turning down a dial on the outside of her head was silly, but she tried it one day and it helped.

Finally, Gwen, who loved shoes, effectively used sole therapy, focusing on the soles of her shoes as she walked, to distract herself from thoughts like "I'll never be happy because nobody could want or love a woman like me with herpes."

It took time and hard effort, but eventually the approaches above were quite successful for Gwen. Her negative thoughts declined about

90 percent over a ten-month period as she used the preceding approaches. We were finally able to speak openly about herpes. Gwen could feel comfortable enough to talk with her doctor to get antiviral medication to use to try to prevent herpes outbreaks. We practiced how she could tell a potential partner that she had herpes and how she might answer his questions. Ultimately, Gwen was able to stop aborting her relationships with men just as they were about to become sexual. She told me about the first time that, with trepidation, she risked telling a man about her herpes. Fortunately, he was sympathetic and accepting of Gwen, and they were able to deepen their relationship, which eventually included satisfying sexual intimacy.

Gwen did have to put in the work to tackle her negativity. I admired Gwen for being willing to face her secret and work it through. Freud wrote that you can't slay a dragon in absentia. Gwen had to look her dragon in the eye in order to slay him, and slay the dragon she did. Eventually, Gwen became engaged to a good man. I was happy to receive a note from her with a wedding picture of the happy couple.

> ACTION PLAN <

➤ **Detach:** Don't fight your negativity. Rather, practice stepping back from your thoughts five times each day.

➤ **Shun the Shower of Shoulds:** Pick one half day per week and notice and total up the number of times you have a thought like "I should . . ." or "I shouldn't . . ." This will help you become more aware of how often you are attacked by these thoughts.

➤ **Practice Gratitude:** Write down three things each day for which you are grateful.

➤ **Have a Laugh:** At least three times a day, find the humor in what your inner critic is saying to you. Laugh at it.

3

Rewriting Your Stories

When I first met Carl, approaching fifty, he'd been an accountant for most of his working life. His accounting work was good, but he never seemed to be able to keep up with the required pace and volume of work that the firm's partners assigned him. The April 15 deadlines were killers every year, especially because of his severe procrastination. Carl was disorganized, lost documents, and never turned in the billing sheets used to charge the clients on time; he often forgot to bill clients for legitimate work as well. Accordingly, Carl's income suffered, and he and his wife never met their reasonable financial goals. Carl's poor attention to detail and inability to concentrate on aspects of work that were less interesting to him curtailed his ability to earn a good income. Carl knew that he was struggling, and he had repetitive negative thoughts about himself. "I'm next to worthless. Why can't I keep up and do my work like everybody else?" he would ask himself again and again. When Carl's son was diagnosed with ADHD, his son's doctor suggested that Carl get an evaluation for himself.

Diagnosing Carl with ADHD was straightforward. Lifestyle

changes like dietary optimization and exercise helped some, but Carl continued to have problems with attention, focus, concentration, procrastination, and other ADHD issues. Carl had the definition of a busy brain. Ultimately, because lifestyle changes were not sufficient to help Carl improve, I prescribed Vyvanse for him. Vyvanse is a prescription medication that boosts dopamine, improving function in the brain's prefrontal cortex, the area often underfunctioning because of ADHD. Vyvanse is similar in action to Adderall and other stimulant medications, just longer-acting and smoother in its effects. It didn't take long to find the optimal dose of Vyvanse, and Carl had a great response with few side effects. Specifically, Carl noted an immediate, marked improvement in focus, attention, and concentration. His procrastination was reduced. His energy increased, and his work performance improved significantly. Carl was now able to keep up with organizational demands like proper completion of client billing sheets; his income jumped.

All in all, after seeing me for only two months, Carl seemed to have a great response. His brain worked better, clearly, and he was more productive and effective at work and at home. But Carl still felt bad about himself. He continued telling himself he was a loser, not worth much, next to incompetent, and unable to match his peers at work in productivity and work quality. Medication had remedied Carl's brain problem. But his old "tapes" kept replaying his unpleasant story.

Carl's case illustrates a fundamental principle. We can often rebalance a brain with ADHD, like Carl's. But even after improving the low functional level of his PFC, the cause of the ADHD, with the Vyvanse, there was another repair that needed to take place. To get Carl's brain to stop playing the busy tapes, we still needed to heal Carl's mind, his spirit, his soul. Carl grew up with ADHD, struggling in school, hearing frequently that "You're not trying hard enough. . . . You are capable of more." Indeed, Carl was bright—his intelligence and hard work took him far in school and in his accounting profession. But because of his struggles, Carl's spirit had taken a big blow. Carl's personal story was of being a defective, inadequate, incompetent individual. And this negative self-narrative lingered even after the brain problem had been treated.

Carl needed more than just an approach that would rebalance his brain with medication. He also needed to go further than just conquering negativity. Carl needed to strengthen his PFC in a much more fundamental fashion: he needed to learn to manage his mind by rewriting his negative stories. Conquering negativity and rewriting our stories are obviously connected. However, rewriting our stories is a more thoroughgoing renovation of our psyche than conquering negativity is, resulting in even more profound change and healing.

The Stories We Tell

How do we become so stuck in inaccurate stories about ourselves? One thing we must understand is that just because we create a story about ourselves and others doesn't mean that story is true. We may get attached to a story if we repeat it enough times. Like Carl, we may convince ourselves we've created a valid picture of ourselves and the world. But it isn't necessarily the case. Our stories are representations of ourselves and the world. But they are not real. These maps, these stories, are simply the best we have. We never can really know the world. The best we can do is to learn to better know our thoughts, our stories.

For some individuals, an inability to generate and to tell consistent, meaningful stories is related to attachment problems early in life. Research shows that children with attachment problems with their mothers or fathers have greater difficulty generating coherent stories when they grow older. Why? Because a poor attachment relationship to one's mother or father makes it difficult to have a coherent sense of oneself in relation to others. Because their mothers or fathers were preoccupied with their own troubles, they rarely experienced their child as a separate, developing individual. These children thus also could not see themselves as a distinct entity and as a result had an underdeveloped sense of themselves. Perhaps no one asked them about their schoolwork or their experiences with friends. Perhaps there were few opportunities for the children to generate narratives, stories that began with "I." Healthy attachment experiences are the foundation for a healthy sense of oneself and others. With unhealthy attachment experiences, we could say that there is less of a "self" there, the "I," about which to generate a story.

An example is Lisa, a woman I know who was raised by a disturbed single mother in a chaotic home in which there was extreme poverty, drug and alcohol abuse, legal trouble, and sexual abuse of all the female children, including Lisa. Lisa does not have ADHD, anxiety, or depression. She is not psychotic. Yet when Lisa talks, it is difficult to understand what she is talking about. Lisa will tell a story, but it is rarely clear if she is talking about herself or another person. Sometimes she will slip from present to past and back to present. It's as if she can't distinguish what happened in the past from a more recent encounter with a family member; or maybe it's more accurate to say that she has little experience telling stories about herself. Her confusions are most likely related to the fragmented and ambivalent interactions she had with her mother. Lisa simply has too little "self" to generate a coherent narrative.

When a lack of coherent story-telling ability reflects a more fundamental lack of coherence in one's sense of self, as it does with Lisa, rewriting your story on your own may not suffice. Psychotherapeutic assistance may be needed to help give birth to and develop a functional self. If you try the storytelling approach that I present in this chapter, and you find that you are stuck or cannot make progress, consider consulting a psychotherapist for help.

Most of us, however, can address the unhealthy stories we tell ourselves and how we generate them. We can rewrite our stories. And by doing so, we'll improve our capacity to function with fewer internal inhibitions and improved overall brain function. We will strengthen our PFC, take a giant step toward reclaiming our brain, and move in the direction of bringing our life back under control.

Trying to know oneself is like being in a fun house full of mirrors! Which makes sense. A perfect, static model of the self *is* overly ambitious. That said, models can be more or less true. The healthiest stories about ourselves emerge from our ability to engage in self-reflection.

The path to self-reflection begins with the prefrontal cortex. In large part, the prefrontal cortex generates our stories. The temporal lobes generate the memory traces that we call upon when we reflect, and the prefrontal cortex takes the memory information and generates cause-and-effect relationships. It is these cause-and-effect relationships that give me so much difficulty when I talk with Lisa; I can never figure out who is doing what to whom in her stories.

When we retell our stories, we thus recruit the PFC to look at itself. Retelling stories does at least three important things:

1. *It counterbalances our intrinsic negative tendencies.* In retelling our stories we take a more complex, more nuanced view of the story, overcoming to some extent the brain's default negativity.

2. *It allows us to see our own thoughts.* In essence, we are thinking about our thinking, thinking about our stories. If we are true to the task of retelling our stories, we necessarily reexamine what we think about ourselves and others.

3. *It strengthens self-reflective capacities.* Story-telling and self-reflection are analogous to lifting weights to build muscle strength. The muscles become stronger through the repetitions. Analogously, our PFC can become stronger through retelling our story exercises. And the stronger the PFC becomes, the easier it becomes to self-regulate, self-reflect, and create even more coherent, nuanced, and adaptive stories for oneself.

This story-rewriting approach freezes our thoughts. It allows us to meditate and focus on the stories as if we have put them under a microscope, and essentially it recruits the help of the prefrontal cortex to modulate the activity of the more primitive limbic brain centers. We are recruiting the thinking brain to help offset the busy, emotional brain.

Being able to self-reflect is not just about adjusting our self-narrative and calming our busy brain. It crucially helps us connect with others. Retelling stories helps integrate us into our social world. And hearing the richly shaded stories of others allows us to identify with their healthy, more balanced worldview. For example, maybe you and your team are down to the wire on an important presentation when you realize that Bob bungled a key piece of data in the PowerPoint presentation. Your first reaction might be fury at Bob's incompetence. Then a colleague explains that Bob is going through a terrible divorce and is under great strain. Your colleague's version of the story is more charitable and compassionate than your instantaneous anger. Suddenly, rather than seeing Bob as a talentless idiot, you might realize that he's a hurting soul in the midst of a personal crisis. It doesn't excuse Bob's mistake per se, but it does help you understand it and put it into a more nuanced context.

Through telling and hearing stories, other people can serve as external brains that we can use to improve our own brain function and improve our capacity to understand the world. We learn to live and let live. To see others' perspectives. To nurture tolerance, empathy, and compassion for others. Being able to see all sides of a story, being able to see the other person's position, is advantageous for social organisms like humans because it allows us to get along better in our social world.

It may sound like magic that after years of telling incorrect stories about ourselves, such as Carl told himself, by rewriting those stories we will suddenly see the light: we will become less negative, more social, more kind to ourselves and to others. But this isn't magic; it works. And the reason it works is that just as healing your brain helps calm your overactive mind, changing the mind—that is, changing the stories that you tell yourself—can also change the brain. How? Because the brain is plastic. In essence, we are talking about self-directed neuroplasticity. The mind, the self, you, can rewire your brain circuits by rewriting your stories. Brain scans show evidence of brain alterations that resemble the changes brought about by medication in people who undertake cognitive behavioral therapy (CBT), which is simply a structured version that teaches retelling of your stories. Other brain scan research also supports this claim of self-directed neuroplasticity from rewriting your story. For example, the work of Jeffrey Schwartz, M.D., at UCLA demonstrates brain changes from mindfulness-based interventions for obsessive-compulsive disorder (OCD). Schwartz's mindfulness approach is close to retelling your story. The key point is that changing how you talk to yourself, changing what you say to yourself, how you tell yourself stories, changes your brain.

By learning techniques to manage our minds and brains, we are breaking old habits and patterns (related to particular brain circuits) and causing newer circuits to form. If our new stories are more nuanced, these newer brain circuits are also more adaptive. For example, if we develop the habit of seeing shades of gray in a spouse's behavior, when our spouse repeats that particular behavior, our mind more naturally goes to those shades of gray rather than a rigid black-and-white interpretation of the event. For example, perhaps at one point we viewed a spouse's unwillingness to talk about their day as a personal rejection. We might come to understand that their quiet doesn't stem from a lack of desire to share. It's simply exhaustion after a long day. Now when our spouse returns home lacking their usual talkativeness, we may ask if it's been a hard day and express compassion. The mind has literally rewired the circuitry of our brain in a more nuanced, more adaptive fashion.

Self-directed neuroplasticity, changing our brains ourselves, is the basis for hope that we can change. But it requires sustained effort to break old patterns and learn new ones. In fact, co-created story revision is the essence of good psychotherapy with a skilled therapist. Intensive psychotherapy may well be one of the best ways to address intransigent maladaptive patterns.

Many story patterns, however, are less deeply ingrained. And you should find success with the techniques I describe next.

Rewriting Our Stories

In order to rewrite our stories we must let go of the negative interpretations of our lives that hold us back. Think of the goal as trying to move from a black-and-white story theme to one that includes a palette of many colors. Rewriting our stories, in thinking, appreciating nuance, being able to *think about thinking*, adds a richness and a dimension to life that would not exist otherwise. The whole point is greater inner freedom—we don't want to be weighed down by inflexible stories.

One of the most important tools for rewriting is self-reflective capacity. We need to be able to reflect on the meaning of our experience and on our stories; we must not take our stories at face value. Self-reflection not only strengthens our PFC—our ability to govern ourselves. It also gives us inner freedom. We are talking about a mindful stance, one that allows us to think about our thinking—awareness of awareness.

Do you have the courage it takes to be one-on-one with your thoughts? It might take more courage than we often realize. A series of studies done by Timothy Wilson at Harvard University and the University of Virginia showed that most people prefer doing something—even hurting themselves—to doing nothing or sitting alone with their thoughts. Remarkable, isn't it? Study participants were asked to quietly be alone with their thoughts for six to fifteen minutes. Many participants found the time alone with their minds to be unpleasant. Two-thirds of the men and one-quarter of the women preferred self-administered electric shocks to sitting quietly with their thoughts. The researchers suggest that the mind's primary job is to deal with the external world. In primitive times the mind was almost always directed outward—for survival reasons, for food, sex, countering attacks, and so on. Once people did not have to worry about such things, the individual had the luxury to begin to look inward, to contemplate the nature of human existence, to create art, literature, and music. But these studies suggest that dealing with the inner world, our minds, is still difficult for many of us.

What to Do: Self-Reflecting and Story Rewriting

If you have the courage, the will, to look at your thoughts, your stories, how do you go about it? Here are the steps that I have found helpful for my patients and myself in trying to sort through the troublesome stories, the soap operas, in the brain.

Write It Down

It is important to write down your thoughts and stories.

I find that writing down my thoughts and stories on paper or on an electronic device helps me freeze my thoughts so that I can assess them. Thoughts are slippery devils. They're here now, gone in a moment. How can we really work with our thoughts if we can't grab them, pin them down, and take a focused look at them? You really need to be able to hold your thoughts still so you can shine a spotlight on them.

You may be tempted to talk out your thoughts instead of writing them down. But grabbing hold of and nailing down your thoughts in writing is key to the process. As Carl, my ADHD patient from earlier, and I began to work together to rewrite his negative account of himself, I explained to Carl that because thoughts come and go so quickly, it would be important to write them down in order to work on them. He wasn't too keen on this initially, but he agreed to try it. As he found it useful, his initial reluctance to write down his thoughts and stories passed.

True or False?

Pick a simple story. Summarize it in a few lines. Write down whether your story is true or false.

You could select any painful thought, feeling, story, or belief. Anything that causes you pain. For example, Carl wrote, "I was a lousy student who didn't try hard enough."

If we are honest with ourselves, we recognize that our stories are incomplete, if not untrue. Have you believed your thoughts? Have you believed your stories? I bet you've done that. I have. What a change it can make to realize that thoughts and stories are fiction, a narrative that emerges from brain activity. "He doesn't like me." Is that really true? Can I really know for sure? If we wait, take the time really to look inside and be truthful with ourselves, the answer is almost always no.

As I worked with Carl to help him rewrite his story, I suggested that he really look at the truth of his statement that he was a lousy student who didn't try hard enough. At first, he was quick to say yes, it was true. I asked Carl to slow down, to really look inward, as if this question were a kind of meditation. This time, Carl said no, this story of being a lousy student who didn't try hard enough was not true. I asked Carl to explain. Carl admitted that he achieved grades of B or B+ in high school and graduated from a well-regarded state university. He couldn't have been lousy. Then I asked Carl about the second part of his statement, that he was capable of more. Again, Carl at first said yes. But I asked him to really reflect on that statement, to look inside to seek the truth. After a few minutes, with tears in his eyes, Carl said that it wasn't true that he was capable of more. In fact, he said, he knew that he always worked much harder than his peers, but he'd never known why. He stayed up late, missing out on sleep. Often he declined social activities to try to study. He'd assumed his problems were because he was less intelligent, but now Carl was realizing that it was the ADHD that was the problem, not whether he was capable of more. I could see the glint of recognition in Carl's eyes as he saw the more nuanced version of his educational experiences. The truth was that he had not been capable of more. He'd figuratively knocked himself out to accomplish what he had accomplished. He'd used every ounce of energy he had. How could he have been capable of more?

After you write down your painful thoughts, feelings, stories or beliefs, examine them for their truth. More likely than not you will spot an error in the thought that is causing you pain and affecting how you see yourself and the world.

Time Traveling

Where are you in time? Is your story about now? Or are you more likely stuck in the past or projecting yourself into the future?

We keep talking about wanting to live in the now. But our thoughts go endlessly into the past or future. Recognizing this in yourself can bring you back to the present.

When Carl dwelled on his school struggles, he was stuck in the past. Yet Carl wanted to be more present for his wife and children. When we discussed his "time travel," Carl began to realize how much of his mental life was spent away from the present. Simply recognizing this made it easier for him to spend less time in the past and more time in the present with the people he cared about most.

Ask yourself: Are you spending the time you want to be spending in the present? Are you living in the past or the future, or are you living in the now?

Judgment

Look honestly at whether you are judging yourself or others in your story.

Christianity and other religious traditions teach leaving judgment in the hands of God. Unfortunately, eschewing judgment is difficult for Christians and most others, given human makeup, especially the way brain evolution and the resulting brain function contribute to our negativity. But it is important to try to avoid judgment. Judgment usually does little good and often stirs you up. Judgment is often in the search for who or what is right or wrong, really an extension of that negative, black-and-white thinking. Think about the common saying about being the peace you want to see in the world. Our judgmental tendencies get in the way of having the internal peace that we need to start with. Why not let go of judgment and just be?

When Carl and I talked about judgment, it really struck a chord. Carl realized that he'd felt judged harshly in school and that he constantly judged himself, and always negatively. Carl was eventually able to move away from this judgmental stance and just be, without criticism or judgment of self and others. It wasn't easy and it took time, but he was able to do it.

Whose Business?

Whose business are you in? In your story, your internal drama, whose affairs are you concerned with? Yours? Somebody else's? God's/the universe's?

We can really only change ourselves, and even that is difficult. We'll never know what is best for others. Parents of my teen patients get worked up if their son or daughter doesn't want to attend college. Can we really know that someone should go to college, even our children? Some people do not attend college and have wonderful and successful lives, sometimes contributing much to society. I don't mean to say we shouldn't talk with our children, calmly and lovingly, helping them consider and think through the pros and cons of attending college. But after that, what can we do? If our child isn't inclined to try college right then, so be it. It's the child's decision, and it should be, after we helped them think it through.

This is akin to the Buddhist concept of acceptance. In the case of the college decision, it's not my business after I helped my child think it through; it's my child's business. But what about God's or the universe's business? Well, that has to do with situations like whether I have a stroke, or whether a meteor falls on my house. I owe it to myself and my family to try to remain as healthy as I can and take care of myself, but that might not be enough—I still could have a stroke. And, if so, that's God's business. It's also God's or the universe's business when a tsunami strikes in Asia. I cannot do anything about that, other than donating money and supplies for relief, which I do. These are horrible tragedies, and they seem to happen far too often. But they are beyond my control.

I asked Carl to consider whose business he was in with his story of being a lousy student who didn't try hard enough. He thought that he was in his own business; after all, who else was there in this story? I agreed, partially, but Carl was a bit surprised when I told him that I thought he was also in God's or the universe's business. Why? Because Carl didn't give himself ADHD. It was through no fault of his that he had it. He couldn't do anything about having it, although he could try to address it via treatment, which he'd done. I agree, it was a bit of a stretch telling him this, but I wanted to gently shake his sense of excessive responsibility for his problems.

Accounting

Analyze the pros and cons of continuing to hold on to and believe that story.

Look at the pros and cons of believing the story and tally up the columns.

Because Carl was an accountant, the notion of a cost assessment appealed to him. He looked at the cost of believing the story that a colleague didn't like him. Carl said that the pro was that if he believed it, he might work harder to be liked. The cons were that he became tense and on guard, didn't sleep well, and was always ready to counterattack in case the colleague said something that could hurt Carl at the upcoming monthly board meeting. What would it be like if Carl didn't hold on to "He doesn't like me"? "Well, I'd feel calmer, happier, really freer. I would not have to worry about what he might do at the board meeting." To total up the accounting, there is a slight benefit from holding on to the story. But there is a significant downside. The negative outweighs the positive. "Better to give up that story if I can," said Carl.

Opposites

Be honest with yourself and think about whether, at least in some ways, the opposite of your story might be true.

Carl considered whether a story opposite from the one that he was a lousy student who didn't try hard enough might be true. Carl had gotten decent grades. But more important he could now see that he'd functioned with a handicap when he was in school. A handicap of a paralyzed leg is visible to everybody. But his handicap was invisible. Realizing he'd done as well as he had despite the handicap of ADHD was liberating. Suddenly Carl could see the opposite of the "I was a lousy student who didn't try" story. He realized that what he'd accomplished in his life before he knew he had ADHD was actually heroic, like climbing a mountain with one hand tied behind your back. You can do it, but it is much more difficult than the usual way.

It may seem like these steps could be accomplished in a few minutes. Realistically, Carl and I did go through all the points in one appointment. However, to move ahead and really rewrite his story, Carl needed to return again and again to the approach I've outlined. Sometimes I helped or even prodded him. Other times, he worked on his own.

You too may need several sessions with this exercise. Always writing down your thoughts and responses to the various steps will help significantly. As you repeat the steps, new insights may appear. And at the same time bonds to old ways of thinking may loosen.

As with Carl, part of what you may be doing is reframing your development. In Carl's case, we took a look back at the story of his childhood and schooling. His understanding of what happened had been incomplete because he had not been aware of having ADHD. My work with Carl helped him reframe and reinterpret his developmental struggles in a more nuanced and much less self-attacking way. Carl no longer judged himself so harshly. Plus, he gained a developmental history that was, in my view, more accurate and more healthy. The stories that made up his newfound developmental history were much more positive and realistic. Ultimately, Carl even could own a sense of pride for surmounting his struggles the way he did. To add a postscript, Carl was made partner in the accounting firm two years after he first came to see me.

I hope that by repeating the exercise, you too will reframe and reinterpret your struggles in a much more nuanced way and stop judging yourself so harshly. Ultimately, you will be able to write stories that are more positive and realistic, find relief from inner attacks, and see your own successes multiply as you do so.

In this chapter on rewriting your stories, I wanted to present individuals for whom rewriting their stories is particularly important and effective, given that their brain function is fundamentally healthy. Because ADHD is so common, and because rewriting their stories and reframing their development can be so helpful for someone with ADHD, we discussed Carl. Let's now look at another condition for which rewriting stories can be extremely helpful, a situation in which there is no diagnosed psychiatric condition: job loss.

Ana, thirty-three, came to the United States from Central America with her parents at age six. Her parents, seeking the American dream, started a cleaning business. They worked six and a half days a week, cleaning the homes and business establishments of the well-to-do. Ana's parents wanted nothing more than for her and her siblings to have a good life: an education, a spouse with similar values, and the ability to make a contribution to society. Ana pursued the goals her parents set for her and did well. Education came easy; she did well in school and graduated from a good university.

After that, Ana, cash-strapped, attended law school at night while working during the day in her parents' business. Her hard work was rewarded by graduating from law school with honors.

Aiming to contribute to society, to give back, so to speak, Ana took a job as a junior associate at a firm that specialized in immigration issues. At first, the firm was flush with work and Ana thrived, working eighty hours per week. Unfortunately, the economy soon fell into recession. Ana was laid off, another of the many job casualties experienced by young attorneys across the country.

Losing her job was quite a setback for Ana. Until that point, her hard work had resulted directly in success, in moving toward her important goals. Suddenly, through no fault of her own, Ana was out of work. Her sense of what to do was shaken. Could she succeed as an attorney? Could she even survive financially? Just as the legal profession was hit hard by the downturn, Ana's parents' cleaning service lost clients for the same reasons that resulted in her being laid off.

Not so much anxious, not so much depressed, but shaken, discouraged, and filled with increasingly negative thoughts and stories about herself, Ana sought my help. In the course of a few sessions, I explained to Ana the principles of rewriting one's stories, which she used to good benefit. I won't give as much detail as I provided with Carl, but I'll sketch some of the key points about how Ana approached rewriting her stories.

First, it was important for Ana to learn to write down her negative thoughts and stories so she could pin them down and work effectively with them. Ana wrote down thoughts and stories like "I wasted years of schooling and tens of thousands of dollars" and "I'm a failure." I asked her to start by clarifying whether these stories were true or false. Ana's initial response was to say that they were true. "Can you know absolutely that these stories are true?" I asked. She replied that she couldn't know for sure that they actually were true.

I asked Ana to look honestly at herself, to consider whether she was judging herself with this story she was telling about being a failure and wasting tens of thousands of hard-earned money. Ana reflected for some minutes. Yes, she said, she was judging herself. She had unconsciously absorbed her parents' immigrant ethos of hard work. She wasn't working hard; in fact, she wasn't working at all. Did that mean she was a failure? No, it didn't necessarily mean that. Ana recognized that she tended to apply to herself an unfair judgment.

Ana had worked hard, but one can't control everything, even through hard work. Economies falter. I asked Ana to consider whose business she was concerning herself with when she told these negative stories about herself. Ana came to recognize that it was God's business, or the universe's, or maybe that of the major banking houses that contributed to or caused the economic downturn that hurt her and so many others. That didn't make her a failure. It didn't mean that she wasted her money on a legal education.

Ana did an accounting, considering the pros and cons of holding on to the negative story of herself. She couldn't find any pros. The cons were that she felt miserable and defeated. And Ana was able to consider whether the opposite of her negative story might be true. She concluded that she was not a failure, that she had achieved a lot overall through her hard work, and that she was likely to find success—somehow—in the future.

Rewriting her story helped Ana. It didn't get her another legal job, of course; that took time. But rewriting her negative thoughts and stories did help her keep up her morale. A few months after we'd ended our work, Ana let me know that she'd been hired by the U.S. Department of Justice as an attorney specializing in immigrant affairs. She thanked me for teaching her how to rewrite her stories, which she said that she'd continue to practice, with good results.

Each life story is different. And the stories we tell ourselves are all different. It's one of the things I love about my work. I am privileged to learn so much as I meet and share the lives of the people I come to know. Because of what we now know about brain plasticity and brain function, the self-reflection and story rewriting that I encourage you to try likely does more than just help you feel better because your negative stories are less burdensome. This approach is likely to change your brain as well, in fundamentally positive ways.

→ ACTION PLAN ←

At least one time a day, take fifteen uninterrupted minutes and work on rewriting one of your stories. Pick any story, thought, or belief that causes you discomfort or pain. Write it down. Then work through the steps in this chapter, starting with "True or False?," writing down your answers as you meditate on each step in the process, attempting to find the truth within you.

4

Becoming Mindful

Have you ever noticed that during periods of high work intensity or stress, at the times when your brain feels busiest, you don't breathe? Of course, that is not literally true, or else you would be in an ICU or worse. But the calm deep breaths, which fill you with oxygen, don't occur. Rather, you breathe shallowly, not quite hyperventilating, but maybe close to it. Perhaps your balance gets out of control. You become decentered. And at these times, you have too much noise in your head; your brain is overactive. You seem to be reacting to life, rather than acting. You are somehow being lived, not living, not managing yourself, not regulating yourself.

This is a condition that affects most everybody I know, patient and nonpatient alike, myself included. I'm talking about living life on automatic pilot. Living mindlessly.

The overstimulation of modern life, with our modern information overload, tugs and pulls at us from every direction. We can't regulate ourselves. We can't regulate our emotions. Our minds are restless. I hear more and more talk about "monkey brains," meaning brains in which thoughts jump around every which way like monkeys do on trees. We are experiencing a mental too-muchness.

Yes, modern life bombards us with external stimuli. We are also, however, being overwhelmed by inner stimuli, by the noise from our too-active limbic systems. The imbalance we see in a busy brain is caused not merely by a PFC that is too weak but by a limbic system that has become too strong. We've already discussed some ways to address the PFC–limbic system imbalance by strengthening our PFC. We can manage our negativity. And we can rewrite our stories. On the other side of the equation, we can also learn to calm our overactive limbic systems.

Learning to calm our limbic systems, we learn to tame our hyperarousal and create new patterns of behavior. And it is through calming the limbic system that we will find more ways to stabilize ourselves within our modern maelstrom. To turn down the noise that keeps us from even hearing ourselves. From finding ourselves. From really knowing ourselves.

There is a rather nasty joke common among medical trainees. It has to do with what the earliest responders need to do at a "code" in the hospital, that is, the crisis when a patient stops breathing or has a cardiac arrest. The joke goes something like this: "What is the first thing you have to do at a code? Answer: Take your own pulse!"

The joke, of course, plays off what one would expect—that is, first take the pulse of the patient. Apart from using humor to help medical professionals manage their emotions related to the powerful life-and-death issues they face daily, this joke underscores a deeper point. We cannot think clearly if our emotions are running wild. The medical professionals running the code need to have their wits about them; their own pulse can't be going a thousand miles an hour. They cannot best help a patient in crisis if their own physiology is out of control. The first—and most important—thing they need to do is make sure that they calm themselves. Only then can they have the best chance of making the split-second decisions that may spell life or death for the patient whose heart has stopped.

Like the medical professional managing a code, those of us

who are attempting to conquer our negativity, rewrite our stories, and improve our relationships cannot do so if our emotions are out of control. We need ways to calm ourselves, to find peace, to be able to think about our thinking. This is what mindfulness provides.

Before tackling the mindful approach, however, I'd like to introduce you to James, an overwhelmed pastor, whose story is almost a parable for our contemporary multitasking era. If anyone was a candidate for a busy brain, it was James.

When I first met James, he was married and in his midforties. He served on the local school board in his community and performed in an a cappella chorus of local renown. He was also continuing the home remodeling business that his father started. And, following a religious calling he experienced as a teen, James became the pastor of a small church. The cumulative demands on James, a people pleaser, were striking. I noticed anxiety within myself as I thought about all the pressures on James. He had four children; the youngest had cerebral palsy and required time-consuming and expensive physical therapy. His wife had multiple sclerosis. The school board demands were significant; budgetary cutbacks created rancor between teachers and the school board, which was reluctant to raise taxes to do more in the schools, including giving teachers a raise. James's remodeling business was successful financially, but it fell to him to deal with customer complaints, of which there were more than a few. Finally, in his church there were the common strains within the congregation, with various cliques and disputes about the overall direction of the church, especially in connection to changes within the national organization, of which James's church was a member.

Not surprisingly, James was stressed to the point of being overwhelmed. He wrestled with anxiety and feeling down but did not have symptoms severe enough to warrant a clinical diagnosis. James did experience insomnia, skin outbreaks, gastrointestinal (GI) problems such as nausea and diarrhea, and heart palpitations. His primary care doctor gave him a clean bill of health; no serious medical problems accounted for James's issues. But James's doctor was concerned about James's level of stress. That was when he referred James to see me.

What bothered James most was that he never experienced himself as being present. Counseling the members of his congregation, he struggled with thoughts about school board conflicts. Dealing with customer complaints in his remodeling business, he found himself worrying about the health of his wife and daughter. James, who loved music, found himself not able to pay attention during the a cappella rehearsals because he was worrying about church members whom he was counseling for marital problems. And so it went. James's busy brain prevented him from ever feeling like he was there, in the moment, with the people with whom he wanted to be present. The restlessness of his mind ensured that he was always in more than one place at one time, and never really *there*, where he needed to be.

James needed help. We discussed whether mindfulness approaches could be useful for him. Many of my other patients had experienced success in calming their busy brain using mindfulness techniques.

What Is Mindfulness?

Mindfulness is an approach. It is a deliberate effort to facilitate the development of an agency, a self, that monitors and regulates our experiences. Mindfulness is a way of being—a way of looking inside oneself, of being aware of awareness, of paying attention nonjudgmentally to the unfolding of experience. It can be a way of being quiet and of quieting a busy brain.

Mindfulness stops you from living life on automatic pilot. You live with more conscious attention; you're more aware of the mind itself. Mindfulness is thinking about thinking, awareness of awareness. Both correlate with self-reflection, reflection on inner life, on the events of the mind. Mindfulness slows down the busy brain, in part through anchoring us in the present moment. Mindfulness and meditation, which is one form of mindfulness, are important approaches for achieving inner peace.

The Benefits of Mindfulness

Mindfulness approaches improve our ability to regulate our emotions. Mindfulness practices reduce our negativity. We find improved relationships in those who practice mindfulness because mindful individuals are better able to read the nonverbal signals of others. Mindful individuals are better attuned to the inner worlds of others and have greater compassion for others and themselves. Intuition is improved. Fear response is modulated. Insight is better. The list could go on and on. Many of these benefits stem from strengthened PFC function and improved PFC–limbic system balance. Brain language networks, especially those that involve evaluation, are tamped down, with resulting greater openness and less judgment. When we engage in meditation, an approach of mindfulness, we turn down the sympathetic branch of the autonomic nervous system and turn up the calming, parasympathetic branch. As a result, we are less defensive, less in a fight-or-flight mode. Thoughtfulness predominates rather than raw feelings and impulses.

The science confirming meditation's benefits is far-reaching. Here's just a snapshot taken from hundreds of available studies:

➤ According to a Harvard Medical School study, 80 percent of hypertensive patients who meditated lowered their blood pressure and decreased medications, while 16 percent were able to discontinue using their medication.

➤ Researchers at Northwestern Memorial Hospital in Chicago found that people with insomnia who meditated fifteen to twenty minutes twice daily for two months all reported improved sleep; in fact, most of them were able to reduce or eliminate sleeping medication.

➤ Individuals who experienced chronic pain due to injury, surgery, arthritis, or fibromyalgia reduced their physician visits by 42 percent, and open-heart-surgery patients had fewer postoperative complications due to a regular practice of meditation, according to studies conducted at the University of Pittsburgh Medical Center.

➤ Researchers at Cedars-Sinai Medical Center in Los Angeles showed that patients were able to lower their blood sugar and insulin by practicing meditation.

➤ The *International Journal of Neuroscience* reports that meditators who have been practicing for at least five years are physiologically twelve years younger than their nonmeditating counterparts. The reasons? Studies show that meditators lower their levels of cholesterol, blood sugar, inflammation, and the stress hormone cortisol—all of which are known to contribute to aging.

➤ Studies done by Yale, Harvard, and Massachusetts General Hospital have shown that meditation increases gray matter in the brain and slows down certain kinds of brain deterioration. The Harvard experiment included twenty individuals with intensive Buddhist "insight meditation" training and fifteen who did not meditate. Brain scans revealed that those who meditated had an increased thickness of gray matter in parts of the brain that are responsible for attention.

➤ Meditation helps to eliminate feelings of anxiety and anger. Using magnetic resonance imaging (MRI) scans, researchers at the University of Wisconsin looked at the brains of meditators and discovered that during meditation their amygdala (the part of the brain responsible for the fight-or-flight impulse) switches off, and the prefrontal cortex (the area of the brain responsible for feelings of peace, compassion, and happiness) lights up.

Other studies show that meditation decreases depression, anxiety, and moodiness and boosts self-esteem, concentration, and relaxation. Mindfulness meditation makes people happier. It can remind us of our purpose in life: to experience joy in the here and now.

Neurofeedback (NFB) and Biofeedback (BFB)

Turning down the sympathetic branch of the autonomic nervous system and turning up the calming, parasympathetic branch may be difficult for those with low-functioning PFCs or active amygdalas. Neurofeedback can help. *Neurofeedback*, also called *neurotherapy* or *neurobiofeedback*, is brain biofeedback treatment that is performed by a neurotherapist trained in the procedure, with the help of an electroencephalograph (EEG). Neurofeedback allows an individual to control their brain wave patterns so that they can learn to generate more calm and focused brain wave patterns, thereby improving mindfulness. Real-time brain tracings from scalp sensors are used to teach self-regulation of brain function. For example, alpha waves in the brain are associated with a calm yet relaxed state of mind, focused and optimally attentive. If an individual has insufficient alpha waves, neurofeedback can increase alpha wave activity, which is linked to meditative states of mind.

There are a number of different NFB approaches; if the approach or therapist you are trying doesn't work for you, consider switching to another neurofeedback therapist or approach.

Biofeedback is another way to help us reduce the burden of mental overload. Biofeedback is an approach that teaches individuals how to influence aspects of their autonomic nervous systems, such as muscle tension and blood pressure. It reduces excessive arousal and is helpful for increasing calm. For those interested in an at-home biofeedback approach, consider the Wild Divine biofeedback system (www.wilddivine.com).

James, our overwhelmed pastor, was a perfect candidate for the mindfulness approach. And he ultimately successfully used biofeedback and other mindfulness practices. But he had some intermediate steps he needed to take first.

Like many of those who have a busy brain, by the time James came to see me for help, he had simply accumulated too much on his plate. In order to resume a higher level of function, he was going to need to clear away some of the demands he had piled on himself. As it stood, James was experiencing "decision fatigue," which refers to the deteriorating quality of decisions people make when they are over-loaded. For example, evidence suggests that convicts up for parole are more likely to be granted parole if their case is heard early in the morning rather than just before lunch, when parole board members are hungry and tired and may well have lower blood glucose and "pooped-out" adrenal glands. Think of the brain as an organ that requires fuel and replenishment. With constant demands for deci-sions, the brain becomes depleted of the resources necessary for opti-mal function. That was the state that James was in all the time.

I explained to James my ideas about his being overwhelmed with decision fatigue. He thought about it and acknowledged the problem. James, people pleaser that he was, hated to give up any of his responsibilities. He asked me to give him a medication to improve his overall function. I told him that no such medication existed. Rather, he needed to look at his lifestyle and his demands and see more clearly how negatively the relationships he cared about were affected.

James was willing to consider my points. During several months of exploration, we discussed all the factors that contributed to his people pleasing and taking on too many responsibilities. James recognized that he would have to reduce his commitments and demands; this was associated with much grief on his part. He hated giving up anything he was doing. But he had to. James saw that although people and relationships were of paramount impor-tance, he would not be able to do justice to these relationships. He was there, but he wasn't. He wasn't present in a mindful sense.

With regret, James decided to resign from the school board, stop his a cappella participation, and speak with the church elders, who arranged for an associate pastor to be hired, one with special expertise in pastoral counseling. These changes, which occurred over a two-month period, significantly reduced the demands that James bore. James's sleep improved, his GI problems remitted, and he no longer had heart palpitations. More important was that James was able to be present with those he cared about, because he experienced fewer competing demands for his time, energy, and attention.

James's story underscores the reality that the brain is an organ that, like any other in the body, can become overtaxed by demands. James had gotten himself into a situation in which ever-present demands wore him down. Simply instructing him in mindfulness approaches would not have been sufficient. He needed to make real-life changes to reduce his distractions. In making those real-life changes, however, James was also able to benefit from the practices of mindfulness: he was better able to find quiet, to slow down, and ultimately to function lovingly and be more present in his important relationships.

Mindfulness and Relationships

James's experience that mindfulness made him a better husband, father, friend, and pastor is not unique. Generally, mindfulness improves your relationship with yourself and with others. Attuning yourself to the present moment may enhance healthy relationships. Evidence suggests that mindfulness may enhance romantic relationships and the communication in these relationships.

Research suggests that mindful individuals are less susceptible to the negative mood states of others, which obviously is useful in romantic relationships. Mindfulness seems to reduce emotional reactivity during conflict. Thus, mindfulness would seem to improve intimate relationships. The overall benefit of mindfulness for relationships seems to be in the areas of empathy, emotional balance, and response flexibility. Moreover, mindful individuals likely do not flee as readily from relationship difficulties, for obvious reasons, increasing the chances for successful relationships. They have more of an "approach mind-set," rather than a mind-set of withdrawal.

Mindful individuals are more present. When we are present, we are relaxed. We don't feel stressed. We don't feel pressure. We don't feel bombarded by stimuli. Extraneous thoughts are reduced. We are open, not defended or defensive. We are able to focus and give our attention to the situation or individual. In the next chapter, when we take a closer look at relationships, we will see that we are much more likely to be present when we are in what I call a horizontal (or equal) mode of relationships. In contrast, we cannot be present in a vertical (or unequal) relationship mode because danger, helplessness, and victimization make it impossible to attain the calm attunement, focused attention, and clear perspective that presence requires.

When we are present with another, we resonate with them and are empathic. We are tranquil and seek truth. We trust. Presence suggests flexibility. The opposite of flexibility—rigidity—makes truth and trust more difficult. Presence is mindfulness as applied to relationships. To apply a mindful approach to a difficult relationship, decide that you are not going to argue with the person. Don't respond defensively. Interrupt your reflexive, self-justifying responses. Rather, when you experience tension in the interaction, take a few moments to reflect before responding. A few seconds is all you need. Get ahold of yourself. Be calm, centered. Don't struggle to be in control of the experience. Instead, focus on first being aware of what is going on in your mind. Notice what you are experiencing. What do you feel? What are you thinking? Does this reaction seem familiar to you? Perhaps your reaction is rooted more in another relationship than in the current one.

Digital Distraction

Mindful living, as James discovered, is not easy in our age of never-ending, always-on, electronic information exchange, which Elkhonon Goldberg has referred to as "digital anarchy." What does this information flow do to our brain, our mind, our spirit, our body, our life? With technology available essentially everywhere, all the time, some fear that we are becoming a society of droids. We read that "digital dementia" is on the rise as young people increasingly rely on technology instead of their brains. My wife, who used to work in an elementary school library, often observed that her young students didn't know how to use a phone book to search for phone numbers; they didn't even seem to know the alphabet well enough to use a phone book. They used Google to find all needed information.

With the Internet, many are expected to check work e-mail regularly on weekends and holidays. Everyone is reachable. Anywhere. Anytime. The line between work and leisure is blurred, if there is even a line that remains at all. Can we relax and refuel in our always-connected world? Are we attention-exhausted? Does the assault of constant new information coming at us all the time put us into a state of chronic stress with an overactive fight-or-flight response? Humans were not built to be "always on" every waking hour. Downtime and disconnection are critical.

More important is what these devices may be doing to our relationships. How present are we with others if we are always thinking of checking our phones to see the latest text, posting, or e-mail? A recent study has linked the use of social media like Facebook to activity in an area of the brain called the *nucleus accumbens*. This brain area is involved with processing rewards in the brain, such as food, money, and sex. It may be more than just words when we talk about the Internet being addictive. I won't even go into how pornography is a distraction and a potential addiction. Suffice it to say that twenty years ago, few of my patients talked about problems with sex addiction. Now it is a common complaint, especially in men with weaker self-regulation due to ADHD and other issues.

Multitasking is likely better in those raised from birth with this technology, but are those immersed in the digital world losing the capacity to sit with an idea, to ponder it, to tolerate the uncertainty of not knowing?

I notice that people fear being left out of the communications loop. An acronym captures this fear: FOMO—Fear of Missing Out. Being in the loop is one kind of relating, but what about mindfulness and presence? Although modern technology allows ever-present connectivity, we wonder whether we're becoming lonelier.

Our modern world gives us many benefits. But we must always be clear about our own personal goals. If being present in important relationships is one of your goals, digital distraction may often interfere. Being present with those we care about is enhanced by less digitalness and more mindfulness.

Given our ever-present digital distraction, it may seem as if the modern world conspires against us to derail our centeredness and further excite our already busy brains. In a way, I think the world really does work against our being at peace. Texting, information overload, politics, advertising: all of these are meant to influence us—usually for purposes that someone else has determined.

Principles of Mindful Living

1. Observation

When we practice mindfulness we pay purposeful attention. We focus on the present moment. And we attend to the unfolding of experience. We do so nonjudgmentally. We have attitudes of curiosity and acceptance. We don't judge ourselves for our thoughts, feelings, urges, and behavior. We try to get away from the "shoulds" and "ought tos." We observe. We try to notice our inner experiences without reacting to them. We seek to be aware, to manifest the opposite of being on automatic pilot. We attend to our behavior and try to tune in to our state of being. Generally, mindfulness helps us attend to our thoughts and experiences, while freeing us from the urge to immediately respond to them. We seek "reflective delay." In terms of relationships, this means: Can you put yourself in the mind of the other person? What is their point of view? Get away from those knee-jerk responses we all have. The goal is less reaction and more reflection.

2. The Power of How

Western societies, in contrast to Eastern cultures, are results-oriented. We seem to act, rather than react. We focus on the goal, rather than the process. Focusing on the goal, although obviously necessary for achievement, moves us away from the process, from the present. In contrast to *The Power of Now*, by Eckhart Tolle, I like to emphasize "The Power of How." How we do something is important. By this I mean: Do I act mindfully, with presence? Do I almost slam the door shut without thinking, or do I gently close it, being aware of the door and my muscles as I do so? Or do I type so fast because I am in a rush that I make more typos than I would if I typed more slowly? How we shut the door or how we type in a rush, really the "how" of any action, can be as important as the end result.

Dedicate yourself to performing more mindfully whatever action you select. Stop rushing when you perform that activity. Close the door gently, almost as if the door were precious. Or walk down the hall more slowly, noticing how your body moves, what your muscles are doing; feel the contact of your feet with the floor as you walk. Be more present. Stop performing this action on automatic pilot.

3. Finding Quiet

Try going to a quiet place and listen to the silence. Have you ever really heard what silence sounds like? How many of us are actually able to be still, to sit calmly, to look inside, and to be clear on who we are and what we want? To be quiet inside and out? Garret Kramer calls the ability to attain this kind of quiet *stillpower*, or "the clarity of mind to live with freedom and ease; the inner source of excellence; the opposite of willpower." A mindful individual is a quieter individual. Such may be anathema to the brash American culture we are used to. It may be hard to escape the endless connectivity and buzz. Yet finding silence and stillness is essential to mindfulness, to inner peace, to calming a busy brain. Increase your quiet time. You need to be alone and undisturbed. Turn off your electronics. No TV, computer, phone, or other distractions. Just be.

4. Slowing Down

Slowing down oneself and the mind undergirds many aspects of mindfulness. When we live in the moment, we live and work with deliberate slowness. When you work with deliberate slowness, at a pace that allows you to pay attention to what you are doing, there is no impatience. You focus more on the moment.

Making movements as small and as efficient as possible also helps. As a young guitar player, it was always my goal to play fast, like my rock idols. However, I soon learned that the only way to learn to play fast was to take small sections of the music, maybe even one measure, and take the time and effort to learn to play them slowly, but perfectly. Only if a guitarist can play something perfectly at a slow rate can he eventually learn to speed up the pace and play fast. There aren't shortcuts, at least not for the guitar, and not for life.

When it comes to meditation and engaging in other mindful pursuits, it is important to emphasize disciplining oneself to keeping things simple and moving slowly. In my own life I've focused on how I open a door by turning the knob (do I do it mindfully, or thoughtlessly by rushing?) or how I type (pounding on the keyboard, or making slower, gentler finger movements?).

5. Breathing

Monitor your breathing. Make sure you are taking slow, calming breaths. Focus on your breathing to help you maintain your observational stance. This is something I practice myself, because as a psychotherapist, it is important for me to monitor and be aware—to be mindful—of what I am experiencing when I meet with a patient. I need to prevent my busy brain from taking over. I consciously try to slow down and not be swept away by the emotional force field that my patient generates. Monitoring my breathing anchors me, and I don't lose myself in the flow of whatever is happening with my patient. As guitar teacher Jamie Andreas says, "The peace I feel as I take this breath is how I measure my success."

Breathing properly is something most individuals with busy brains must master. Practicing breathing, even just a few times each day, can make a difference.

Breathing Exercises

Breathing is a way to cleanse ourselves from unhealthy emotional and physical conditions and calm the busy brain. This concept is worth repeating because breathing is involuntary; most of us take it for granted—and we do it all wrong. In one year an average adult with bad breathing habits inhales about four to five tons of oxygen, but only a thousand pounds of it are actually used; we don't get enough of the oxygen we need and we expel only half the carbon dioxide we should, and we end up robbing ourselves of energy.

This high level of carbon dioxide in the blood can cause the body's fight-or-flight mechanism to kick in. On the other hand, when we breathe freely and deeply, the diaphragm, belly, and chest undulate with the rhythm of each breath, and the whole body is energized with oxygen. Watch a young child or an animal breathe and observe how the body moves when the breathing is natural and relaxed. As adults, most of us have lost this knack. We breathe shallowly. We don't make full use of our diaphragms.

Muscular tension that has evolved over years of poor posture contributes to our shallow breathing, although sedentary work postures and restrictive clothing contribute as well. But we may also unconsciously restrict our breathing as a way of suppressing painful emotions, because the depth of our breathing is also related to the richness and intensity of our feelings. In the process of distancing ourselves from feelings of sadness, anger, or fear, we also block the free flow of purifying energy in the body and diminish our capacity for pleasure.

The following exercises will help you to relax and cleanse your system. With practice you may be able to change your negative breathing patterns, gain vitality, and achieve a calmer state of mind.

➤ For full breathing, lie on the floor, resting your hands on the sides of your rib cage just above the waist, and exhale completely. Inhale slowly through the nose, letting your abdomen rise as much as possible for five seconds, expanding and filling your rib cage. Hold for five seconds. Now slowly exhale through the mouth for ten seconds, expelling all the air from your chest down to your abdomen.

➤ Or, lie on your back with your upper body propped up on a pillow at about a thirty-degree angle. Place a book on your stomach, watching the book rise and fall, to make sure you're breathing with your abdomen and not just your chest. Focus your attention on your nostrils and gently inhale, concentrating on the feeling of taking air in through your nose. Next, gently exhale, and completely relax one group of muscles (shoulders, arms, legs), letting them go limp and heavy. Once you've exhaled fully, breathe in again, continue the process, and switch muscle groups for eight to ten minutes. Try this exercise once a day for optimum effects.

6. Mindfulness Meditation

There's an old Zen saying: You should sit in meditation for twenty minutes a day, unless you're too busy; then you should sit for an hour. Mindfulness meditation is a practice of concentrated focus on a sound, an object, the breath, or attention itself, in order to increase awareness of the present moment. Studies show that it tames the runaway busy brain, increasing creativity, pumping up energy and vitality, reducing muscle pain, lowering stress, boosting organizational skills, and contributing to mental and physical flexibility.

Although meditation has profound effects on our well-being, it doesn't have to be a complicated process. Advanced meditators may prefer to sit on a cushion in a lotus or half-lotus position and focus on their breathing or on a particular chakra (one of the seven centers of spiritual energy in the human body according to yoga philosophy).

Mindfulness Meditation for Beginners

Try these basic steps:

1. Sit in a quiet, comfortable place on a straight-back chair or floor cushion. Relax your muscles; do not lie down.

2. Select a syllable, phrase, or word, such as *one, peace, love,* or *om* to focus on.

3. Close your eyes and follow the rhythm of your breath.

4. Repeat your chosen word, either silently or aloud, as you breathe in and out. If your mind wanders, don't quit. Just let your thoughts go and refocus by repeating your chosen word.

5. Continue for ten to twenty minutes.

When you finish, sit quietly for a minute or two—first with eyes closed, then with eyes open—and perhaps notice how differently you are experiencing your body, mind, and emotions.

———→ ACTION PLAN ←———

The following approaches will help you increase your presence, your mindfulness. It takes discipline to carve out the time to pursue these approaches. But they are worth the effort, and you will reap the benefits as you make the following more and more a part of your daily life.

- **Mindful Meditation:** Take fifteen to twenty minutes daily, first thing in the morning or later in the evening before going to bed.

- **Practice Breathing:** Three times a day—midmorning, midafternoon, and early evening—take a few moments, say five minutes, and practice breathing.

- **The Power of How:** Each week, select a different action that you tend to perform mindlessly and focus on slowing down, being minutely aware of how you perform that action. The action you select should be a simple one—closing a drawer in your kitchen or putting down your hairbrush on the counter in the bathroom.

- **Relationships:** Each day, select one interaction with somebody—ideally an individual with whom you've experienced stress, tension, or anger—and practice interacting with them mindfully.

- **Digital Distraction:** Make a conscious effort to turn off—or at least minimize—your electronic immersion: TV, radio, mobile phone, texting, Internet, Facebook.

5

Righting Relationships

Many of our most joyful and meaningful moments come about through our relationships with others. We gather at weddings and, with tears in our eyes, celebrate the joining of two people; we feel a moment of pure bliss holding our children for the first time—and feel equal joy witnessing many of their antics thereafter; we sneak off early from work to see the old friend who has unexpectedly come to town and we revel in our shared memories over a good meal. Bonds with others add depth and great pleasure to our lives. And we are happier when we feel connected—to family, to friends, to colleagues, to our fellow citizens.

From a more basic point of view, one could even say that the lone individual does not exist in the world. Why? Because humans are social creatures. Eons of evolution have woven social relations into the fabric of our beings. A significant part of brain function is dedicated to regulating our social relations. Throughout our lives we need others to help us feel safe, to be interested in us, and to understand us. Good relationships can make us feel valued, needed, and accepted. A sense of belonging to a community or group increases our well-being, diminishes anxiety, and even boosts our immunity. Connection to others can help soothe our stress and calm our busy brains. We need others to thrive.

Social relationships are key to brain function, and the relationship goes both ways. That is, all things being equal, those with healthier and appropriately balanced brains are more likely to have good relationships; those with unhealthy and less well-balanced brains are more likely to have relationships that are poor. Moreover, healthy relationships have a positive regulating effect on the brain, calming brain activity and reducing the tendency to have a busy brain. And less healthy relationships exert a destructive impact on the brain, causing inner tension and turmoil and an increased risk of a busy, unbalanced brain. It is no wonder that some say that the human brain cannot exist in isolation, underscoring the significant impact of relationships—for good and for ill—on the brain.

Starting at birth, the human brain is prepared to absorb and learn from contact with caretakers. Even as we grow older, safe and healthy attachments to others help us develop our prefrontal cortex; brain growth is activated through positive interactions and relationships. We then are more likely to regulate ourselves properly, control our impulses, understand others, maintain positive expectations, and use our intellectual endowment as a foundation to strive for and achieve appropriate goals and aspirations.

By contrast, less healthy or unsafe relationships can be both physically and psychologically destructive. Brain development is literally stunted; one's psyche, one's spirit, may be gravely damaged. When we are in an unhealthy relationship, we feel the need to be on guard; the world seems like a dangerous place. We have urges to protect ourselves or retreat. We are suspicious, ill at ease; we may distort who we are and what we do. We may be hostile or manipulative. The fight-or-flight system remains on high alert. Basic concerns for safety predominate, rather than drives to grow, explore, and reach for our goals.

Individuals in unhealthy relationships often experience not just psychological but physical symptoms. They have a busy brain that is related to the stress of the unhealthy relationship. The lack of safety in the unhealthy relationship calls into action the sympathetic nervous system, which is always on guard in case of danger situations. The adrenal gland produces epinephrine and cortisol to help the body prepare for possible fight-or-flight responses. Arousal increases, and the amygdala revs up. We feel stressed. We don't focus and concentrate as well. We are prone to multiple psychosomatic issues, such as irritable bowel problems, headaches, and skin eruptions. We don't sleep well. We're more on edge. Even in rather innocuous situations such as when a clerk rings up the wrong item at the grocery store, we overreact with irritation and distrust.

At their worst, unhealthy relationships can be controlling, emotionally invasive, and abusive. They are the opposite of the healthy social integration discussed earlier. Rather than strengthen our confidence and ability to actualize ourselves, bad relationships erode those capabilities.

In fact, the danger that we will erode our capabilities as much as strengthen them is why, as fundamental as relationships are, we tackle them *after* we have worked on some mastery of our inner states. As anyone who has gotten into a screaming match with a colleague or a spouse knows, much of our ability to manage our relationships depends on our own good impulse control. If we have good impulse control, our actions and reactions are mediated by our PFC, which allows us to regulate ourselves and calm our own limbic system first, a crucial step in a high-conflict situation. Without that self-mastery of our inner states, our ability to master our external relationships is that much more difficult. We must first manage our own negativity, rewrite our stories, and work on our mindfulness if we expect to succeed in attaining healthier relationships.

That said, that our brain is as plastic as it is—that we can, as discussed earlier, effectively change our self-narratives—should give us great hope that we can change our relationships. If we can rewrite our stories, we can also improve our relationships. If we can regulate our minds and ourselves, we can better regulate our interactions with others.

The first step, as in managing negativity, is to distance ourselves enough to be able to construct more accurate accounts of what our relationships are. As difficult as it is to construct full, truthful narratives of who we are, constructing accurate accounts of our relationships can be equally difficult. Getting perspective on ourselves is tough. Gaining perspective on ourselves plus others can be even tougher. Yet lacking perspective on our relationships can be costly. Both parties contribute to unhealthy relationships. If we do not understand the relationships we are in, we may stick with adversarial relationships and partners who harm our health rather than improve it. Distinguishing between healthy and unhealthy relationships is a skill many need help with.

The Horizontal/Vertical Model of Relationships—How to Think About Your Relationships

How do we recognize an unhealthy relationship? Let me present a helpful model, one that will help you look at your own relationships and become clearer about what is going on.

We all know what actors do. They play roles. A good actor can play different kinds of roles. Well, we all play roles, too. There is a difference between the roles we play and those that actors play. When an actor takes on a role, it is a conscious and deliberate choice. The roles we play are less conscious, often outside our awareness. In what follows, I'll ask you to think of yourself as an actor, playing various roles, and to be more aware of the roles you assume.

Interestingly, we can play different roles at different times, with different people and in different situations. For example, although I am generally a mild person, in the presence of a friend who is particularly passive I notice that my behavior becomes strong. I am bold with him almost to the point of bullying. I don't like this part of myself, but something about my friend's passivity seems to evoke this strong reaction in me that can bring out some of my less desirable behavior. And it is not just my friend's passivity that is the issue; I am not blaming him. Rather, I am aware of certain aspects of my own psychology that contribute to my acting in this strong, almost bullying fashion. I'll spare you the details, but the key point is that I, like everybody, am capable of shifting between playing roles that are weaker and those that are more powerful.

The horizontal/vertical relationship model helps us think about these points. Imagine a barbell shape—two circles connected by a line. The two circles represent you and another person. The connecting line represents your relationship. If the barbell is horizontal, the relationship is a safe one. There is openness and honesty. The relationship partners are equal. The relationship is cooperative. There is no need to distort the other person, who is accepted as he or she is. Truth can exist in this relationship. These relationships grow and develop. Neither party dominates; there is a safe equality. There is a cooperative give-and-take of two subjectivities.

Now consider when the barbell is vertical. This represents a hierarchical relationship, one in which there is a real or imagined power imbalance. The parties are seen as unequal. One party is above the other and dominates the weaker party. A vertical relationship is adversarial and competitive. Think of top and bottom, winner and loser. The roles are opposites. Top represents winning, dominating, controlling the bottom. Bottom is losing, dominated, submissive, controlled, and subordinate. Each category (top, bottom) defines the other.

In a vertical relationship, it is difficult to break out of this adversarial pattern. The words that competitors use in a contest (top, bottom) are shaped by their need to eliminate truth—in an adversarial relationship, where competition and struggle exist, opponents jostle for the upper hand. In a vertical relationship, we behave like spies trying to outmanipulate one another, or like poker players hiding the truth, the cards we're holding, from the other players. It's an adversarial, zero-sum game. If we don't win, we lose. Language used in vertical relationships is used not for the sake of truth but as propaganda, designed to mislead the other. We try to exploit others, to make them helpless by confusing them with lies and uncertainty.

The adversarial vertical mode engenders danger, which often is unconscious. In a vertical relationship, we behave as if the other is an enemy. The tendency is for a black-and-white, fixed relationship. Our brain function regresses. We don't use the PFC to manage nuance but to come up with schemes to protect ourselves or trick the other, or at least to hide the truth. We regress to a more primitive, limbic system way of functioning—aggression, struggle, lying, self-protection. Our fight-or-flight system is activated because of the struggle inherent in vertical relationships, and a busy brain can be the result.

Here are some examples of vertical relationships: The critical boss who always has negative comments about your work, no matter what (critic/criticized). The telephone solicitor calling elderly people trying to get their bank account numbers to steal money from them (predator/prey). The charismatic—but emotionally and physically violent—male who manipulates his girlfriend into taking the blame for all relationship problems, even when he hits her (victimizer/victim). The enmeshed mother who manipulates her adult children through guilt; "You're breaking my heart," she says, in response to their natural efforts at separating and defining their own lives, especially if they find a partner from a different race or religious tradition (guiltor/guilted). The television preacher who presents teachings and dogma in a black-and-white fashion; he is pure and holy, and unbelievers are dirty sinners (pure/impure). Politicians who devalue their political opponents, not recognizing their opponents as sincere human beings (idealized/devalued). We could come up with more role patterns, but you get the point. Vertical relations involve a power differential and an adversarial stance. Manipulation is always just beneath the surface.

Emotional Manipulation
and Predatory Others

The idealist in me wishes that emotional manipulation were not a fact of life. But the reality is that our interactions with others are intended to create a certain emotional state in the other person. Often this occurs partly or wholly out of awareness, for one or both of the parties.

We must recognize that such manipulation is ever-present, in ourselves and others. We try to influence one another because of the needs we have as social creatures. We are emotional manipulators. And we are all susceptible to the impact of such manipulation.

Why are we susceptible to emotional manipulation and abuse? Because we all have basic human needs. And because we all have more primitive aspects to our functioning: the reptilian and limbic brain areas that can make us experience the world in black-and-white terms. In part, we are attracted to others (and their influence and emotional manipulation) who seem to be able to give us what we lack. Cult members are likely attracted to their cult because it promises to give them what they feel they lack (belonging, esteem, self-actualization, etc.). We are strongly attracted to others who seem to offer us safety and certainty. In a less problematic example, you may even idealize your mentors (they are all-powerful, know everything, have all the answers . . .) and devalue yourself. The world is complex, at times frightening, and can feel unbearable. A pied piper can come along, promising us fulfillment for all of our unmet needs, and we may find him irresistible and follow blindly.

Lest I be presenting things too simplistically, let me take a moment to underscore that relationships are always co-created. Each party, each actor, contributes to the evolving drama. Problems in early attachment relationships can predispose an individual to significant difficulties later in life, including major problems in relationships. If one has no history of solid relationships, a healthy give-and-take—horizontal—relationship pattern is much more difficult to achieve. One will most likely have to overcorrect for stunted development of both brain and psyche, and a template of a safe, healthy relationship must be created from scratch. No mean feat.

Emotional abuse is an extreme example of vertical relationships. Humans can and do prey on one another, emotionally and physically. Often, in modern, "civilized" society, human predators are well camouflaged, making our recognition of them problematic. Most of us are aware of emotionally abusive relationships between a powerful partner and a dependent partner with fewer resources—emotional or financial. The dependent partner has low self-esteem, which is further attacked by the predatory, emotionally abusive partner who passes up no opportunity to debase and further lower the dependent partner's poor sense of self. Everything is the dependent partner's fault. The abuser isolates him or her from others, further solidifying the abuser's hold, strengthening the dependence, and deepening the vicious cycle. The victim of the abuser minimizes the problems and refuses to see the nature of the extremely unhealthy relationship in which he or she is trapped.

The cycle may not stop there. Emotionally trapped people may go on to manipulate others to solidify their sense of control, which seems to have spiraled away from them. Sera's story below provides an illustration of how difficulties with early attachment figures and the violation of a child's innocence can jump-start a vicious cycle of unhealthy relationships.

Sera's Courage to Heal

Sera was in her early thirties when she came to see me because of troubles at work. Specifically, although she was bright and capable, her subordinates, especially male subordinates, experienced her as devaluing, harsh, and excessively critical. She knew that behind her back, the men called her a "castrating bitch." Sera could own that she contributed to troublesome interactions at work, but she did not understand why. Intelligent, with a quick wit and a sharp tongue,

Sera, who was single, grew up in a third-world country dominated by strong patriarchal and religious traditions that clearly put women in second place. Longing to escape her native country, Sera studied hard, won a scholarship to attend university in the United Kingdom, and eventually made her way to the United States, where she worked for a think tank in Washington, D.C. The quality of her analytic and written work was superb; it was the difficulty with male subordinates that was the problem.

In our initial meetings I could see, in her relationship with me, what she enacted with her male subordinates. She could be critical with me, quickly dismissing what I had to say to her. I began to feel helpless and angry, but I held my tongue until I thought we had a strong enough relationship that I could call Sera's attention to what she was enacting with me. I began to comment, gently at first, on the harshness of her comments toward me and the way she rejected nearly everything I had offered her.

Sera eventually was able to acknowledge that there was something valid in what I was pointing out. She began to wonder why her first impulses were to attack me and reject anything I said.

Soon thereafter, Sera told me that she had something horrible that had happened to her during her childhood; she had never told anyone about it, other than her parents when she was a young girl, and they minimized and rejected what she told them. She told me that she didn't know if she could trust me enough to tell me. Sera said that if she shared this horrible thing and I didn't believe her or react appropriately, she couldn't bear it. She would have to break off our treatment.

Sera worked up the courage to tell me what horrible thing had happened to her. What she told me was that she was sexually abused from ages five to eleven by a prominent older man from her village. He told her that he would kill her and her entire family if she breathed a word of the abuse to anyone; she had reason to believe him. Week after week, month after month, year after year, the abuse continued, ceasing only when the perpetrator died suddenly of a heart attack. Sera, relieved, then worked up the courage to tell her family, but they completely rejected her story, saying that this respected man would never do such things. They told Sera that something was wrong with her for making up such wild accusations.

Devastated by her family's rejection of her when she shared the abuse with them, from that moment on Sera never trusted another soul. She vowed to escape her family and her country, which she did through devotion to her studies, using her high intelligence and rage as motivation.

Established in the United States, Sera started at the think tank. But there was more to the story. In the U.S., Sera began cruising bars to pick up men. This was her pattern: Sit at the bar, alone; exchange glances with a man; and accept his offer of a drink. Simple banter progressed to sharing of personal details. Soon, Sera indicated that she would be receptive to spending the night with this man, and back to Sera's condo they went. At the condo, there were more drinks, and they would move to Sera's bedroom. Apparent romance continued, clothing was removed, and soon both parties were naked in Sera's bed. Foreplay continued, the man was erect, and then it happened. Sera would sit up, turn on a light, look at his penis, and say, "You call that a penis? I've seen clitorises that are bigger than that!" With that castrating comment, the man became deflated, literally and figuratively. "Get out of here," she'd shout. "Leave, and take your microdick with you." The man would grab his clothes and leave. The astonishing thing was that Sera, who enacted this drama with dozens of men, was never physically assaulted by any of them.

Healing the Hurt

Reading this drama, you may wonder, "What now?" What are the keys to healing such a deep hurt like Sera's? What are the keys to healing your own deep hurt? Healing requires courage. It involves being able to acknowledge, bear, and put into perspective the pain we have experienced. There is no growth, no healing, without pain. And we need courage to face our pain.

We also need courage to begin to give up old patterns. As dysfunctional as they can be, our old patterns worked for us in some ways. These patterns arose because they were the best we could do at the time. Beginning to give up old, unhealthy patterns throws us into a state in which we can feel defenseless. For example, as Sera contemplated what it would be like to give up her predatory pattern with men, she feared that she would revert to the position of a helpless child, again threatened, taken advantage of, and exploited by all men. It was difficult to realize that there could be another way, a way of living and being in which she would be neither predator nor victim.

Sera's Recovery

I helped Sera understand how she had turned the passive experience of being the victim of childhood sexual assault into the active experience of being the perpetrator. I drew for her the diagrams of horizontal and vertical relationships. She could understand more clearly that as a child she had experienced the passive, helpless, bottom side of a vertical relationship. Now, as an adult, she had been enacting the top part of the vertical relationship in her sexual drama and also, in more muted form, with her male subordinates at work. I was also able to point out how earlier with me and to some extent even up to this point, she symbolically castrated me by rejecting most of my comments, making me experience a muted form of the helplessness she experienced as a little girl.

Having laid herself bare, having put all her pain and trauma on the table, so to speak, Sera asked me, "What now?" I had some ideas, but I reflected Sera's question back to her: "What do *you* want now?" It was important for Sera to find some answers within herself. And it was important that Sera find within herself a wish for things to be different, a wish for change.

Sera told me that she wasn't sure that she wanted to change. Part of her did, but it seemed risky. Without her abrasive, attacking stance toward men, not to mention the sexual dramas that she acted out, she might feel helpless and might be destroyed by men. She wondered, though, could there be another way? Could there be a way in the middle, between predator and victim? Could she find that within herself? Would she want to try?

A psychotherapist is often tempted to help a patient by offering advice, urging, prodding, and the like, to help the person move toward more healthy and adaptive behavior. At times it is useful for a therapist to do all these things. But this was not what Sera needed. What Sera needed from me at that point was someone who was there for her, who cared, but who could allow her the space and time to struggle, to find the truth about her own wishes and desires. In essence, I was enacting a horizontal relationship with Sera, neither attempting to control her nor accepting her intermittent attempts to control and devalue me. Indeed, although we had reached the point of a trusting relationship that offered Sera the safety she needed, Sera still at times behaved toward me with her old attacking and rejecting style. Because we had a good treatment relationship by this point, I was able to point out to Sera those "There you go again" moments, and she could accept my interventions and analyze the motives behind her behavior.

Over a number of months, Sera and I were able to look at what she might want for herself in relationships toward men and women. What kind of life would she want? Sera, who really had not been close to anyone in her life, said that she thought she would want a life partner, probably a husband. She wasn't sure about children, given her own childhood experiences, but she might be willing to consider children in the future.

By this point in our treatment, I began to hear from Sera that her relationship toward men at work seemed to have changed. She had become more and more aware of the critical, devaluing, and indeed psychologically castrating behavior she enacted toward men, and she wished to try to change. Her coworkers and supervisor began to comment that Sera's relationships with her male subordinates had improved. They no longer dreaded working with her. She began to have more lighthearted moments at work and began to show an interest in the personal lives of her employees. All of this affected the work output of her unit, which showed increased efficiency and improved quality of the written analyses that they provided.

Words are the tools we use in a book, but words cannot easily convey all the nuances of Sera's path toward healing. There was no quick fix. We worked together for months, going back and forth as she dared to make changes and step ahead, only to pull back, returning to her negative thoughts and stories. But eventually she remained more often in a psychological posture in which she felt positive about her capacity to have healthy, horizontal relationships with others, especially men.

Out of town for a conference, Sera met Steve, a man who did similar work for another think tank. They met during a cocktail hour, seemed to hit it off, and Steve signaled his interest and definitely pursued her. Here was an opportunity. Could Sera find a new way of being with a man? Would she revert to the old ways with Steve? Or would she flee from Steve, feeling unprotected if she dropped her previous predatory stance? Sera felt scared but took some time and realized that she felt safe and secure enough to try a new way.

Sera took things slowly with Steve. No quick sexual encounters, no castrating comments about his penis. Rather, she took the time to get to know him. She found him to be outgoing, friendly, modest, and athletic. Steve was not academically brilliant like Sera, but he was smart enough, and his social and emotional intelligence were good. He laughed easily, which Sera liked, never finding that easy herself. That Steve lived in another city seemed to help; there was less pressure to move things along quickly in the relationship. They kept in touch by phone, Skype, and frequent texting for more than a year. Once or twice a month, one would fly to the other's city, where they spent a long weekend together. When winter came, they took a weeklong trip to the Caribbean, the longest time they'd spent together. It was a success, Sera told me.

As Sera's relationship with Steve continued to deepen, they discussed living together. Eventually Steve decided to move to Washington, D.C. When Steve relocated and moved in with Sera, she felt panicked. What if this was a mistake? Maybe it was better to be alone and safe than to risk intimacy and being controlled or controlling him. Although Sera had an upsurge of her old fears, she was able to use the tools she had acquired in our work together. Living together was not a mistake. In fact, she enjoyed the additional closeness that cohabitating brought to the couple. Their sex life continued to be gratifying for both; Sera never acted out with Steve the devaluing and castrating behavior she had with her previous conquests several years earlier. Two years after he moved in, Steve proposed, and Sera and Steve married six months later.

Sera and I stopped meeting regularly after the marriage, but I get a note from her now and then. Things continue to go well, and she continues to express gratitude for my help. Sera talks about being reborn through our work. As for me, I have silent gratitude for being able to participate in, witness, and learn from the struggles on the path toward healing of someone who was severely wounded as a child yet had the courage to face her fears and risk a better way of living and being. Sera had changed from having a predominantly vertical relationship style to a horizontal one, in which truth and intimacy abounded, without excessive control, predation, or victimization. A remarkable transformation.

The hurts we suffer early in life can be so severe that they can warp our capacity to have anywhere near a normal, healthy horizontal relationship. This was the case for Sera, who was fortunate not to have been assaulted or killed during her repetitive, compulsive reversal of passive to active in her sexual acting out.

Development always involves a mixture of nature and nurture. Nature is what we are born with, which includes our physical, intellectual, and genetic endowment. Nurture refers to our life experiences, including the important relations we develop. Nurture can influence which aspects of our nature get expressed. Good attachment relationships and nurturing can help us overcome even suboptimal natural endowment. Less good nurturing and attachment relationships can cast a dark shadow over the rest of our lives. The good news is that healing is possible. Rewriting your stories and replacing vertical relationships with horizontal ones—through self-reflection or psychotherapy—can help you overcome locked-in brain-behavior patterns and improve your life.

Hopefully you did not endure the deprivations and traumas that Sera experienced. Hers is an extreme case. I described Sera's story in such detail to show how healing occurs when early wounds are so severe. Insight-oriented psychotherapy or psychoanalysis can be important in helping severely wounded human beings heal and grow, actually lifesaving at times. But not everybody needs intensive psychotherapy. Many people can heal themselves and their relationships without the aid of a therapist, especially if the wounds they carry from early life are less deep than Sera's.

Here are approaches to help you better understand your relationships, heal the hurt, make positive changes, and move from vertical to more horizontal relationship patterns.

Relationship Assessment

Recognize and understand the kinds of relationships you have. Be curious. Think in terms of vertical and horizontal relationships. You'll naturally want to focus on vertical relationships because they are the ones that give you problems.

Critic/Criticized

Are you a critic, constantly berating your young adult daughter, who seems helpless? Or in your marriage, are you the criticized one, often feeling powerless against your dominating spouse?

Susan constantly berated her teen son Kyle. He didn't study enough. He wasted his time on video games. Kyle's girlfriend wasn't smart enough. Susan insulted Kyle by saying that he must be a dummy himself to have such a stupid girlfriend. Susan wasn't used to looking inside herself, to understand that she had absorbed her own father's critical nature. She took her criticisms of Kyle as statements of truth, not her own subjective interpretations. In reality, Kyle was much like any teen, mature at some moments and less mature at others. Susan's constant criticism did nothing to help him develop into the confident, functional adult that he needed to be.

Susan, like many critics, justified her disrespect of Kyle by saying she thought that her critiques were helpful to him. After all, he probably should study more. What she needed to do, however, was to reassess her motivation for the constant criticism. Was she criticizing to help him or because somehow she felt disrespected by his inattention to her suggestions? Was she trying to help him improve his behavior, or did she want to affix the blame on him and away from herself for his failures? Could Susan look at it from Kyle's point of view? Could Kyle look at it from Susan's? Was there a real disagreement between them? If there is a genuine disagreement in approach, rather than blaming the other person (or merely accepting the blame if you are the criticized one), it's important to see the relationship as a two-way street. Disagreements naturally arise in any relationship. They should be discussed in a way that the relationship and each party can grow and deepen.

In a healthy relationship, both parties intrinsically respect and value the other. They talk out their differences. The fundamental relationship currency in a healthy, horizontal relationship—as opposed to vertical relationship—is honesty.

Parent/Child

Think about your early life experiences that contributed to your having unhealthy, vertical relationship patterns. Were your parents overbearing, making it difficult to find and develop your own strength? Did your father devalue you, calling you stupid, because your undiagnosed ADHD made it difficult to succeed in school? Were you a "parentified child," forced to grow up too early, needing to reverse roles and parent your alcohol-abusing mother?

Recognizing the roots of this unhealthy, vertical relationship pattern can help us catch ourselves from repeating the same pattern in other relationships. Keep in mind that adults do not need to parent one another. In fact, a nonrescuing stance, a horizontal relationship pattern, is a much healthier way to live. If you are someone who goes through life trying to rescue people, recognizing this can be a major step forward in permitting yourself to play the part of an equal rather than a parent. Stephan, one of my patients, assumed the adult role early because he needed constantly to rescue his family from his father's gambling disasters. For Stephan, acknowledging that he was always trying to rescue the people he cared about allowed him to make a major shift, liberating him from the unconscious prison in which he'd been jailed.

Dominant/Dominated

Are you troubled because you are always the dominant one in relationships? One of my patients, Cecily, was an extraordinarily successful entrepreneur. She drove her colleagues and employees to great heights of success. Cecily didn't want to have to play the same role at home—yet her children and husband all seemed incompetent, virtually demanding that she be a hard-driving executive of the family, all the while rebelling against her efforts. Cecily wanted a more horizontal relationship with her family, at least with her husband and older teen children. Recognizing this pattern, she realized that the only person she could try to change was herself. She closely monitored her behavior within the family, consciously deciding not to give too much, so that her husband and children needed to take on more of life's responsibilities themselves. Pulling back from her previous do-everything-for-everybody-in-the-family stance, although not so easy to do, gradually helped her husband and children to begin to flower themselves as competent, responsible human beings.

Note that complete equality in marriage is most often a mirage. And in fact, some researchers have found that marriages with one dominant partner are often more stable and successful than marriages in which both partners refuse to ever take a subordinate role. Asymmetry can guarantee that decisions on everything from where to go on vacation to what television program to watch are made with minimal conflict and upset. The key here, however, is that the dominant person is tolerant and respectful of his or her partner and that the dominant partner's efforts are dedicated toward the welfare of the couple or of the other person. Abusive dominance should never be tolerated, in marriage or in other relationships. Signs of an abusive relationship include threats, intimidation, insults, and humiliation. If these occur regularly, the relationship is at least an unhealthy one, if not unsafe.

Victimizer/Victim

One of the most striking things about vertical relationship patterns is that our behavior can be strongly shaped by our experiences, and yet we may not be fully aware of the roles we play or why we play them. This was the case for Jessica, who I would eventually learn was unconsciously caught up in her victimhood. In an attempt to avoid victimization, she tried to keep everyone at arm's length, resulting in a barren life.

Jessica had trouble getting close to anybody. An engineer, forty-three, accomplished in her field but lonely, Jessica had no friends and no romantic interests. On paper Jessica was a good catch. But we don't live our life on paper.

Only with trepidation did Jessica come to see me for help; she'd heard from a coworker that I'd helped the coworker's wife. Jessica wasn't even sure what she wanted from me. All she knew was that she felt as if she were going through the motions. Although not really depressed or anxious, Jessica realized that her life felt empty and she wanted something different.

I met initially with Jessica for several sessions to begin to get to know her. What was remarkable was how barren our meetings were. Jessica, if not quite boring, seemed almost robotic. She told me about her work, the projects, her supervisor, her coworkers. But nobody ever came alive in her descriptions; they all seemed like cogs in some big machine. When I commented to Jessica that I had difficulty imaging the people she described, she said she often felt the same way about the people in her life. This seemed like a good opportunity to look more at her intimate relationships, or lack of them. I learned that Jessica wasn't dating anyone currently. She'd date from time to time, but there was no closeness, no attachments. Out loud, I wondered why. Jessica said that she wondered too.

Our curiosity resulted in Jessica's telling me more about her mother, who was deceased. She had been a cranky woman, even bitter, miserable, complaining constantly. I learned that when Jessica "misbehaved," as punishment her mother put dead insects on Jessica's pillow and shoved her face into the pillow. I found this difficult to believe, or maybe I didn't want to believe that parents could be so cruel with their children. Regardless, this story seemed legitimate and was one of numerous episodes of cruelty at the hands of her mother that Jessica recounted.

As a child, Jessica tried to stay away from her mother. Often she was successful, but not all the time. Jessica's father, who traveled out of town often for business, was rarely present to buffer Jessica's mother's cruelty.

As Jessica grew older, she kept her mother at arm's length, taking every opportunity to stay away from her. Applying herself to her studies, she won a full scholarship to an engineering school hundreds of miles from home. Jessica felt liberated by her college experience away from her mother and rarely visited her parents.

I was pleased that we seemed to be getting to the bottom of Jessica's issues. She was able to acknowledge, bear, and put into perspective the challenges she faced growing up in the clutches of her cruel mother. And she began to understand more clearly why she kept other people at a distance.

It was at that point that something curious happened in our relationship: Jessica canceled three appointments in a row. Then she left a curt message about needing to put her work with me on hold; she said that she would call me back at some point in the future.

I value the autonomy of my patients. Yet I also know from experience that patients often develop fears and flee therapy when things start getting "hot." I called Jessica and we spoke briefly. I told Jessica that I wanted to respect her wishes but that I also suspected that something was going on between us that was important to try to understand. I asked if she would be willing to return, at least for a session or two, so we might think together about what was going on. Jessica told me she needed to give it some thought, which she did. The next day, Jessica called back, telling me that she would see me the following week at our regular time.

At her next appointment, Jessica told me that she had been having upsetting dreams, really nightmares. Anxiously, Jessica began to describe the nightmare she'd been having for the previous few weeks. In the dream, Jessica enters a classroom. She is the only one there; she waits for the instructor. Soon, the professor enters, and it turns out that the professor is a female cannibal. Jessica is horrified and runs from the classroom. She usually woke up after this dream, heart pounding.

I asked Jessica if she had any thoughts about the dream. As a psychoanalyst, I've helped patients analyze thousands of dreams over the years, and it is useful to begin exploration of the dream with a simple open-ended question. Jessica said that being the only student in the classroom seemed connected to the fact that she was the only child in her family. Indeed, a classroom in someone's dream could represent the learning situation a child faces in his or her family of origin. We talked about how Jessica might have felt as a child that her mother wanted to devour her. In fact, in a broader sense, Jessica's mother was so overbearing that she seemed to want to consume her life.

Psychotherapy can be a powerful relationship, in which old and new emotions and urges are re-created and become directed toward the therapist. I had an inkling that there was more to the cannibal image in Jessica's dream. Because Jessica had more or less fled from our therapy, I decided to take a leap. "Any thoughts about

'C Annibal'?" I asked. Jessica paused. "C Annibal, C Annibal," she said. And then, suddenly, "Oh my God, 'C Annibal' means 'see Annibali'!"

With that realization, we were able to look at how Jessica's relationship with a mother who was likely disturbed and psychologically cannibalistic had warped her expectations about all future relationships, including the relationship with me. She needed to keep away from everybody because she unconsciously expected them to try to make her a victim and consume her, much as she had experienced with her mother. She unconsciously felt she needed to flee from therapy—from me—to save herself. Jessica could not imagine that she could have an independent existence as a human being if she had a relationship with anyone else. She thought that she could exist only as a separate individual apart from others.

Jessica's cannibal dream, to which we would often return, was the real opening for Jessica's healing and growth. Over the next few months we were able to deepen our understanding of what the cannibal theme meant to Jessica. I explained to Jessica that we can think about relationships in horizontal and vertical terms. Could she even begin to imagine having horizontal relationships, in which there would be honesty and openness, and neither party controlled or took advantage of the other? This was difficult for Jessica to imagine. She had never before had a horizontal relationship. The only relationship pattern she knew was the vertical one in which she tried to fend off being devoured by a troubled other person like her mother. Yet Jessica had courage, which I admired. Life had little zest for Jessica, little meaning, and no passion; she was just going through the motions, as she'd done all her life. She vowed to try to change.

Healing, change, and growth take time. But Jessica was able to continue in treatment with me, to acknowledge and put into perspective her fears of the all-consuming control of others. She was able to move beyond a reflexive expectation of being a victim in a relationship toward a position in which she could accept and even be open to positive, mutually satisfying experiences with others— horizontal relationships. Jessica started to do volunteer work teaching English as a second language, which she found gratifying; helping yourself by helping others is often a good strategy. While teaching in the program, Jessica met the director, who was fresh off a nasty divorce. He was wounded but experienced Jessica's personality as naturally gentle and safe. They would go on to form a long-term, mutually satisfying romantic relationship.

How might you recognize your tendency to play the unconscious role of a victim, like Jessica? Here are some indicators:

➤ When around other individuals, you find that you can't tap into your wants, needs, and values. You can't find them within yourself.

➤ Around other people, you can't think clearly, as if your brain is partly frozen.

➤ You have an urge to run away—literally or figuratively—when you are with other people.

How can you stop being a victim? Try these suggestions:

➤ If you find that you cannot tap into your wants, needs, and values, stop and reflect on what is happening. What is going on in the relationship that seems to be causing you to lose touch with important parts of yourself? See if you can identify subtle factors in the relationship that are closing you down. Is it a veiled threat? Intimidation? An ultimatum? Identify what the subtle communications are, get clearer on your contribution, and decide how and what you can change.

➤ "Strike while the iron is cold." Reflect on the relationship when you are not so caught up in the heat of the moment. What specifically is being asked of you in the relationship? How are you responding and possibly contributing to your experience of being a victim? I often say that there can be activity in passivity. For example, in being passive and excusing a partner's emotional or physical abuse—"because of his work stress"—we enable the victimizing behavior toward us to continue. Take responsibility for your feelings and behavior; be open about what is not healthy for you in the relationship and how you need things to be different.

➤ Identify events or relationships from the past that have shaped you and your victim role. Imagine that you could rewrite those events and relationships. How would you change the old script of victimhood into a healthier one?

➤ Imagine and play out in your mind how you want to change your victimhood role. What kinds of limits can you set? How can you own and communicate your feelings? How can you respond differently to a situation that frustrates you or makes you angry? How can you use "I can" and "I will" statements to empower yourself or to stop being passive in a situation that requires you to step up and be more active? In twelve-step programs, they say, "Fake it till you make it." That's not a bad strategy as we seek to grow.

Manipulator/Manipulated

Kurt was a young but brilliant manager of a financial services firm. His keenly honed empathic understanding allowed him to manipulate others, almost without their awareness. Overworked, underpaid employees would schedule a meeting to discuss their work frustrations with Kurt, including being underpaid and wanting to request a raise. But Kurt was so perceptive and skilled at manipulation that the employee would leave the meeting without a raise but with increased responsibilities. They never saw it coming. Only the savviest individuals were able to figure out afterward what Kurt had done to them so masterfully.

In an unhealthy, vertical relationship, the other party is interested in themselves, not you. They might even threaten you as leverage to get what they want. The threats could be of harm to you physically or otherwise. Kurt, of course, was so skillful at his manipulations that he never needed to utter threats of any kind.

The actions and behavior of others seem naturally to cause us to act in a certain way, sometimes because of our own psychological makeup. Think of the saying "He brings out the worst in me." If the other person is a manipulator, do you too easily fall into the role of the manipulated? Once you have recognized another's manipulations, you must recognize and claim the power within yourself to reassert your own desires and interests.

If someone in your life plays the role of manipulator, try these steps:

1. Create physical distance. Imagine holding out your hand and keeping the other at arm's length. Perhaps even shout "Stop" to them in your play-acting scenario.

2. Assert your priorities. Once you have established imagined physical distance between the two of you, imagine asking the other person what they want. Then respond with your feelings about what they want and tell them what you want. Imagine another demand that they would make. "Stop" them. Give yourself some space. Then respond with what you desire in the pretend scenario. Remember, you have the right to say no, to assert your needs and desires, to be treated with respect, and to want something different in any given scenario.

3. Put the spotlight back on them. Practice asking the other person if what they are asking of you sounds reasonable or fair. Often forcing them to consider their own request will highlight its unreasonableness in a way that makes them back down or back off.

4. Learn to say no. Be polite but firm. Stand your ground.

Remember that though some of this involves play-acting, just the practice of articulating what you want in a situation will empower you the next time that someone tries to manipulate you into doing what is good for them rather than what accords with your own values and priorities.

It is important to maintain hope. People can change; you can change. Healing and growth are possible. Remember that change is rarely quick and healing takes time. Be gentle with your expectations of yourself. Find the goodness within yourself and others and build on that. Keep in mind that good things come from difficult experiences, such as a more profound understanding of yourself and of all human beings as illuminated by the efforts to improve your relationships. By rerighting unhealthy relationships, you turn down your fight-or-flight alarms, calming your busy brain.

ACTION PLAN

➤ Think of yourself and the other person as actors in a play. Write down the roles you and the other party are playing. Are you the guilted child to the guilting mother? Are they the idealized to your more devalued self? How does the other person evoke that role in you? Remember that you can play both parts at different times, depending on the situation and the people with whom you are involved. You are shining a spotlight on each actor in the drama to clarify who is doing what to whom. And now that you've recognized the dynamic, what can you do to equalize it?

➤ Think about what roles you would like to play in relationships. What would your behavior and life look like if you moved toward more horizontal relationships?

➤ Evaluate your actions and motivations. What actions are taking place in the relationship? What are you doing? What is the other person doing? Think of the words that you and the other person speak as actions designed to do something. If I complain or praise, I am trying to affect the other person emotionally, regardless of whether my actions are a conscious decision. My words and the emotions attached to them are designed to create a certain emotional state in the other person.

➤ Identify and assert your values. Defend yourself from manipulative others by being aware, monitoring yourself. Always remember that you have a choice. Determining what is for you in your life is probably the most important thing you can do. Know who you are; know what you want. Decide on and write down the values that are key in your life. A healthy relationship is one in which there are commonly shared values and beliefs. Reflect on your core values when you feel the gusts of other people's emotional influence. If a relationship is consistently toxic, end it. We would never eat rotten food. Why should we absorb the toxicity of others if we have a choice?

➤ Seek sounding boards. In less severe cases, turning toward a trusted friend or mentor can help you clarify what you need to do to improve a relationship, to turn one that is vertical into one that is more horizontal. In some cases, you might use your friend's or mentor's support or borrow their strength to bring an end to a toxic relationship.

➤ Seek professional help, if needed. Sera had profound early traumas and severe disruptions in early attachment relationships. In cases of relationship difficulties rooted in such early problematic relationships with caregivers and other significant individuals, like Sera's abuse, treatment with an experienced psychotherapist who understands how to create a safe place to bear, explore, understand, and master issues can make all the difference.

➤ Maintain hope. People can change. Growth and healing are possible.

ADDRESSING SPECIFIC ISSUES

6

Bored Brains, Excitable Brains: ADHD

Jeremy was a bright student who worked hard and succeeded academically. He was bored easily, but he loved to learn and had done exceptionally well at a prestigious university. As a result, Jeremy attained his dream of being accepted to med school. He expected that medical studies would be an extension of the smorgasbord of intellectual challenges he had experienced in college. But Jeremy was soon disappointed. Rather than learning information essential to patient care, Jeremy had to memorize by rote an extraordinary amount of uninteresting information such as the number of proteins on the outer surface of a certain virus. The memorization of more or less unimportant facts made Jeremy and his brain feel half asleep. He resorted to simultaneously listening to both the television and the radio to remain awake enough and have sufficient attention to commit to memory what he needed to for his exams. That Jeremy's brain began to fall asleep when confronted with uninteresting information was an important sign that Jeremy had attention deficit/hyperactivity disorder (ADHD).

Over more than a century, several different labels have been used to describe ADHD. Years ago, the term was *minimal brain dysfunction*. After that it was called *attention deficit disorder* (ADD). Later, we used the label ADD for the inattentive subtype, and the label of ADHD for the subtype with hyperactivity. Now, officially, it's all called ADHD, with ADHD subtypes for inattention, hyperactivity/impulsivity, and inattention and hyperactivity/impulsivity combined. Confusing, I know.

Using brain SPECT, we can even carve the ADHD pie into smaller slices, depending on other aspects that can be present—such as overactivity in different areas of the limbic system, temporal lobe problems, and low cerebellar function. Interested readers should refer to the revised edition of Daniel Amen's *Healing ADD* for more information on ADHD subtypes. For the sake of our discussion here, I am going to focus on ADHD with inattentive features that may or may not be accompanied by hyperactivity and impulsivity. ADHD is a legitimate brain disorder that results in problems with low stimulation and boredom. Because the PFC, or governing system of the brain, is impaired in ADHD, there is also often difficulty with *executive functions* or common forms of self-regulation, including focus, attention, concentration, goal-setting, planning, organization, and impulse control.

Many people assume that individuals with ADHD have overactive brains. After all, people with ADHD often seem scattered; we hear them leaping from one topic to the next in conversation or see them darting around the room rather than settling in one place. Yet in many cases, the exact opposite is true. Many individuals with ADHD feel understimulated, even bored because the activity in the front of their brains is too low. Think of Jeremy, frantically pumping up the volume on his radio and television, all in order to stimulate his brain sufficiently to commit boring facts to memory. Brain SPECT imaging of individuals with ADHD typically shows low function in the prefrontal cortex—what we've called the governor or the CEO of the brain. Other brain areas can be affected as well.

What I'm about to say may surprise you. Even though these

individuals have low stimulation in the front of their brains, they can still have a busy brain. How is that? Well, remember that when the PFC is understimulated, it is underactive and less able to rein in the wild horses of the limbic system. And a busy brain results precisely when the PFC and limbic system are imbalanced. Thus, we commonly find that individuals like this do experience busy brains, because the limbic system is poorly regulated by the PFC. Their governing systems are inadequately regulating the wild horses of emotions and impulses that have too much free rein.

Some individuals with ADHD experience low PFC activity and understimulation to an extreme degree. Activities that would make most of us tremble with anxiety—such as motorcycle racing or skydiving—seem to calm these individuals, probably because these exciting activities boost the low activity in their PFC. For a man I knew who was an airplane wing walker, an extreme amount of stimulation was required for him to feel calm and comfortable. Most of us would be paralyzed by anxiety walking on the wing of an airplane midflight, but this man, who normally experienced boring situations as remarkably intolerable, was optimally stimulated when engaging in his hobby. He stopped being distracted and became simply mindful, alert, and fully aware in the present moment. Why? you might inquire. Well, the adrenaline pumped out by his adrenal glands boosted his typically very low-functioning PFC, so he felt calm and focused walking on wings instead of rattled by his normal state of intense boredom. To each his own, to be sure. Some individuals, who are more "normal," like my son Chris, are attracted to action movies containing high-speed car chases, combat scenes, and explosions. Chris also loves roller coasters and other thrill rides. Thrill rides and action movies probably optimize for Chris what I suspect is mild underactivity of his PFC.

This is the important point I want to make: Many people with ADHD have difficulty tolerating boredom, and many seek out experiences in which intensity or stimulation is high. Sometimes the stimulation is extreme. The wing walker overcame his intolerable boredom by walking on the wings of an airplane in midflight.

But the stimulation can also be of a different order. Think of those who are "addicted" to their iPhones and other mobile devices, because the constant pings alert them to new information; novelty stimulates and relieves their boredom.

Every moment of every day, whether awake or asleep, you are bombarded by sensory input that stimulates you—sometimes a little stimulation, sometimes a lot. Stimulation means anything that requires the brain and nervous system to pay attention. In its simplest form, stimulation acts like a knock at the door. When we hear a knock, we become mentally aroused no matter the outcome. The knock alerts us to a possible need for action. We might decide not to answer the knock, to first look out our peephole before answering, or to open the door to let the person knocking enter. Regardless of our ultimate decision, we become activated in response to the knock on the door. We need to pay attention to the stimulus of the knocking and decide what, if anything, to do about it.

Stimuli can come from the environment (think of the iPhone), from inside our body (e.g., hunger, pain, and sexual urges), or our brain (e.g., thoughts, plans, goals, and memories). When stimuli are present, attention needs to paid. We call arousal the increase of attention and brain processing that stimuli demand.

Many individuals with ADHD who could barely spend ten minutes doing boring activities such as paying bills or doing their taxes can easily lose themselves for many consecutive hours playing exciting video games. The constant change and feedback they receive by playing overcomes their boredom. The stimulation, novelty, and excitement gets them paying attention. Without it, they are apathetic, fatigued, or spacy. Some patients with ADHD even become bored in their relationship with a romantic partner after several months; they break off the relationship, not because it is a bad one but because they need a new relationship, a new person, someone fresh, novel.

Considering the need for novelty and stimulation, no wonder so many children with ADHD have difficulty in school environments that are boring and repetitive. And no wonder so many adults have difficulty performing the routine aspects of their jobs, like completing expense reports. Taking a broad view, many of the mundane but important tasks that we all need to accomplish in modern society are not very interesting. Completing tax returns is a prime example. Many of my adult ADHD patients cannot or will not complete their taxes until the last minute because the work is so uninteresting. The last-minute deadline of April 15 provides just enough adrenaline to help them overcome their boredom and inertia. We see the same pattern in students with ADHD, who wait until the night before to start their term paper or to study for the final.

Overstimulation

For every individual like Jeremy—those who have problems with understimulation—there are individuals on the other end of the stimulation spectrum. Twenty-two-year-old Penelope and her mother, Lucinda, were barely speaking to each other when they first came to consult with me. Emotionally, Penelope took after her historian father; she was quiet and reserved and preferred solitude over what she found to be superficial interactions with her peers. Lucinda had a different emotional style altogether. She was intelligent, quick, and witty, and her outgoing personality and sociability had helped her achieve great things in the business world. Yet those same traits worked against her attempts to connect with Penelope.

Lucinda's emotionality and her perceived intrusiveness pushed Penelope away. The more Lucinda turned up the emotional volume, so to speak, the more Penelope withdrew, trying to reduce the excessive stimulation caused by contact with her mother. It quickly became clear that Penelope couldn't stand talking with her mother, not because Lucinda was a bad person but because Lucinda's intensity so destabilized her. Penelope said that her father seemed to know intuitively how much or how little to say, especially when it came to questions about her research in her Ph.D. program; her mother's questions, on the other hand, visibly annoyed Penelope.

Moreover, given Penelope's extreme sensitivity, Lucinda's questions made Penelope feel unpleasantly stimulated, really bombarded. Lucinda, it seemed, simply couldn't tune into Penelope's sensitivity or wavelength.

Penelope tried to withdraw from her mother to reduce her excessive stimulation, but the withdrawal resulted in Lucinda chasing her emotionally, which evolved into an unfortunate vicious cycle. Lest Penelope's story be seen as yet another example of unwarranted blaming of mothers, let me point out that Penelope was exquisitely sensitive to being bombarded by everybody, not just her mother. For example, I had to watch what I said to Penelope, more so than with nearly every patient, so easily did she become overstimulated and fragmented.

Those of us like Penelope who need just a wee bit of stimulation to become aroused and pay attention are often sensitive individuals who become overwhelmed with more than the small amount of stimulation we need to pay attention. We are rarely bored, because we so often feel overactivated by stimuli, with our fight-or-flight responses triggered excessively. When overstimulated, we feel flooded, excessively excited, anxious, irritated, or fearful. A busy brain par excellence.

Optimal Stimulation

People vary greatly in how much their nervous systems are aroused under similar situations of stimulation. Each of us has a kind of set point, meaning how much environmental stimulation we can optimally handle without feeling understimulated (bored) like Jeremy or overstimulated (overwhelmed) like Penelope.

Most of us find ourselves between Penelope and the wing walker; we need a moderate amount of stimulation to be optimally aroused, to feel awake and alert, and to pay attention. Too little stimulation and we feel bored, underaroused, dull, drowsy, uninterested. We search for something to jazz us up, maybe caffeine.

Too much stimulation and we feel distressed, overloaded, and overwhelmed. The goal is to find the sweet spot. Attention levels are optimized when our degree of mental arousal is just right. We are relaxed and our minds are alert, but not overloaded. This often correlates with the state of flow described by Mihaly Csikszentmihalyi.

Optimal states correlate with sufficient stimulation—but not too much—so that you are not flooded with adrenaline and other stress hormones. You feel motivated, confident, and interested, and your capacity for attention gives you a clear mind that allows you to focus on whatever is necessary. Note that what may be too much stimulation for one person is too little for another. The goal is for each of us to become aware of our individual patterns with regard to stimulation and then to reclaim our state of optimal stimulation.

Stimulation and Temperament

Developmental psychologist Jerome Kagan studied *temperament,* which means one's inborn, biologically based arousal and behavior patterns. Kagan's research showed that about 20 percent of infants reacted strongly to novel, unfamiliar stimuli. Interestingly, the infants in the high-reactivity group were most likely to become quiet teens who had serious, careful personalities. Infants in the low-reactivity group tended to develop into relaxed and confident teens.

In essence, what Kagan had found was how to predict in infancy who would become an introvert and who would become an extrovert later in life. *Introvert* and *extrovert* are terms that Carl Jung had coined years earlier. Introverts are thought of as self-reflexive, bookish, sensitive and maybe thin-skinned, having a strong conscience, dreamers with a vivid imagination, idealists, thoughtful, serious, calm, modest, shy and preferring solitude, and tending to avoid risk. Sensitive to the environment and overwhelmed easily, they tend to be contemplative individuals. Introverts react strongly to stimuli.

Extroverts (sometimes written as *extraverts*) tend to be outgoing, social, talkative, excitable, lighthearted, assertive and even dominant, active, practical, realistic, and thick-skinned. They are people of action. They tend to be risk takers who like or even crave the spotlight. Extroverts tend to be understimulated individuals who require greater amounts of stimuli than do introverts to achieve their sweet spot of optimal stimulation.

We now have a good idea about some genetic underpinnings of these arousal differences. The source of these differences is amygdala activity. Remember that the amygdala is a key center for detecting danger, responding to potential dangers instantaneously but rather primitively. If while hiking you notice a shape that could be a snake, your amygdala causes you to jump back immediately. Only milliseconds later does your more nuanced prefrontal cortex recognize that what you saw was not a dangerous snake but a stick; all is well. But if it had been a snake, your amygdala reaction, which occurs reflexively and instantaneously without thinking, might have saved you.

The amygdala is overactive in the easily overstimulated group. Genetic studies have correlated amygdala overactivity with the presence of the "short" version of the serotonin transporter gene (in contrast to the "long" version); the presence of the short version increases depression and overarousal in affected individuals. We can now understand how, with amygdala-based threat detection on high, genetically prone individuals become more overstimulated and highly stressed than others in new situations.

Think about people you know. Some love and even crave new situations, events, and experiences. Others prefer the same old thing, day after day. What we are discussing is a biologically based attitude toward novelty, mediated by amygdala reactivity. A highly reactive amygdala will keep you on edge, on guard, chronically overstimulated. You will tend to avoid novelty. An amygdala with low reactivity doesn't keep sending up warning alarms; if anything, the individual instead is likely to be understimulated. An understimulated individual will tend to seek out new and exciting activities to increase brain activity. Maybe this individual would try their hand at wing walking. Or rock climbing with nothing but their bare hands and feet. Or skydiving.

Stimulus tolerance, as determined by amygdala activity level, can affect a person's choice of profession. Highly reactive individuals from educated backgrounds often select intellectual professions in which they are in charge—such as teachers, writers, artists, scientists, and thinkers. They can close the door, manage external stimulation, and get to work. Novelty for them, if explored in an intellectual pursuit, is encountered in a controlled fashion, more or less on their terms. Highly reactive individuals from less formally educated backgrounds may become file clerks or truck drivers for the same reasons.

Please keep in mind that I am painting with a broad brush. Not every overstimulated or understimulated individual has all of these traits. Some individuals have combinations of features of both overstimulation and understimulation. With optimal nurturing early in life and fortunate life experiences from which one can learn and grow, an overstimulated individual can blossom and learn to tolerate greater stimulation, and an understimulated person can learn to become more quiet and contemplative. And somebody who is mildly overstimulated might become much more so in the face of significant stress or life changes; the situation is likely vice versa for those who are understimulated.

Optimal States

How can you know if you are in an optimal state—neither understimulated nor overstimulated? Remember that the optimal point will vary greatly from one individual to another, and probably from one day to another in the same individual. But consider the following.

Someone who is optimally stimulated will feel relaxed, not tense or strained. They will be able to calmly accept interruptions and frustrations. An optimal state can be easily maintained. One should feel interested, pleasantly challenged. The individual is acting, not just reacting, in pursuit of clear goals that they have defined for themselves.

How can we begin to manage our stimulation? Here are steps you can take.

Strategies to Increase Stimulation

➤ Accepting: Your physiology is not defective, just different in that you require high stimulation and novelty.

Phil, twenty-three, took a job following college graduation as a claims processor for an insurance carrier. The problem: he found the work as boring as work could possibly be. After six months, it was clear to his supervisors that his performance was mediocre at best. He was given notice—"shape up or else." That was when he came to me. I quickly realized that we were dealing with a misfit. Phil wasn't the misfit, but there was a misfit between Phil, an action-oriented, excitement-loving fellow, and his job. With encouragement, Phil found another job, as a kind of problem solver in an information technology (IT) department, where the unpredictability and frank crises were more than enough to help him achieve an optimal state.

➤ Mentally Preparing: When you anticipate understimulating situations, plan ahead. What strategies could you use to "survive"?

Phil did much better in his new position. However, even he had to endure periodic "all hands" meetings that most everybody found dry and boring, if not painful. No way to escape them. Phil planned ahead by deciding which seat to select (in the back in order to be less conspicuous) and by bringing written material to review to pass the time.

➤ Increasing Stimulation: Notice your body state. How are you experiencing the low-stimulation situation? Notice your negative thoughts and stories. Multitask if bored (like Jeremy, although hopefully you won't need to take it to such an extreme). Play upbeat, energetic music. Take frequent scheduled breaks. Munch on a healthy snack.

One way that Phil coped during the "all hands" meetings was by taking multiple restroom breaks so he could stretch his legs and pace off nervous energy. Munching on healthy snacks like apple slices or small carrot sticks also helped and was acceptable behavior in meetings at his company.

➤ Releasing the Tension of Boredom: Exercise vigorously or work on a challenging intellectual task.

Phil found that an hour of mountain biking was enormously helpful.

➤ Make Expectations Realistic: Be realistic. Don't overexpect or overpromise. Say no appropriately.

When he could, which wasn't all the time, Phil tactfully bowed out of boring meetings by offering a legitimate excuse about pressing work that needed to be attended to. That he was responsible for IT emergencies gave him plausible cover for his excuses.

Strategies for Reducing Stimulation

➤ Accepting: Your physiology is different; not defective, just different.

It took some time, but eventually Penelope could accept that she was not defective, just more sensitive than most people. In fact, she could appreciate the benefits of her heightened sensitivity, which helped her appreciate art, music, literature, and nature— but always on her terms, so that she would not be flooded with excessive stimulation.

➤ Mentally Preparing: Because you easily become overloaded, plan beforehand how to try to overcome your discomfort in a potentially difficult situation.

Penelope, who was in grad school when she consulted with me, mentally prepared as best as she could for situations in which she would have been overstimulated. For example, if her study group was planning to meet for lunch or dinner in a restaurant, she gently tried to steer the restaurant choice to one that was quieter than others. In the restaurant, she expressed her preference for a table at the back of the room, which was less crowded, and she sat with her back to the wall because she felt more grounded and less stimulated that way.

➤ Managing Difficult Situations: Calm your breathing in difficult situations. Notice your body state; be in tune with your body. How overstimulated are you? What are your thoughts? What negative story are you telling yourself? Decide if you need to reduce your excessive stimuli. Focus on calming yourself and taking things one step at a time.

By focusing on how and where Penelope experienced excessive stimuli in her body, and labeling it with self-talk ("I feel it in my neck. . . . I feel it in my jaw. . . . I feel it in my lungs"), she gained some distance from her excessive stimulation and calmed herself.

➤ Recharging: Make sure you have adequate time to rest and recharge. You need downtime, alone time. Meditation can help. Use calming music. Take frequent breaks. Go outside. Walk.

Penelope used walking outside while listening to calming music to great advantage.

➤ Make Expectations Realistic: Don't overschedule.

Once Penelope could accept that she was just different, not defective, she could more easily decline meetings and events that were not essential and not feel inadequate or guilty. In this way, she reduced the depletion she experienced in social situations.

Advantages of Understimulation and ADHD

Lest we focus only on the negative, proneness to understimulation and ADHD can have an upside. Individuals with these traits are often curious, adventurous, open to exploration, passionate, and good with people. They can excel in times of challenge. Some claim that the United States may have more than its fair share of individuals with ADHD. After all, many of us are descended from ancestors who took the bold step of leaving behind their original countries and cultures to forge a new life in a new land. These people would not have been as overwhelmed as their peers by the challenges they faced emigrating. Rather, they may have been more likely to be excitement-seeking individuals, revved up by change and deadened by boring situations. In brief, such individuals would have been comfortable with high levels of stimulation, maybe even seeking it.

Life Problems in ADHD

Individuals affected with ADHD, especially when it is untreated, often have difficult lives, filled with learning struggles, speeding tickets, job failures, divorce, legal difficulties, substance abuse, and poor self-esteem. In fact, without adequate treatment, one-third of those with ADHD never finish high school, half abuse drugs or alcohol, and three-quarters have significant relationship problems. Some develop a pattern similar to post-traumatic stress disorder (PTSD), due to living a life of chronic dysfunction. One issue that rarely gets discussed: the problems that ADHD causes in the bedroom.

Sexual Problems in ADHD

Terry was a thirty-two-year-old woman with ADHD. She had a good job as a buyer for a major department store chain. Always somewhat distracted, always a little anxious because of her distractibility, she nonetheless did well in her work because the excitement of new fashion styles and the give-and-take with the buyers at the major fashion houses revved up her understimulated PFC.

Although she was in a stable marriage of four years to Stu, an outgoing dentist, Terry complained that she never enjoyed sex. She could not become sexually aroused. It wasn't her husband; Terry had experienced problems in a number of previous relationships, too. Terry convincingly told me that she had no history of sexual abuse or other sexual violations.

We talked about her marriage. Terry was faithful, as was Stu. Their marriage seemed good, with mutual devotion, sharing of household responsibilities, and mutual caring. What I came to learn was that because of Terry's ADHD, it was impossible for her to relax and focus on the pleasurable aspects of sex. It was a classic busy-brain problem. Her underfocused brain was going here, there, everywhere, just not where she needed to be in the moment with Stu. Although it may sound like a paradox, it's not: her understimulated PFC led to her being underaroused sexually.

I told Terry that medication for ADHD would boost the activity of her understimulated PFC, resulting in her greater ability to be more sensitive and receptive to sexual arousal with Stu. Terry was afraid of medications; the few prescription medications she'd taken in her life—for nonpsychiatric reasons—caused strong side effects. Terry asked about alternatives to medication.

What helped Terry was neurofeedback training, in which she was able to learn to control her brain wave patterns so she could improve her baseline understimulated PFC. Twenty neurofeedback sessions with a trained neurotherapist made a big difference, helping Terry learn to regulate her own brain wave patterns and improve her ability to focus. Terry felt calmer and more focused when doing less interesting tasks, even at work. During sexual encounters with Stu she began to notice improved sexual arousal, but it still was not enough.

Having benefited from neurofeedback, Terry was then able to use mindfulness techniques such as relaxation breathing to anchor herself in the present moment. The previous cacophony of thoughts in her brain during sex was quieted. She was able to be present and could fully enjoy sex with Stu. And she noticed that her increased ability to be present with Stu improved their intimacy outside the bedroom. Stu appreciatively commented on her improved presence with him.

Causes of ADHD

Although we understand much about what happens in the brain of an individual with ADHD, the causes of ADHD are harder to pinpoint. There is not one cause for ADHD but likely many, which can vary case by case. Some individuals with ADHD likely have a developmental "lag" in which the prefrontal cortex matures several years later in those with ADHD than those without ADHD. Genetics play a role; there are increased rates of ADHD in biological relatives. For a child with ADHD, at least one parent usually has ADHD, and often both. Some, though not all, children with ADHD are exquisitely sensitive to food additives, colorings, and preservatives. This is why some do better on the Feingold diet, which emphasizes eliminating food additives from the diet. A number of children with ADHD have what is called a "leaky gut," a malfunctioning GI system likely resulting from a less-than-optimal diet and antibiotic exposure. Diets low in fish oil seem to increase ADHD in teens.

Some children and adults with ADHD have low iron (as measured by a blood test for ferritin) or low zinc levels. Sam was a married man in his forties who came to see me with longstanding ADHD and low energy. Sam's ADHD made him scattered and disorganized. He never felt calm. Sam had a moderately good response to one of the common stimulant medications, but we never seemed to hit the nail on the head and get Sam to where he wanted to be. His low energy really never budged. Sam told me that he had yearly checkups with his primary care doctor, but I decided to seize the bull by the horns and order my own lab work for Sam, which revealed low testosterone, low B12, and low iron. We then had targets we could aim at to try to improve the function of Sam's brain and body. DHEA supplementation boosted Sam's testosterone. Sublingual B12 increased that vitamin, and iron pills increased his low iron. Ultimately, with these additions, we were able to get Sam close to 100 percent. Only by focusing on these previously undetected hormonal and metabolic issues were we able to help Sam improve. Ultimately, he felt less scattered and disorganized. He became calmer and simultaneously more energetic. This is a good place to mention that ADHD for which a woman showed little evidence earlier in life may become unmasked during and after menopause, because declining estrogen production indirectly reduces dopamine levels, thereby negatively affecting PFC function.

Toxic exposure may play a role in bringing about ADHD in some. Maternal smoking during gestation, elevated heavy metal levels (such as mercury, lead, and aluminum), pesticide exposure, and sensitivity to mold all seem to be contributing factors, at least in some individuals. Thyroid dysfunction can mimic ADHD. Tick-borne infections, such as Lyme disease and related conditions, can also be a factor. We need to check whether any child who snores and seems to have ADHD is really having apparent symptoms of

ADHD because of sleep apnea. Finally, using brain SPECT imaging, we can detect evidence of brain injury caused by physical trauma that can mimic or contribute to ADHD issues.

Treatment of ADHD

➤ **Diet:** A gluten-free, dairy-free, sugar-free diet helps many. Avoid processed food. Eliminate artificial colors, flavors, and preservatives. High protein intake with low carbohydrates keeps blood sugar levels stable. Often, these diet changes need to be a family affair.

➤ **Substance Use:** Minimize caffeine, which many use as self-medication to activate their low prefrontal cortex. Caffeine reduces blood flow to the brain and dehydrates. Don't abruptly stop a high level of caffeine use—tapering is often needed to reduce caffeine withdrawal symptoms. Alcohol and marijuana, which are often used to calm a busy ADHD brain, should be minimized or avoided, because of their detrimental impact on brain function.

➤ **Exercise:** Daily intense aerobic exercise is often essential for those with ADHD, especially those who are hyperactive, to burn off excess energy and help calm mental and physical hyperactivity. One of my patients with severe ADHD deteriorated significantly when he broke his ankle and could not continue his intense daily workout routine. Consider yoga, which has been found to help ADHD.

➤ **Sleep:** Good sleep is essential. Mornings are often difficult for those with ADHD, in part because getting to sleep at night is typically a problem. Brain function is worse when we don't sleep well. Attention to "sleep hygiene" and use of nutritional supplements and medication to assist with sleep can be essential.

➤ **ADHD Coaching:** Coaching helps resolve the organizational issues that plague those with ADHD. Coaching for ADHD involves a collaborative relationship with a professional who understands how an ADHD brain works and who helps you address the specific challenges and opportunities that someone with ADHD faces. A coach is not a therapist; rather, they offer support, guidance, and accountability, so that things change and the individual with ADHD progresses. Coaches help individuals with ADHD learn new ways to solve problems and accomplish goals, moving life forward in important areas such as work, family life, relationships, health, education, talents, and interests.

➤ **Psychotherapy:** Various kinds of counseling and talk therapy are useful to help individuals with ADHD to understand why they had the difficulties they had and to reframe their development. Marital and family therapy can improve the relationship issues that arise so commonly in ADHD.

➤ **Neurofeedback and Biofeedback:** See the information in Chapter 4 ("Becoming Mindful").

➤ **Accommodations for School and Work:** Accommodations often help at work and school. School accommodations are often essential. Tutors can help parents get out of the toxic loop of struggling with their child over homework.

➤ **Parent Training:** Parent training is often important. Parents need to be able to set clear limits and have clear structure. Family life often degenerates into a constant focus on negativity. Parents need to be able to focus on what their children do well so they can escape the constant spiral of negativity that is so common.

Nutritional Supplements/Brain Boosters for ADHD

➤ **Multiple Vitamin:** Use a daily high-quality vitamin and mineral supplement to help optimize brain function in ADHD.

➤ **Fish Oil:** Fish oil is good to help heal injured brains, reduce over-activity, and minimize inflammation. Studies show that fish oil alone is helpful for ADHD. EPA and DHA are the two main omega-3 fatty acids that we want to boost by using fish oil. Children should take about 1,500 mg/day of the total of EPA and DHA. Adults should take about 3,000 mg/day of the total of EPA and DHA. Look on the label of your fish oil product to determine the amount of EPA and DHA each dose contains.

➤ **Cognitive Activators (to boost the front of the brain):**
  • **L-tyrosine:** This amino acid shows some benefits, but they may be short-term. Take it on an empty stomach. Use 500 mg three times a day for three days, then 1,000 mg three times a day for three days, then increase if needed to 1,500 mg three times a day.
  • **Ginkgo Biloba:** I recommend 120 to 240 mg/day in the morning. Ginkgo can thin your blood, which is usually a good thing. Mention that you are using it if you are going to have surgery.
  • **SAMe:** SAMe is a compound found naturally in the body. It plays a major role in a number of important chemical reactions, including your body's synthesis of chemical transmitters. Start with 200 to 400 mg twice daily on an empty stomach. Increase every few days as needed by 200 mg at each dose. The maximum total daily dosage is about 2,000 mg. Be careful if you have an underlying bipolar-type condition.

➤ **Phosphatidylserine (PS; to boost temporal lobes/learning/ memory):** Take 300 mg/day. Many PS products are derived from soy and may cause reactions in those sensitive to soy.

➤ **Supplements for Sleep:** These include gamma-aminobutyric acid (GABA; 750 to 1,500 mg), melatonin (0.5 to 10 mg), 5-HTP (50 to 200 mg), and L-theanine (100 to 200 mg or more).

Medication Used for ADHD

➤ **Stimulants:** Vyvanse, Adderall XR, Adderall, Concerta, Focalin, and others increase dopamine and boost function in the prefrontal cortex. They are often quite effective. Some teens and young adults abuse these. They have some side effects (insomnia, appetite suppression). With severe abuse, one could become psychotic.

➤ **Provigil/Nuvigil:** These are used primarily for narcolepsy and fatigue in multiple sclerosis. They function somewhat like stimulants for patients with ADHD but are less effective.

➤ **Strattera (atomoxetine):** This drug is effective in some cases. It has low abuse potential. In my experience, it is not very useful and often has side effects.

➤ **Wellbutrin (bupropion):** Wellbutrin is a stimulating antidepressant of some usefulness, with limited abuse potential.

➤ **Desipramine:** This older antidepressant is somewhat useful for ADHD. Children should have an electrocardiograph (EKG) before use because desipramine can affect heart rhythms, and we need to determine that a child's heart is in good shape prior to taking the medication.

➤ **Amantadine:** This drug is less effective than stimulants.

➤ **Blood Pressure Medications:**
  - **Tenex/Intuniv (guanfacine):** These reduce brain overactivity and help with calming ADHD. They are not as useful as stimulants. They provide some benefit for sleep in ADHD.
  - **Clonidine:** This drug is useful for sleep and overall calming.

ACTION PLAN

➤ **Stimulation Sweet Spot:** Know your stimulation sweet spot and take steps to implement it. Plan ahead so that you can manage over- and understimulation as necessary.

➤ **Diet:** Try a gluten-free, dairy-free, sugar-free diet with no food additives, no artificial colors, and no preservatives for one month. If you see improvement in ADHD symptoms, continue this diet if you can. Not everyone will benefit, but this dietary regimen is often helpful. Emphasize protein in your diet, including having several small snacks with protein during the day to keep blood sugar levels stable.

➤ **Sleep:** Make sure that you get eight hours of sleep each night. Remove electronics from the bedroom. Use sleep aids like melatonin, 5-HTP, or Benadryl if necessary.

➤ **Exercise:** Try to exercise daily for at least thirty minutes.

➤ **Electronics Diet:** Minimize electronic distraction. Children and teens should not spend more than one half hour each day on video games.

➤ **Nutritional Supplements:** Take a high-quality multivitamin and fish oil daily.

7

Heart Matters: Anxiety

David was a hardworking, decent man who came to me for help with anxiety and stress. Single and thirty-six, David was a rising star at a major bank. His colleagues and superiors appreciated his attention to detail; in his line of work, overlooked details could result in financial disaster. A perfectionist, David naturally understood the importance of being detail-oriented and worked hard at his job yet experienced anxiety and stress because of the responsibility placed on his shoulders. A common story. Many of us find ourselves in similar situations.

David sometimes had difficulty falling asleep because his busy brain wouldn't turn off. David coped at work by making sure to dot every *i* and cross every *t*. His hard work paid off and he was promoted to a senior position at the bank. In his new position, David needed to manage six subordinates, which added to his stress. His previous coping mechanisms were not adequate; he couldn't possibly make sure that his six subordinates dotted all their *i*'s and crossed their *t*'s. Following his promotion, David's insomnia worsened and he began to have panic attacks. He began dwelling on the financial catastrophes that would occur if important financial information was missed. That was when he came to see me.

When you are experiencing anxiety as David was, your body is chronically and excessively aroused. Those with anxiety tend to predict the worst. They look to the future with fear. They may be shy or startle easily. Worrying drains their happiness. Brain SPECT imaging of anxious people often reveals excessive activity in the basal ganglia—areas of the brain that correlate closely with anxiety, worry, fear, and panic attacks. We often say that an individual with anxiety has basal ganglia that have a high "idle," almost like a car that idles too fast when it is not well tuned. In addition to overactivity in their basal ganglia, those with anxiety often have excessive activity in the amygdala and frequently low activity in their prefrontal cortex. The weaker PFC cannot rein in the wild horses of the basal ganglia and amygdala, which is why the person has a busy brain.

The Highly Sensitive Person

Elaine Aron has studied the highly sensitive person (HSP), an easily overaroused and overwhelmed individual who is sensitive and often anxious. Aron believes that evolution has favored the careful, reflective style that tends to accompany the highly aroused individual, and not high arousal itself. If understimulated and sometimes impulsive people like those with ADHD, whom we looked at in the previous chapter, live by the mantra "Ready, Fire, Aim," sensitive, reactive, easily overaroused HSP individuals have a strategy of observing carefully and reflecting before acting: "Look before you leap," but probably even stronger than that, more like "Think long and hard, explore all the angles, before you leap. And maybe don't leap; perhaps take it a small step at a time."

When humankind functioned as nomadic hunter-gatherers, more impulsive, underaroused, action-oriented individuals probably were the first to find food. Once humans developed agriculture and began living in settlements, it is likely that overaroused, more reserved, less action-oriented, less impulsive individuals would survive preferentially. Easily overaroused individuals would be better able to detect and warn of potential danger, better monitor animals and other humans, and more able to pass along cultural wisdom.

A number of the strategies in *Reclaim Your Brain* assist HSP individuals with calming their overstimulation, including the butterfly hug described shortly. Here are additional strategies that may be particularly helpful for HSPs:

1. Accept your feelings of being overwhelmed; don't fight them. They, too, shall pass.

2. Rewrite your negative story of being flawed or defective because you become overwhelmed so easily.

3. Reframe your coping style as not lack of coping ability but rather a different way of coping.

4. Remind yourself of the good qualities that accompany being an HSP—such as sensitivity, feeling deeply, being empathic, understanding others, and being sensitive to art.

5. Get enough rest so you can recharge effectively after being particularly overstimulated.

Anxiety isn't all bad. Anxious individuals tend to be more sensitive, which can aid in developing relationships. Anxiety drives us to keep our children safe. We may anticipate problems better if we're on the anxious side. And anxiety alerts and mobilizes us. Yet when it is too strong, too painful, we need to find a way to deal with our anxiety. How can we manage anxiety when it's severe? How can we better regulate ourselves and aim for better harmony within?

Though anxiety, like most of the issues we explore in this book, originates in our busy, unbalanced brain, one less remarked-on solution for anxiety lies in our hearts—specifically, in our heart rhythms. Optimizing our heart rhythm is one way to manage anxiety, control stress, and rein in our busy brains. Let's look at how managing our heart rate helps us control emotions like anxiety.

The Heart: More Than a Pump

The brain and autonomic nervous system affect the cardiovascular system, especially the heart. Sympathetic nervous system (SNS) activity causes the heart to beat faster, while activity of the parasympathetic nervous system (PNS) causes the heart to slow down. The SNS is like stepping on the accelerator. The PNS is like stepping on the brake. This cardiac balance is delicate and important. While most people know that the brain influences the heart, what is less well-known is that the heart can affect the function of the brain and the rest of the nervous system. Heart rhythm patterns directly affect the brain and the mind, as we'll see.

Many older cultures and faith traditions have considered the heart to be the source of positive emotions, including joy, compassion, and love. The Bible describes God's creating a new heart for those seeking spiritual change. Some speak of having God's word written on their heart. In our everyday lives, most of us have a sense that the heart is involved with our most profound positive feelings. We experience these "heartfelt" emotions as being localized in our chest, in the area of our heart.

Yet around the sixteenth century, likely with the study of anatomy, the view of the heart as being the source of positive emotions began to change. Henceforth, the heart was to be considered only a pump, circulating blood. Have we lost something by viewing the heart as simply a pump? I think we have. The view of the heart as only a pump is likely mistaken; the innate sense most of us have that the heart is involved with our positive emotions is correct. The heart can be at the core of our being, if we know how to use it.

The Heart and Our Emotions

Research suggests that the heart plays a key role in regulating emotional experience. The heart has more than forty thousand neurons that sense, process information, regulate body physiology, and even remember—the equivalent of almost a little brain of its own, which can function more or less independently of the much larger brain in our head. The heart has the most extensive neural connections with the brain of any body organ. It also manufactures and secretes neurotransmitters like norepinephrine and hormones that can have widespread effects on the body, including oxytocin, the so-called bonding and love hormone. Some evidence suggests that oxytocin can have a calming effect. Thus, because of its own "brain" and its secretion of hormones and neurotransmitters, the heart is in a unique position to regulate our emotional states. This is why we can recruit the heart to help us manage our anxiety states.

Heart rate variability (HRV) can be a key factor in helping us regulate ourselves, so let's take a closer look. Heart rate variability means the beat-to-beat changes in heart rate that result from nerve signals sent back and forth between the heart and the brain. HRV patterns vary with emotional states. A "coherent" HRV pattern is a smooth sine wave, with gradual increases and decreases in heart rate. The coherent HRV pattern results from synchronized brain and autonomic nervous system (ANS) function; coherent patterns reflect the action of calming nervous system activity. We see a coherent HRV pattern with positive emotions like joy, gratitude, love, and compassion. A coherent HRV state is associated with calmness, emotional balance, and optimal alertness and responsiveness, a state similar to that described as *flow*.

Negative emotions, such as stress, anger, anxiety, and frustration, give rise to chaotic HRV patterns. Chaotic HRV patterns are jagged, not the smooth sine wave pattern we see with coherent patterns. This is an unhealthy pattern that has a negative impact on our overall physiology. During stress, anxiety, depression, anger, or even typical day-to-day worries, heart rate variability is chaotic, with a negative impact on brain function, including cognition and ability to regulate one's emotions.

Self-Regulation and the Heart

HRV patterns not only reflect one's emotional state, they also play a direct role in determining emotional experience. This is key. In other words, by focusing on and being able to make our HRV more coherent, we reduce anxiety and increase our positive emotions. Well-being is increased, with feelings of peace and harmony. Our busy brains are calmed. Making shifts in HRV is called *HeartMath* or *Heart-Focused Breathing*. We will look at how to do this in a moment.

How to Increase Cardiac Coherence

We can't usually change the stressful world or the difficult people in our lives, but by learning to better improve our physiology by improving cardiac coherence, we are in a better position to master our inner being. Computer-assisted programs, such as those available through the HeartMath website (www.heartmath.org), teach how to increase cardiac coherence. However, there are exercises one can do without using a computer that give the same result.

Improving heart coherence draws on approaches from yoga, mindfulness, and relaxation strategies. Here's how to improve cardiac coherence with Heart-Focused Breathing. Remember David from the beginning of the chapter? I taught David Heart-Focused Breathing, with good results. I've included his approach in *italics*.

1. Recognize that you are feeling stress from a troublesome situation. Take a mental time-out so you can put your thoughts and feelings on hold.

David had no trouble at all recognizing that he was experiencing stress and anxiety. I asked him to find a quiet place and just let his feelings be. Don't fight them. Don't argue with them. Put them on hold, so to speak.

2. Start by taking two slow, deep breaths, each one about five seconds in and five seconds out. Continue breathing this way during the next steps. This approach to slow breathing activates the parasympathetic nervous system.

David was glad to hear that there was a part of his nervous system that worked to calm him and that slow breathing could activate it. He was able to start with two slow, deep breaths, and to continue that way through the next steps. Just doing this gave him a sense of control and he already felt a little better.

3. Shift your focus from the troubling feelings your busy brain is generating to the area around your heart. Continue breathing slowly, as if your breath is flowing in through your heart and out through your stomach.

David was easily able to imagine his breath flowing in through his heart and out through his solar plexus. No problem there.

4. Think of a positive, pleasant, fun experience or time and put yourself back in that situation to try to reexperience how you felt then. It could be appreciation or caring for someone. Really try to feel the feeling, not just think about it.

David easily came up with a number of positive situations. A particularly special time came to mind—he was seven, and the family just got its first dog, a wonderful pup named Max who was only eight or ten weeks old. Max was full of life and ran and ran in the family's backyard as he explored his new home. Max seemed so free, and David felt almost then as Max felt. It was a wonderful time, and putting himself back in that situation, still breathing in and out slowly, filled David with warmth and love for Max.

5. Sincerely ask yourself what would be a better response to the difficult situation you're in, one that would reduce your stress. Try to come up with a less stressful way of seeing the situation, even if you can't yet feel it.

David bathed in the delight of his experience of getting to know Max. "What would be a better response to my needing to make sure that I don't miss important details than imagining that I'll miss something and cause financial catastrophe?" he asked himself. His question to himself was sincere. What came to mind was this: "I usually don't miss things. I have a knack for this work. My new position will help me grow as a manager. I might even find a way to be at peace with needing to avoid overlooking important details. Maybe I'll learn better ways to process the large volume of financial information I need to master. Maybe I'll learn to ease up on my perfectionism, which is rather harsh. And anyway, nobody is perfect." It seemed as if focusing on Max was able to give David a greater perspective on the situation, one that reduced his stress. He felt free as a kid with Max. David seemed to again experience moments of freedom now as an adult, even in the face of his stressful work demands.

6. Be open to what you come up with in response to the question you ask yourself in step 5. Notice any change in the way you think or feel about your difficult situation. Try to hold on to the new thoughts and feelings for as long as you can.

As David continued to be open to the answer to his question in step 5, he laughed. It seemed ludicrous to be so worried about the financial details at the bank. "Life goes on, regardless," he thought. His thoughts went next to Karen, a young woman he had been seeing. Their relationship was new but developing nicely. "Loving relationships, that's what makes life worth living," he thought. "Crunching financial numbers pales in comparison."

David achieved significant benefit the first time he used Heart-Focused Breathing. As he used Heart-Focused Breathing in his appointments with me, and on his own, his stress and anxiety gradually—but significantly—declined. He slept better. Plus, David came to realize that even before his promotion he was driving himself too hard. He especially appreciated that steps 5 and 6 seemed to give his heart, his intuition, a chance to speak to the rest of him about what was really important.

Heart-Focused Breathing is similar to the approaches we've covered previously to deal with the busy brain. The key difference is that Heart-Focused Breathing is directed more at balancing the nervous system than the brain. It focuses on changing our emotions. What happens in the heart doesn't stay in the heart but affects what happens elsewhere in the body, including the emotional activity in the brain. Heart-Focused Breathing improves cardiac coherence, reducing cardiac chaos, which positively affects the limbic centers in the brain, signaling that one's physiology is in working order. The net result is improved balance between the sympathetic and parasympathetic nervous systems. Coherence increases inner calmness, but improving coherence is not meant primarily for relaxation. Cardiac coherence improves our capacity to take appropriate action, because our body physiology is more balanced. Thomas Merton wrote, "Happiness is not a matter of intensity but of balance, order, rhythm and harmony."

Heart-Focused Breathing is not the only way to decrease anxiety, reduce stress, and calm a too-busy brain. Let's turn now to some other techniques that can help.

Butterfly Hug

The butterfly hug technique was developed in Mexico to work with a group of children following the trauma of a hurricane. It has since been used all over the world to help increase the same positive feelings of "a safe place."

How to Do the Butterfly Hug

1. Cross your arms in front of you with your right hand on your left shoulder and your left hand on your right shoulder.

2. Close your eyes and envision a safe or calm place.

3. Slowly tap your hands alternately on each shoulder four to six times.

4. Open your eyes.

5. If the calm state increases, repeat the process.

Butterfly hugs were especially helpful for Rachel, who experienced extreme panic attacks. By all accounts Rachel, twenty-four, had been a precocious child. Inquisitive, bright, musical, she seemed to have everything going for her. But she was having panic attacks, bad ones, including attacks that awakened her from sleep. As happens often for those with panic disorder, Rachel became almost totally homebound, unable to drive or even go out because she was afraid of having a panic attack in a situation in which no help would be available. And like many people with panic problems, Rachel had significant chronic anxiety, likely biologically based and also related to her legitimate fear of having attacks. Indeed, panic attacks can be frightening and overwhelming. During an attack, the person experiences significant shortness of breath, chest pain, dizziness, and nausea and can feel like they are going to die or go crazy. Notably, Rachel selected me as her psychiatrist because my office was located one block from her home. She could walk to my office in two minutes, and Rachel imagined that she could run back home quickly if she had an attack during our appointment time.

Medication (Zoloft) and cognitive behavioral therapy were

effective in stopping her panic attacks within three or four weeks. Rachel then worked to gradually extend the boundaries of her life. After three months, she was back to going out and driving, except on the Beltway, which is a nightmare for everyone in the D.C. area. And she started going back to her work at a public interest lobbying firm; she had worked from home for six months because of her panic problems.

One would think that all was well in the world for Rachel. She had improved significantly. But Rachel believed that she was a defective individual because of her panic attacks. I had educated her on our understanding about how and why panic attacks arise. An area of the brain, the locus coeruleus, functions like an anxiety thermostat. If too sensitive, as hers was, it fires too often, setting off an unwarranted alarm, causing the panic attacks. Rachel understood my explanations, but the belief that she was defective persisted nonetheless. This is not surprising. Panic attacks are really anxiety seizures. They are powerful, overwhelming events. They come on suddenly, and the victim of a panic attack feels totally out of control.

Thus, it was no wonder to me that Rachel continued to believe that she was defective, even though her panic attacks and generalized anxiety were gone. The question was how to help Rachel get to the next level, a level at which the fundamental sense of defectiveness—which was not present prior to the onset of panic problems—could be addressed. What we are really talking about is self-control. Each of us needs to feel in control of ourselves, our bodies, our experiences. If we don't have control, we fear that we will be strongly buffeted by any stray wind gust that life brings.

What Rachel needed was a way to feel more in control of herself. That way turned out to be simple—Rachel used the butterfly hug. She closed her eyes and crossed her arms and placed her hands on her shoulders. Rachel then imagined being back in the safest place she knew: on the lap of her grandfather, who had seemed huge and strong to the little girl she had been. Rachel imagined being back in that place and time, protected by her grandfather's love. As she imagined that, she tapped several times on her shoulders. Rachel could do this quickly and easily whenever she needed to, to increase her sense of being safe and in control of herself. After doing butterfly hugs many times a day for two weeks, Rachel had calmed her too-busy brain and reestablished the feeling of safety and self-control she had before her panic attacks started.

Cranial Electrotherapy Stimulation (CES)

An example of cranial electrotherapy stimulation (CES) is the Alpha-Stim device (www.alpha-stim.com). This device, about the size of a small mobile phone, runs on a nine-volt battery. You attach two clips to your earlobes, through which the device passes a small current through your brain. Used for twenty to sixty minutes daily, it is useful for anxiety, stress, depression, and insomnia. I've tried an Alpha-Stim with benefit, as have family members and patients. An apparently similar device, with which I am less familiar, is the Fisher Wallace Stimulator (www.fisherwallace.com). Some of my patients have found it useful for the same issues as an Alpha-Stim.

Cognitive Behavioral Therapy (CBT)

Cognitive behavioral therapy (CBT) is a structured, short-term psychotherapy directed toward solving problems and modifying dysfunctional thinking and behavior. Research and clinical experience show its usefulness for anxiety, depression, and other issues. CBT has much in common with the rewriting-your-stories approach I've already presented. It has the advantage of working collaboratively with a therapist who helps structure the sessions and can make sure that you thoroughly learn and follow the approach. To find a therapist with expertise in CBT, visit www.abct.org or search on the *Psychology Today* website: http://therapists.psychologytoday.com.

Acupuncture

Some of my patients find acupuncture helpful for anxiety. My impression is that it is useful for mild to moderate anxiety and excessive arousal.

Essential Oils

Increasingly, my patients are turning to essential oils for calming, anxiety reduction, sleep, and other conditions. We've known for years that lavender is calming. Essential oils go way beyond using lavender. An appeal of essential oils is that these are natural products, derived from plant sources. One source of essential oils is found at http://do-essential-oils.com.

Nutritional Supplements Useful for Anxiety

Many individuals find nutritional supplements appealing because they are natural and they are useful for calming an anxious, over-aroused, busy brain.

Jill, a sensitive teen, had school phobia. She had been out of school for two months when she came to me. The only thing that seemed to help Jill was marijuana, which she used daily with her parents' consent because they knew that Jill's anxiety was over-whelming. I knew that anxiety ran in Jill's family; both parents and a brother experienced severe anxiety. Jill's parents also had thyroid problems. I checked Jill's labs, and she too had thyroid issues. Stabilizing her thyroid with medication reduced some of her anxiety about school, but not enough. Only when I calmed Jill's overactivity with magnesium supplements and the supplement GABA was she able to consider returning to school and reducing her marijuana use. I then sent Jill to a counselor, who helped prepare Jill for her return to school. Jill worried about what she would tell her classmates when they asked why she had missed school for two months. Jill and her therapist addressed Jill's negative thoughts and developed strategies to help her deal with the difficulties she anticipated, such as explaining to her classmates why she had missed school for so long. Eventually, Jill did return to school without much difficulty and was able to stop using marijuana to self-medicate for her anxiety.

Robert, thirty-nine years old, worked third shift in a busy machine shop. He had a busy brain, with racing thoughts, social anxiety, and difficulty approaching women because of his anxiety. Robert was lonely. Robert's school history suggested learning problems, and he remarked that his memory was not good. Even with me, Robert seemed to have difficulty finding the right words to express what he wanted to say. Robert likely sustained a brain injury during an auto accident at age eight in which he was thrown through the windshield, which could explain his learning, memory, and word-finding struggles.

Robert had been strongly influenced by his mother, who was leery of medications; she insisted on natural remedies for herself and her family. Because of his mother's attitude, Robert wanted natural healing approaches for himself. He read about using L-theanine for anxiety and decided to try it himself. Starting with 100 mg twice daily, Robert obtained a little relief. He increased the dose of L-theanine to 200 mg three times each day, and an extra dose when needed for anxiety. His relief was about 60 percent. It was then that Robert decided to try essential oils, which his mother had learned about from a neighbor. Using lavender oil, Robert noticed a marked calming that he'd never experienced before. With the combination of lavender oil and the nutritional supplement L-theanine, Robert's social anxiety and his busy brain's racing thoughts were markedly reduced; he found himself able for the first time to approach women and talk. What Robert really appreciated about this approach was that he could be in control of what he used to reduce his anxiety and when he used it.

After significantly mastering his anxiety, Robert next used the supplements ginkgo and phosphatidylserine (see Chapter 6 or the Appendix material for information about these supplements) to boost his brain function and to address the learning problems he had that seemed related to his auto accident at age eight. In our meetings he did seem to have an improved memory and he didn't struggle so much to express himself. Once his brain functioned better, Robert could then benefit from rewriting his stories, and he used mindfulness approaches such as meditation and even yoga to further reduce his anxiety and calm his busy brain. He met a woman, started dating, and to my amazement even returned to school.

Supplements That My Patients Have Found Effective for Anxiety

➤ **Fish Oil (Omega-3 Fatty Acids):** Preliminary research suggests that omega-3 fatty acid levels may be lower in those with anxiety; to my knowledge, this has not yet been confirmed. Anecdotal evidence suggests that high doses of omega-3 fatty acids (8 to 10 grams daily) may help anxiety by calming excessive limbic system activity, reducing inflammation, and helping brains heal. Side effects can include bloating, loose stools, and "fish burp." Individuals taking omega-3 supplements may also experience increased bruising and mildly prolonged bleeding times—it is a blood thinner, which is why cardiologists recommend it. Individuals using blood thinner medication can still take omega-3 supplements, but they should consult their physician prior to starting omega-3 supplements. I recommend obtaining a fish oil product that contains both EPA and DHA, the two omega-3 components that we want to boost. Aim for a more or less 3:2 ration of EPA:DHA. Add up how much EPA and DHA is in a capsule or a dose of the liquid concentrate. Take 3,000 mg/day of the total of EPA and DHA.

➤ **GABA:** Gamma-aminobutyric acid (GABA) is an amino acid that also functions in the brain as a neurotransmitter. It is reported to work in much the same way as do the antianxiety and anticonvulsant medications. GABA has a calming effect for people who struggle with anxiety, temper, and irritability. It reduces limbic system activity. GABA does not seem helpful for every patient, possibly because it is not always well absorbed and has difficulty crossing the blood-brain barrier. Side effects are few, it is safe, and doses can range anywhere from 100 to 5,000 mg/day, divided into two or three daily doses. The large dose range is likely due to variable absorption from one person to another.

➤ **Lemon Balm:** Helpful for anxiety, lemon balm is an herb from the mint family. It has no significant side effects. The daily dose is 600 mg.

➤ **L-theanine:** The active ingredient in green tea, L-theanine is an amino acid that promotes relaxation and sleep, reportedly by increasing alpha waves in the brain. The usual dose of L-theanine is 200 mg three or four times per day. You can take higher doses if you find it useful. There are no known adverse reactions. Keep some at your bedside to use in the early morning if you wake up too early. Metabolic Maintenance (http://www.metabolicmaintenance.com) is a good source for L-theanine. Pregnant women and nursing mothers should avoid L-theanine supplements. Children over age six can use L-theanine, but start with 100 mg twice daily.

➤ **Magnesium:** Chronic stress depletes the body of magnesium. And some suggest that most Americans are magnesium deficient. Magnesium is a relaxing mineral that lowers anxiety, calms, and assists in obtaining the deep sleep needed for rest and restoration. I often recommend Tri-Mag 300 (by DaVinci Labs). Start with two capsules twice daily and increase the dose every day or two until your stools become loose. Then reduce the dose slightly.

➤ **Melatonin:** Useful for mild to moderate insomnia associated with anxiety and possibly even anxiety and depression apart from insomnia. Melatonin is a hormone produced by the pineal gland deep in the brain. It is generally safe and easy to use. Occasionally there can be a "hangover" the next morning; other side effects can include headache or vivid dreams, but these occur rarely. Doses typically range from 0.5 to 10 mg taken thirty to sixty minutes before bedtime. Melatonin seems more useful for difficulty falling asleep than difficulty staying asleep. Those who have difficulty staying asleep should use a melatonin preparation that is formulated for extended release.

➤ **Passionflower:** Approved in Germany for use in treating nervous restlessness, passionflower contains a compound that binds to benzodiazepine receptors. Preliminary studies suggest that it reduces anxiety. Side effects are minimal. The dosage is 90 mg/day.

➤ **St. John's wort:** Derived from a flowering herb named after St. John the Baptist, St. John's wort may be the most potent of all the supplements for increasing brain serotonin and thereby calming mild to moderate anxiety and overarousal. It also is beneficial in depression. The starting dosage is 300 mg daily for children, 300 mg twice daily for teens, and 600 mg in the morning and 300 mg at night for adults. Sometimes the dose in adults is increased slowly to 1,800 mg daily. It is important that the preparation of St. John's wort contain 0.3 percent hypericin, the active ingredient. Those taking St. John's wort are more vulnerable to sunburn, so extra sun protection is needed. Other side effects can include nausea and loose stools. St. John's wort can decrease the effectiveness of other medications, including birth control pills and blood thinners. It can bring on mania in individuals who have bipolar disorder.

Medications

Lower medication doses are often needed in those with anxiety, especially when medication is started, because those with anxiety and overarousal can be exquisitely sensitive to medication side effects. Start with one-third to one-half of the typical doses that one would use for conditions other than anxiety. The following are some of the common medications used for anxiety:

- **Selective Serotonin Reuptake Inhibitors (SSRIs):** Examples include Prozac, Zoloft, and Lexapro. The most common side effects are sexual, including lower sex drive and difficulty with sexual arousal and orgasm. Other side effects include nausea and headaches. We think of SSRIs as antidepressant medications, but they work equally well for anxiety.

- **Serotonin-Norepinephrine Reuptake Inhibitors (SNRIs):** Examples include Effexor, Pristiq, and Cymbalta. In addition to their usefulness for anxiety, they are also used for depression. Common side effects include difficulties with sexual function and gastrointestinal effects. Effexor can be difficult to stop because some people experience significant withdrawal symptoms.

- **Benzodiazepines:** Examples include Xanax, Ativan, Klonopin, and Valium. Ideally, they are used only on a short-term basis. Physical dependence can develop when these medications are used regularly for a few weeks. Xanax, in particular, can cause "rebound" anxiety and insomnia when it wears off. Common side effects of the benzodiazepines include sedation and coordination problems. These medications also negatively affect memory.

- **Buspirone:** I find buspirone (brand name BuSpar) to be useful in cases of mild anxiety when the individual has never used a benzodiazepine medication. Side effects are generally minimal. Unfortunately, the therapeutic benefit for anxiety is also minimal.

- **Beta Blockers:** Beta blockers are medicines like propranolol (Inderal) that are used for public speaking and other instances of performance anxiety. Used primarily as blood pressure and cardiac medications, the beta blockers have few side effects because the doses we use for anxiety are usually lower than the doses used for blood pressure and heart problems.

➤ **Anticonvulsants/Mood Stabilizers:** Neurontin, Lamictal, and Trileptal are the medications in this class that are used most commonly for anxiety. Neurontin probably has the most usefulness for anxiety among the medicines in the category. Its major side effect is sedation. Neurontin's dose should be started low, often at 100 mg at bedtime, and increased slowly.

ACTION PLAN

With multiple options, you may wonder what to do to help your anxiety. Here is what I suggest:

➤ **Heart-Focused Breathing:** Take a mental time-out at least twice each day and practice Heart-Focused Breathing.

➤ **Butterfly Hug:** Use it at least three times each day, especially when you are feeling anxious or stressed.

➤ **Calming Nutritional Supplements:** Try GABA, L-theanine, and magnesium, one at a time or together. They may be used daily if needed and tolerated for anxiety and stress.

➤ **Diet and Exercise:** A high-protein, gluten-free, dairy-free, sugar-free diet is often helpful because blood sugar swings that contribute to anxiety are reduced. Caffeine contributes to anxiety, so minimize its use. Minimize alcohol and avoid drug use. Aerobic exercise is a sure anxiety reducer. Exercise every day and work up a sweat; your anxiety will be lower.

➤ **Obtain Professional Help:** When these approaches are not enough, consult a professional to try CBT, biofeedback, neurofeedback, acupuncture, or medication.

8

Mood Matters: Depression

Jeanette came to me for help with depression. A single mother, age forty-five, she worked as a legislative assistant on Capitol Hill. Jeanette told me that she had long-standing moderate depression, which had been present all her life. She functioned well enough at work, where she was highly regarded. At home Jeanette seemed to devote whatever free time she had to her two young daughters. She was by all accounts a good mother.

The problem was that Jeanette had no joy, no spark, no zest, no happiness. She felt as if she were going through the motions. Jeanette's dark mood was always there, but she didn't cry, didn't take to her bed, and certainly had never been so bad off that she couldn't function. She was a trouper who, despite her depression, bit the bullet, put her head down, and kept on going. Before consulting me, Jeanette had tried to reduce her depression by optimizing her diet, exercising, answering back her negative thoughts, and taking nutritional supplements. Unfortunately, the results were not what she had hoped for. Her depression remained more or less unchanged.

Jeanette was afraid of medication and wanted to be treated for her depression with psychotherapy. We began meeting weekly for psychotherapy. After a few months, I noticed a curious pattern. Whenever I had to cancel our regular appointments for personal reasons, such as a professional meeting or my planned vacation, Jeanette's depression worsened, often significantly. For a week or two after my return she was *really* down in the dumps. We'd talk about it, but it was difficult for Jeanette to understand what was going on when I was absent. After some months, she was able to articulate that it was something about my being away that was related to her flare-ups of depression. What Jeanette didn't suspect, but I began to, was that her worsening periods were related to her difficulties forming attachments.

As we've underscored, relationships are key for humans. We're not like one of my favorite animals, sea turtles, whose mothers dig a hole on the beach, deposit hundreds of eggs, and then leave forever. That's the extent of reptile maternal care—building a good nest for the eggs. After that, baby turtles are on their own. They must hatch and make their way immediately to the sea with no parental assistance.

Not so for us humans. Humans are born helpless and experience a long period of caring, learning, and growth with their parents, at least in optimal circumstances. You will recall that I've underscored the importance of early attachment relationships in forming a healthy sense of self as well as allowing for optimal brain development. To better understand the connection between early attachment relationships and depression in terms of what's going on in the brain, we must look at the thalamus.

Early on we talked about the thalamus as one of the major components of the limbic system, the other components being the anterior cingulate, the basal ganglia, and the amygdala. The thalamus is located deep within the brain beneath the cortex and serves a number of important functions. It is a relay station, collecting and sending information to the cortex. The thalamus is involved with bonding, appetite, sleep, pain conditions, and sexual desire. It colors your emotional mind and provides the filter through which you interpret life experiences. The thalamus is thus key for attachment and bonding and mood regulation.

As you may already be beginning to suspect, if the problem in depression is a problem with what's going on in the thalamus, and the thalamus is a key component of the limbic system, then perhaps depression is related to yet another imbalance between the PFC and the limbic system. You would be right. Excessive activity in the thalamus is often at the root of serious mood disorders like depression, bipolar disorder, and even premenstrual problems. We feel and function better when the thalamus is at a lower level of activity. Individuals with mood disorders have a busy brain because the excessive activity in their thalamus cannot be checked or reined in adequately by the PFC.

Note that I said the problem or brain imbalance is with excessive activity in the thalamus, not underactivity. This is not a typo. Somewhat counterintuitively, many forms of depression do not occur because our brains are going too slowly. Rather, it's because our thalamus is going double time. We may feel like we are trudging through sludge when we're depressed, but in unipolar depression, activity in the thalamus has speeded up. As with many busy-brain problems and imbalances in the PFC–limbic system, the PFC has difficulty reining in its limbic brethren.

When we speak of overactivity of the thalamus in depression, we are usually talking about unipolar depression. A *unipolar mood disorder* is a mood disorder with just one pole—depression. *Bipolar mood disorder*, by contrast, refers to two poles—an individual experiences depression at some times and an elevated, irritable, or expansive mood ("mania" or "hypomania") at other times. Depressions in a bipolar mood disorder outnumber periods of mood elevation by three or four to one; that is, depressive periods are much more common.

In unipolar depression, overactivity in the thalamus tends to be diffuse, or evenly spread out. In bipolar depression, thalamic activity is also increased. But—and here's the kicker—in states of bipolar mood elevation or mania, the increased activity in the thalamus tends to be "focal," meaning localized to one side of the thalamus, not throughout the whole thalamus. In addition, in states of bipolar mood elevation, focal thalamic overactivity is typically accompanied by excessive activity throughout the cerebral cortex. The whole brain is too active, which parallels the individual's manic behavior—he or she is too active.

Returning now to unipolar depression, I left out a piece of the puzzle. Those with depression also often have underactive prefrontal cortex function on the left side. Remember that the left hemisphere tends to be more positive than the right side; lower activity on the left, in the prefrontal region, seems to allow the more negative right side to dominate. So we might even view depression as the prototype of the key brain imbalance I've been discussing in this book—the PFC is not functioning at full strength and cannot hold in check overactive limbic (thalamic) activity.

Considering the thalamus, why would depressed individuals have too much activity? We've just touched on one reason—their PFC is not functioning at full strength. Indeed, this corresponds with what we often see in individuals with ADHD—they have an increased prevalence of depression as compared with the general population. The PFC of an ADHD brain can't always hold the wild horses of the thalamus in check.

Why else? Well, genetics can play a role. You may recall from the ADHD chapter that the serotonin transporter gene comes in two forms: "short" and "long." The short version of the serotonin transporter gene is associated with overarousal, serious depression, and PTSD. Why is the short version associated with these problems? Likely because it results in lower serotonin levels; serotonin is a key chemical transmitter. SSRI medications address depression and other problems by increasing serotonin levels. Interestingly, having the short version of the serotonin transporter gene causes the thalamus to be enlarged, and treatment with antidepressant medication reduces the size of an enlarged thalamus.

Another reason for an overactive thalamus can be early attachment difficulties. Previously, we saw that early attachment disruption caused excessive activity in the brain and that affected individuals were more prone to later psychiatric difficulties, which include depression. Remember that the thalamus is intimately involved with bonding and close relationships. It makes sense that depression could thus be both a result of difficulties in key relationships and a cause of relationship problems. With a malfunctioning thalamus, there would be less drive to connect to significant others, given the thalamus's role in bonding.

Recognizing the connection between an overactive thalamus, early attachment disruption, and depression, we now can put together the pieces of the puzzle of Jeanette's depression, which worsened significantly each time she was separated from me. She reacted each time almost as if she had lost me for good. I tried to explore with Jeanette what developmental factors could have contributed to her strong reactions to my absences. There were no significant overt traumas in her history. No physical abuse, no sexual abuse, no emotional abuse. Reading between the lines, however, what I detected was a kind of benign neglect in her childhood. Jeanette was raised in a wealthy, socially prominent family, the kind of family in which much of the child-rearing was performed by hired help—nannies.

You might wonder where Jeanette's parents were in her story. Although Jeanette's mother did not work outside the home, her mother was not very involved in raising Jeanette or her siblings. Jeanette's mother would show up now and then and evince interest, but whatever maternal instincts she had were not very nurturing. Rather, Jeanette's mother's interests centered on managing the household staff and coordinating social and charity events. Jeanette's father was not involved much in her early life, either; he was always occupied with running the large family business, and when he wasn't working at the business he played golf. As a result, Jeanette was raised by nannies, some of whom were well suited for nurturing a child, others less so.

Although Jeanette never could verbalize her developmental history in these terms, I think what happened is that she lacked consistent nurturing when she was young. Some of the nannies were warm and loving, but they didn't stay. Some left abruptly or were fired. Replacement nannies were not always suited to the task of raising a young child. Childhood was a series of broken attachments and losses for Jeanette. I even came to suspect that Jeanette's parents may have prematurely terminated some of the more loving nannies because of jealousy over their nurturing relationship with Jeanette; they were able to give to Jeannette what her parents could not give.

Note that I began the previous paragraph with "Although Jeanette never could verbalize her developmental history in these terms . . ." This is significant. Jeanette's attachment disruptions were so early that she did not have language to describe what happened then because it occurred so early in her life, before she had a capacity to understand and use language. Jeanette really couldn't describe why she became so depressed when I went away either. She knew that she became depressed, of course; she felt it. But she didn't know why. This is an example of enacting what she could not remember. It was only through the enactment with me that I could begin to develop a hypothesis about what was going on.

Jeanette and I continued to meet, week after week, month after month. I continued to try to explore with Jeanette what was occurring with her when she became depressed, but I never felt that we could make headway, at least not enough to bring her relief from both her chronic depression and the more severe depressive periods when I was absent.

After about eighteen months of her more severe depressive periods repeating over and over when I went away, I suggested to Jeanette that she ought to reconsider her initial rejection of medication for depression. I had in mind that an SSRI medication would likely help. Jeanette seemed to be suffering greatly, and I wanted to relieve her suffering, and I suspected that using medication for depression might help her make progress in psychotherapy. Eventually, Jeanette agreed to try medication and we started Zoloft, an SSRI.

Jeanette's chronic depression gradually began to lift after she began taking Zoloft. Imperceptibly at first, but more clearly after six weeks, it was as if Jeanette had had new life breathed into her. She smiled more, seemed to have less of the emotional heaviness I had seen previously, and seemed more optimistic. The first time I needed to cancel appointments, about ten weeks after she started Zoloft, Jeanette had a bit of a mood dip, but not nearly as deep as before. After that, Jeanette had little negative emotional reaction to my absences.

In fact, we initially overshot the mark with Zoloft. It turned out that Jeanette is sensitive to medication. I prescribed a normal dose of 50 mg for her. What happened was that Jeanette became emotionally numb. She didn't feel sadness, but she didn't feel anything else either. A normal dose of Zoloft turned down her thalamus so much that she couldn't feel anything. Once we realized this, we cut the dose in half, to 25 mg. On that dose, she was able to experience a full range of feelings, including positive ones, but depression didn't hang over her, as it had for most of her life.

Psychotherapy proceeded better after Jeanette started Zoloft. We continued meeting weekly for a couple of months, and then we decided to put our regular meetings on hold because she was doing so well, except for infrequent meetings to make sure Jeanette's medication continued to work effectively. Her Zoloft continued to be of great benefit to Jeanette, as illustrated by her lack of a crash when we stopped meeting regularly.

From a brain systems point of view, what happened when Jeanette improved? My hypothesis is that the optimal dose of Zoloft reduced Jeanette's thalamic overactivity but didn't turn it down too much, as the inadvertent higher dose did. She felt less bad emotionally and was less reactive. When we turned down her overactive thalamus, the approaches we used to strengthen PFC function—psychotherapy, rewriting her stories—had a better chance of being successful. Jeanette's PFC was no longer outgunned by the thalamus, as it had been before we started Zoloft.

Jeanette's case illustrates the complexities of depression. Why was she depressed? Was it lack of consistent attachment and attunement early in life? Did she have a short version of the serotonin transporter gene? Were there other factors? We don't have all the answers. Practically, it is clear that the fundamental intervention that turned things around for Jeanette was medication. Which is not to say that medication is the solution for everyone, but it can be an important part of treatment for those with serious depression. For bipolar disorder, treatment by a medical professional is typically essential. I list my preferred treatment options for bipolar disorder in the medications section of this chapter.

As much my aim in *Reclaim Your Brain* is to discuss steps you can take on your own, I have written about Jeanette in detail because I want to underscore the importance of psychotherapy and medication in healing depression for some individuals for whom other strategies are not sufficiently effective. Our current knowledge of how the brain works—of how people work—remains incomplete and will likely continue that way for a long time to come. I must say, however, that the changes I have seen brought about by SSRI medications and other antidepressants in some patients have been remarkable, far different from what one reads and hears so often that these medications are no better than a placebo. That does not accord with my experience. Because this point is so important, and so poorly understood, I have chosen to present the story of Jeanette to underscore for readers that one should strongly consider antidepressant medication when other approaches for moderate to severe depression are not sufficiently effective. Antidepressant medicine, when used thoughtfully and appropriately, can make life worth living or even save lives.

Depression's Upside?

The treatment of depression through antidepressants has many supporters in the medical community. Antidepressants also attract their fair share of controversy. Why does the prescription of drugs such as Zoloft cause so much controversy when they can be so effective? Some of this may have to do with depression's familiarity.

We psychiatrists call depression the "common cold of psychiatry," because it is common, very common. Depression goes beyond mere sadness. Sadness is a state of mild to moderate unhappiness. It is not an enduring state that colors most or all of life, as one would experience with a serious depressive episode. Depending on the situation, if you are sad, you can be capable of smiling and being happy. In contrast, if you have depression, you have difficulty being happy, because unhappiness pervades everything, as if you are looking through darkly colored glasses. Sadness and its relative, grief, both of which are related to life changes and loss, can merge into depression. On the other hand, we often find in cases of serious depression that there is no change or loss; in these serious cases there is no easy answer to the question, "Why are you depressed?" An individual with clinical depression, which means depression that is severe enough to warrant professional help, experiences persistent feelings of sadness and loss of interest in life's usual satisfactions, among other symptoms.

Because depression is so common, many argue that it is too common for an automatic reach for prescription meds. One concern is that we may be medicating away normality, trying to make everyone the same. As if there were a pharmacological Big Brother. I don't hold that view, but let's consider potential upsides of depression.

Because depression is so widespread, it's led some scientists to consider whether depression might be beneficial to us. Paul W. Andrews, postdoctoral fellow at Virginia Commonwealth University, and J. Anderson Thomson, Jr., staff psychiatrist at University of Virginia Student Health's Counseling and Psychological Services, are researchers who have studied depression's evolutionary upside. They propose that rumination, a negative mental loop common in depression, is actually an evolved response to complex problems; its function is to minimize distractions. That is, in depressive rumination we become stuck on dealing with the problem at hand, avoiding getting distracted by other issues. Rumination, they found, not only reduces the desire to engage in distracting activities but also produces psychomotor changes (the relationship between thinking and physical movement) that reduce exposure to unnecessary distractions. Moreover, research suggests that depression may improve analytic thinking and persistence, qualities useful in complex tasks, by breaking down problems into smaller components.

Anecdotal evidence suggests that people with depression are more sensitive to the needs of others. Thus, if you're feeling blue, you are likely to be more empathic and sensitive. Also, in some cases, those with depression are able to tap into their emotional pain and use their feelings to create powerful artwork, profound literature, or heart-opening music. Indeed, my own observation is that those who are prone to depression are often sensitive individuals. Some philosophers and psychotherapists believe that experiencing depression can help us grow. "Sorrow is the vitamin of growth" is a quote from the late eminent psychoanalyst Elvin Semrad, M.D.

Finally, some posit that depression is an evolutionary strategy used to reduce the sense that one could be a threat to others. Energy, motivation, and emotional strength are all reduced. Moreover, if this hypothesis is true, depression could also be adaptive in eliciting help from others.

Whether depression is an evolved response to everyday problems or not, we can be certain that it's a painful disorder for those who experience it. Seasonal and circadian rhythms provide some keys to strategies that may help lift depression.

Seasonal Affective Disorder (SAD)

Brenda, forty-three, a well-respected attorney, came to see me because she was frustrated about not being able to control her depression. A careful evaluation showed that Brenda worsened significantly each fall and winter. She did function during the fall and winter, but life felt like a constant struggle. She isolated herself, cried frequently, lost interest in her usual activities, and had low energy and low motivation. During these winter periods of low mood she slept twelve to fourteen hours each day and ate too much. Because of her seasonal worsening, I questioned Brenda about her function during the spring and summer. It became clear that Brenda had elevated moods during these times. Why were her moods so drastically different between winter and summer?

That many individuals experience worsening of mood in fall and winter attests to the human organism's evolution in concert with our natural environment. Most—but not all—people notice mood dips and worsening as the days become shorter and temperatures become colder. When your energy, motivation, and mood dip too low in fall and winter, you may well have SAD—seasonal affective (mood) disorder.

Those with SAD are hypersensitive to changes in the natural light in fall and winter, much more so than are most people. Moreover, research suggests that individuals with SAD have a distinctive relationship between light and altered emotional responsiveness that individuals without SAD do not have. Finally, SAD seems related to serotonin availability, with evidence of lower serotonin function in the thalamus like we often see in non-SAD cases of depression. Thus, although there are differences between SAD and non-SAD depression, there are important similarities.

The treatment of choice for SAD is light treatment, which was pioneered by Norman Rosenthal, M.D. Light treatment mimics exposure to natural sunlight and artificially extends the solar day, resetting circadian clocks. That individuals with SAD often need to sleep too much, crave carbohydrates, and experience fatigue suggests that fundamental circadian rhythms have been thrown off kilter in SAD, supporting the importance of interventions to regularize circadian rhythms for seasonal depression. These same strategies to regularize circadian rhythms are useful for treating bipolar disorder; in fact, a significant proportion of individuals with bipolar disorder have SAD. Finally, because many nonbipolar, non-SAD depressions involve unhealthy alterations in energy expenditure, activity, sleep, and nutrition (so-called vegetative functions), interventions to normalize circadian patterns are helpful in these cases as well and likely ultimately have a downstream effect on thalamic overactivity.

Mood stabilizer medication and light treatment during the fall and winter gave Brenda great relief. I helped Brenda understand that she needed to carefully manage her sleep and diet. With these treatment interventions, Brenda has done well, without the typical worsening in the fall and winter she had in the past.

Though people with SAD are almost always affected in fall and winter, I did have one surprising case where the pattern was reversed. Neil, forty-one, an attorney, was the son of well-off parents. His father was a highly sought-after political consultant. Neil's mother was a well-known actress, his brother was a prominent engineer, and his sister was a leader in the tech industry. They were all bright and accomplished, including Neil. Unfortunately, this was a family with a strong history of mood disorders. Neil's mother, for example, experienced repeated bouts of disabling depression. One time she had to be hospitalized. Neil himself had significant mood fluctuations. Most of the time he had a low mood, with no energy, no motivation, and hopelessness. Occasionally, Neil experienced highs lasting from several days to a couple of weeks. During these times, he had racing thoughts, thought he could solve fundamental world problems, didn't need to sleep, and juggled several different women at the same time. Neil rarely experienced a normal stable mood. His depressions were very disabling. He'd lie on his couch for weeks at a time, not working, not bathing, rarely eating, and speaking with no one. Treatment with mood stabilizer medication and interpersonal and social rhythm therapy (discussed next) eventually helped Neil become much more stable. I educated Neil and his family on the signs and symptoms of potential relapse—for Neil, disrupted sleep was a key indicator. Interestingly, Neil had reverse SAD; that is, he typically became depressed in the spring and summer and had mood elevations in the fall and winter. To help Neil address his reverse SAD, I instructed him to avoid sunlight as much as possible, wear sunglasses when outside, and run his air conditioner at a low temperature all the time during the spring and summer. In essence, we were trying to trick his body into thinking that spring and summer had not arrived. These unusual interventions were helpful for Neil and added to his mood stability.

Interpersonal and Social Rhythm Therapy for Mood Issues

Interpersonal and Social Rhythm Therapy (IPSRT) was developed by Ellen Frank, Ph.D., at the University of Pittsburgh. IPSRT addresses the disruption in circadian rhythms found often in recurrent depression and bipolar disorder. The goal of IPSRT is to prevent new episodes of illness or to extend the duration of time between episodes of illness. By focusing on medication nonadherence, stressful life events (especially relational issues), and disruptions in daily routines, IPSRT attempts to help individuals cope with a potentially lifelong propensity to have mood disruptions. Altered daily rhythms and routines are likewise related to mood problems. Dr. Frank found that addressing relationship issues and maintaining regular daily rhythms in sleeping, waking, eating, and exercise help reduce relapses. In severe cases, IPSRT cannot replace medication but is a useful approach for individuals with mood disorders.

Relationship issues are often related to a downward spiral into an episode of a mood disorder, which is why IPSRT pays such close attention to them. The challenges to a relationship are great when one of the partners has mood issues, yet precisely because the relationship itself can negatively affect the mood disorder, it's important to confront those challenges head on and halt the negative spiral before it spins out of control.

Kathy, forty-eight, married with three children, was a competent IT specialist who came to see me because she was frustrated about not being able to control her moods. Kathy's mood worsened significantly each fall and winter, when life felt like a constant struggle. She isolated herself, cried frequently, lost interest in her usual activities, and had low energy and low motivation. During these winter periods of low mood she slept twelve hours each day and ate too much. When her mood was low she gave her children less attention and was irritable toward her husband, Ken, who tended to pull away in response. I suggested to Kathy that she try a light box during fall and winter. She sat in front of the light box for a half hour each morning. Light treatment helped improve Kathy's mood significantly, but we soon learned that their marriage had been negatively affected by Kathy's depression.

Ten Suggestions to Improve Relationships When One of the Partners Has a Mood Disorder

1. Look at the people you spend time with. How do they make you feel? What are the interactions like? Do you feel buoyed up when you are with them? Do you feel dragged down? Take stock. When Kathy's husband, Ken, looked at his relationship with Kathy, he recognized that he felt beaten down by her irritability toward him. Plus, her low energy and low motivation felt like a heavy weight around his neck, pulling him down. You need to begin to recognize and evaluate your own feelings before you can communicate to your partner.

2. Make sure you are clear yourself about what you want in the relationship and discuss those wants clearly with the person you care about. Ken wanted peace, without Kathy's irritable attacks, and he wanted a wife who was present emotionally. Kathy wanted help at home and with their children. They were able to communicate these things to each other.

3. For troublesome relationships, recognize your contribution. Own your part. Commit to change. Ken owned that he withdrew from Kathy when she became cranky and irritable. Kathy owned that her irritability pushed Ken away and that her low energy and motivation were a drag on everybody in the family.

4. Tell the other person, specifically, what they are doing that is hurtful. Focus on their actions, not them. Ask them to change. If they can't or won't change, reduce your involvement or end the relationship. Kathy and Ken each were able to be clear with the other, without needing to reduce involvement or end the relationship.

5. To develop more positive relationships you may have to make changes to meet new people: take a class, do volunteer work, go to lunch with your coworkers, contact an old friend whom you've not spoken with recently, or try a new hobby. Kathy tended to withdraw from her friends during fall and winter depressions. With encouragement, she reconnected with friends with whom she had been out of contact.

6. Make your important relationships a priority. Do you spend adequate time together? This was a problem for Ken and Kathy due to their busy lives and Kathy's withdrawal and isolation during her depression. They needed to commit to more time with each other.

7. Focus on the positive in relationships. Watch out for the creeping negativity that seems to be our default stance. It's so easy to be negative and critical. It was easy for Kathy and Ken to be critical of each other. However, it wasn't difficult for each to recognize positive traits in the other, like Kathy's good mothering skills, or how Ken was good at keeping the family cars running well.

8. Encourage the personal growth of those who are important to you. Support them in new endeavors like career change, more education, or pursuing a hobby. Ken was interested in pursuing photography, and Kathy was able to support him in his new pursuit.

9. If your relationship is a sexually intimate one, make sure that you nurture that aspect of the relationship. It's easy to get into a rut. With Kathy's irritability, lower energy, and withdrawal

during her depressed periods, sex fell by the wayside. Ken and Kathy needed to carve out time to rekindle their intimate relationship.

10. No matter what, always keep the lines of communication open.

Relationships suffer when one of the parties has depression, but attention to relationships can help with healing. Helping someone who is depressed doesn't only have to be about the relationship.

Suggestions for Helping a Depressed Loved One

1. Encourage your depressed loved one to get professional help, if needed. Seek therapy as a couple or family as appropriate.

2. Don't tell your depressed partner that you understand. You may not understand.

3. Respond to your depressed partner as if they were recovering from a serious illness. They are.

4. Don't take the depressed individual's loss of interest in sex personally; it's typical for depression.

5. If you have a depressed individual in your life, you need to make sure that you don't end up beaten down. The nondepressed individual needs to focus on taking care of himself or herself. It's your job to make you happy, not the depressed person's.

6. Take a walk together with the depressed person. It's time together, and exercise can improve mood.

Recommendations for Mood, Sleep, and Circadian Rhythms

> **Sleep:** Good-quality sleep is essential. This is true for all individuals, and even more true for those with a mood disorder. Go to

bed and get up at the same time every day. This helps keep your biological clock regular. Keep your bedroom temperature moderate. Minimize liquids in the evening. Avoid alcohol in the evening; it fragments sleep. Also avoid caffeine. Avoid naps during the day. Eliminate exposure to bright artificial light two hours before you go to bed. Make sure you are more than six feet away from the television if you watch before sleeping. If needed, take an over-the-counter supplement or medication. Ask your doctor for a sleeping medication, if necessary.

➤ **Light Exposure:** Try to expose yourself to bright light outdoors between eight a.m. and noon; twenty to thirty minutes of morning light is enough.

➤ **Work:** If possible, avoid shift work and select a workplace that provides exposure to natural light and a view of the outside. If your workplace does not have natural light, try to get outside for twenty to thirty minutes during daylight, mornings preferred.

➤ **Electronics in Bed:** Avoid light-emitting devices in bed.

➤ **Light Boxes:** A number of companies sell light boxes; some rent them. A light visor does the same job as a light box but can be more convenient. Start light treatments gradually; the box should be used first thing in the morning, for five minutes the first day, and then for periods of time increasing by five minutes a day, until a treatment period of thirty minutes is reached. A second treatment of fifteen to thirty minutes, usually no later than midafternoon, is often helpful. Late second doses of light therapy can cause insomnia. Light therapy is generally more effective the earlier in the day it is performed, so if you can do it at about six a.m., light treatment may be most helpful. In some cases, light treatment has made susceptible individuals hypomanic, causing mild mood elevation. When that occurs, reducing the duration of the light exposure is usually sufficient to remedy the light-induced hypomania.

- **Light Precautions for SAD:** Besides light box treatment for SAD, here are recommendations that one might call "light precautions" for SAD: Increase your exposure to light as much as possible, go out for a walk at noon for up to an hour without sunglasses, and sleep with all the blinds up.

- **Light Treatment for Non-SAD Depression:** Importantly, depressed individuals with non-SAD depression often respond well to light treatment. This intervention is often not considered, but should be more often.

- **Dialectical Behavior Therapy (DBT):** Those with severe depression not responsive to other treatments should consider DBT (websites to check to find providers include www.dbt-therapists .com and www.dbtselfhelp.com).

- **IPSRT:** If you have recurrent mood problems, investigate IPSRT (www.ipsrt.org). Working with your clinician on the principles of IPSRT can be of significant benefit.

Nutritional Supplements for Depression

A number of nutritional supplements show promise for treatment of mild to moderate depression.

- **Omega-3 fatty acids:** The dose is at least 3,000 mg/day of the total of EPA and DHA.

- **SAMe:** People who have bipolar disorder or manic depression need to be careful with SAMe, because it may cause unwanted mood elevations. Take it before breakfast and lunch on an empty stomach. If taken later in the day, it may interfere with sleep. Start at 200 or 400 mg/day and then increase the dose gradually, if tolerated. Some people may require 1,600 mg or more per day.

- **5-HTP:** We generally start 5-HTP at 50 mg twice a day, increase the dose after several days to 100 mg twice daily, and then if needed increase again to 150 mg twice daily, based on response. This supplement begins to work quite quickly, in most cases within several days.

- **L-tyrosine:** This amino acid helps with focus, energy, and motivation. For the first three days, take 500 mg before breakfast, midmorning, and then midafternoon. After three days increase to 1,000 mg before breakfast, midmorning, and midafternoon. Thereafter, some people increase to 1,500 mg at each dose. Take it on an empty stomach.

- **St. John's wort:** Adults start at 600 mg in the morning and 300 mg at night. Sometimes the dose may be increased slowly to 1,800 mg daily. Wear sunscreen—St. John's wort increases the risk of sunburn.

- **L-theanine:** L-theanine promotes relaxation and mood modulation. The usual dose is 200 mg three or four times per day. You can take higher doses if you find it useful. There are no known adverse reactions. Pregnant women and nursing mothers should avoid L-theanine.

- **Vitamin D:** The dose is 5,000 to 10,000 IU/day.

Although most people with a bipolar disorder require medication in order to have stable moods, some do well without medication. Elaine was a psychologist who wrestled with disorganized, distracted thoughts. Her brain never felt calm and she never acted calmly. Previous doctors had diagnosed her with ADHD, but she never responded well to what seemed to me to be reasonable treatment approaches. In fact, she often became depressed, moody, irritable, and anxious when she took stimulant medication.

I had the advantage of being able to perform a thorough assessment of Elaine, including gathering a detailed longitudinal history.

What became clear was that Elaine actually had a previously undetected bipolar disorder. Worsening of mood stability in bipolar disorder is common when stimulants are given. With this new information, I explained to Elaine that we needed to calm her overactive limbic system before we could boost her prefrontal cortex. This all made sense to Elaine, who then started using high doses of fish oil and the supplement GABA to calm her overactive limbic areas. We could have used a medication like Lamictal or Depakote, but Elaine preferred natural supplements. Having calmed her limbic areas, we could then have Elaine try L-tyrosine to boost her PFC, which she tolerated well, without the worsening of mood stability.

On this new treatment approach, Elaine was finally able to successfully use relaxation breathing and other stress-reduction approaches to calm her busy brain, approaches that previously had never worked for her because her brain had not been sufficiently well balanced. She also paid close attention to daily rhythms, sleep, exercise, and diet. Though Elaine's case illustrates some approaches that can be useful for those with less severe mood swings, her case is highly unusual. If you have a bipolar disorder, please do not stop your medication without discussing the matter extensively with your doctor. As I have mentioned above, it is the rare bipolar patient who can do well without medication.

Medication for Depression

We now believe that antidepressant medication changes gene expression (turns genes on and off) in the hippocampus and likely other brain areas. Antidepressant medication actually seems to cause new cells to grow in the hippocampus, reversing the hippocampal cell death seen with depression and stress. Keep in mind that we try to treat episodes of bipolar depression without antidepressant medication, because of the risk of causing more rapid mood cycling. If an antidepressant is needed for bipolar depression, Wellbutrin XL may be the best choice.

Medications used commonly for depression include the following:

➤ **SSRIs:** Lexapro, Zoloft, Prozac, Celexa

➤ **SNRIs:** Effexor and Cymbalta

➤ **Wellbutrin XL:** More energizing and activating than most other antidepressants; lack of sexual side effects is a big advantage over SSRIs

➤ **Abilify:** Not strictly an antidepressant, but helpful as an add-on to antidepressants in some cases

Medications for bipolar disorder:

➤ **Bipolar Depression:** It's best to attempt to treat bipolar depression without antidepressant medication, because antidepressants may bring about more rapid cycling and mood instability.

➤ **Bipolar Mood Stabilization:** Lithium is the gold standard treatment, likely the most effective medication. Anticonvulsant medications are often used alone or added to lithium. Atypical antipsychotic medications, such as Risperdal, Zyprexa, and Seroquel, are effective but can have significant side effects of weight gain and increases in blood lipids and blood glucose. Most individuals with bipolar disorder require more than one mood-stabilizing medication.

ACTION PLAN

➤ **Exercise:** Moderate aerobic exercise can be as helpful for some as antidepressant medication. The trouble is, we don't feel like exercising when we are depressed. If you can, exercise five times a week for thirty to forty-five minutes. As I tell my patients, you don't have to run marathons or climb mountains. Find something you enjoy that raises your heart rate and makes you sweat. Walk briskly as if you are in a hurry. Ride a bike. Swim. Play tennis.

➤ **Supplements:** Try SAMe or 5-HTP. They can be used together, but make sure you start one at a time.

➤ **Light Therapy:** Get outside every day, if you can, and expose yourself to the natural elements. Consider using a light box or light visor even if you don't have SAD. Definitely use light treatment if you do have SAD.

➤ **CBT:** CBT provides a structured approach for dealing with the negative thoughts in depression.

➤ **IPSRT:** Anyone with recurring depression or bipolar disorder should familiarize themselves with the principles of IPSRT. Regular daily rhythms, especially sleep, are essential for someone with a serious mood disorder.

➤ **Medication:** Do not be afraid to use medication if these steps do not give you enough help. Individuals with bipolar disorder typically require the care of a psychiatrist and should give serious consideration to using medication.

— → 9 ←—

Getting Unstuck: OCD

Have you ever felt stuck on a thought? Nagged by a worry you simply can't seem to banish from your mind? Walked down the street with a difficult conversation constantly replaying in your head? Sometimes our busy brains play a scenario over and over again, without a solution. Often we imagine the worst. That ache in our shoulder could be serious; maybe it's cancer. Maybe the boss's comment means that our job is in jeopardy. Bedtime is often a particularly bad moment—the quiet and lack of distraction allow our ruminative thoughts to go wild. With such a busy brain we can't fall asleep, or we awaken in the middle of the night with the cracked record of worries playing over and over again. We're stuck. And the image of being stuck, as it turns out, is a useful way of understanding what's literally happening in our brain.

Error Detection and Incapacitating Stuckness

Our brains are hardwired to detect mistakes. We have error-detection circuits in the brain that constantly search for potential mistakes or dangers, orienting the organism to take steps to protect itself. This error-detection capacity, which happens automatically, is thus for a good reason: it optimizes our chances of survival.

Think of the antivirus program on your computer. It scans each website, download, and e-mail for threats. When the antivirus protection works well, it's almost invisible—working in the background, holding things up for just a few milliseconds as it scans for unwanted intruders. However, imagine that the antivirus program is not functioning well; in that case, it might flag nearly every website, e-mail, and document as being a potential threat, even when no threat is there. The flow of your work on the computer would be slowed down immensely. Eventually, the computer might become paralyzed, and with it your ability to work. That's what happens when the error-detection circuits in your brain are overactive. You become slowed, sometimes to the point of paralysis, needing to check and recheck and yet check again. Stuck, sometimes to the *n*th degree.

Error checking matters. Our ancestors from many thousands of years ago needed to constantly scan for threats to their existence. Whether in matters of hygiene (think cleanliness and contamination obsessions such as repetitive and excessive hand washing) or the safety of one's family and dwelling (think lock-checking compulsions), checking and even double-checking likely improved the chances of staying safe and secure, of surviving.

Obviously, survival behaviors have their place, and mild stuckness on these behaviors may be a good thing. Regular hand washing reduces the risk of contamination and the spread of infection. Some of the religious traditions regarding food in Judaism and Islam may well be variations and extensions of genetically determined behaviors to optimize cleanliness. However, more severe obsessions and compulsions are the mistake-detection circuitry run amok. The antivirus program flags every little thing, paralyzing the computer and blocking you from doing the work you need to accomplish.

Brain Anatomy and Circuits in Stuckness

There are three key players in the brain's error-detection circuitry: the caudate (a component of the basal ganglia), the anterior cingulate, and the orbital-frontal cortex.

The **caudate,** part of the limbic system, seems to generate the emotional anguish connected with the error messages, announcing that there is imminent danger that needs to be attended to immediately. This emotional anguish is the sense of an impending catastrophe.

The **anterior cingulate** is the brain's gear shifter, which, if functioning well, allows us to shift smoothly from one thing to another. When the anterior cingulate is working well, one can cooperate with others, see options, have cognitive flexibility, and go with the flow. When it isn't working well, we are stuck, rigid, and cannot transition our thoughts and attention easily from one thing to another; we're stuck on the perceived danger, just like the antivirus program is stuck on and keeps flagging that innocent e-mail you're trying to download.

The **orbital-frontal cortex** is the error-detection center; this is the antivirus software, so to speak. When it works well, it appropriately sends error messages about problematic or dangerous situations, just as properly functioning antivirus software does. When it doesn't work well, when it is too sensitive, it flags situations it shouldn't flag, just as a malfunctioning antivirus program flags files that really are safe.

Brain SPECT of individuals prone to stuckness typically shows excessive brain activity in the anterior cingulate and caudate areas. The notion of being stuck and of an excessively busy brain may seem at first to be a contradiction. It's not. The excessively busy brain of somebody who is stuck typically manifests excessive cingulate and caudate brain activity that cannot be adequately reined in by the PFC. Remember how with depression, excessive thalamus activity sent the delicate balance between the PFC and limbic system (of which the thalamus is a part) topsy-turvy? It's the same with stuckness. Only this time the limbic system culprit is excessive anterior cingulate and caudate brain activity rather than excessive thalamus activity. In both cases the apple cart of PFC–limbic system balance has been upset, leading to classic busy brain.

When the PFC inadequately regulates the excess cingulate and caudate activity, individuals who are stuck feel keyed up, needing to do something to relieve their inner tension, but no matter what they do, the tension remains. An individual with stuckness or OCD cannot "gate" or appropriately filter the information flow from lower centers (anterior cingulate and caudate) to the cortex. Too many disturbing thoughts about potential errors keep reaching the prefrontal cortex, which is not able to control these error messages, motivating us toward activity in response to the error messages, just like the malfunctioning or oversensitive antivirus program keeps flagging safe files, making us spend time checking the files—a busy brain par excellence caused by anterior cingulate and caudate wild horses run amok.

Activity of the error-detection circuit that is a bit overactive, but not extremely high, causes us to appropriately check and organize. Organization is a key to success in modern life. I could not function well as a physician if I could not organize my workload; developing systems and routines for things I do repetitively saves time, ensuring that I take care of all of the details and that I am the best doctor I can be to my patients. Most physicians have a little bit of stuckness, which helps. Wouldn't you want your doctor to double-check? I would. High motivation to do the right thing, even perfectionism, can enhance function and survival.

Slightly elevated activity of the error-detection circuitry results in conscientious and effective individuals. Maybe they are even perfectionistic. This is the good part of higher activity in the error-detection circuit. But where does perfectionism merge into obsessive-compulsive behavior? Problems arise when double-checking becomes triple-checking and then becomes stuckness carried out ad infinitum. There is no hard and fast dividing line that determines when checking—or any other potentially dysfunctional stuck behavior—becomes a problem. Practically when a behavior—say, checking—causes distress (think emotional pain) or disability (think interfering with day-to-day function), then we call it pathological, a problem, a disorder—a malfunctioning antivirus program inappropriately flagging nearly everything.

Stuckness, difficulty shifting our mental gears, includes OCD and a number of less obvious problems. My clinical experience and brain SPECT have taught me that in addition to OCD, a number of other conditions join in the pantheon of stuckness, including oppositional defiant disorder (ODD), scrupulosity (pathological guilt about imagined moral or religious failings), autism, eating disorders, pathological gambling, and addictions to alcohol and drugs. Because they are special cases of stuckness, we will cover addictions in Chapter 11.

As I have suggested, stuckness and OCD-type behaviors exist on a spectrum, from rumination, mild double-checking, perfectionism, and conscientiousness at one end to severe, disabling OCD on the other that renders an individual absolutely nonfunctional. With milder cases of stuckness, we find that the feared problems and dangers are usually social. In modern society, we don't need to occupy ourselves as much with literal survival issues as our ancestors did. Rather, the potential threats and dangers we face have to do more with our relationships. Am I attractive enough? Will I be accepted? Will I be admired? Will I be loved? Will I be rejected? Will I be successful? Individuals with these milder stuckness issues ruminate on perceived social dangers and social mistakes, of potential faux pas. They ruminate about failure, embarrassment, humiliation, and social rejection.

OCD and ADHD Compared

Individuals with ADHD and OCD/stuckness are both flooded with stimuli, but for different reasons. In ADHD, the individual cannot properly filter external stimuli. Their busy brain jumps around from one thing to another. The individual is distracted by his or her inability to properly filter *external* stimuli. In OCD, as we pointed out earlier, the individual cannot properly filter *internal* stimuli. It is as if they are recipients of constant error messages, with each message jarring them as a result. Stuckness is a daytime nightmare of repeatedly needing to try to address what is "wrong," to turn off the error-detection circuit. But because the error-detection circuit malfunctions, one can never be at peace. The error alarm sounds continuously, no matter what. The antivirus program continues to inappropriately flag as dangerous the innocent file your grand-daughter e-mailed to you.

Let's consider how distraction by internal and external stimuli results in problems with focus. In ADHD, there is too little focus; one is scattered, distracted. Important issues are not attended to or missed because the mind can't stay with something (especially "boring" things) long enough, even when important. Many individuals with ADHD need novelty in order to generate interest. In OCD, there is too much focus on the perceived dangers generated from the malfunctioning error-detection circuit, albeit in a narrow, nonproductive, possibly dysfunctional area. With stuckness, important issues are not attended to or are missed because the mind is stuck on relatively nonessential things (contamination, for example). Individuals with OCD and ADHD do have in common that they have poor self-regulation; in OCD, there is excessive self-regulation because of unimportant error messages. In ADHD, there is weak self-regulation because of distraction and focus problems with external factors; these individuals have difficulty selecting and sticking with the most important issues they face.

Genetics and Life Changes Predispose for Stuckness and OCD

There is some genetic predisposition for OCD; it does seem to run in families. Moreover, although we rarely find a psychological "meaning" behind the symptoms, we often do observe the onset of OCD symptoms following a life change or a period of stress, as if the life changes and stress destabilize a previously stable equilibrium. Those with OCD find that their symptoms wax and wane through the course of their lives, similar to how someone with a predisposition for mood problems such as depression has periodic symptomatic recurrences.

OCD is when our brain takes error detection to the extreme and is best treated with professional help. But many of us experience a more common version of feeling stuck. We ruminate, we unhealthily return again and again to a small slight. When this happens, there are strategies that you can use to reduce commonplace stuckness. These strategies divert attention away from mental stuckness and recruit the PFC to offset the brain's overactive error-detection circuitry. Ted's and Barb's examples illustrate how to use these strategies yourself.

Ted, thirty-four, had worked since his college graduation for his father's successful real estate firm. He'd done well. However, although his father was a good and decent man and employer, Ted yearned to step out of his father's shadow. One way to do this was to take a position with another real estate firm, in which he hoped that he could spread his wings and fly—if not solo, then more under his own power. An opportunity arose in a nearby city, but Ted would have to interview for the position. That was the problem.

After arranging the interview, Ted began to ruminate. What if the owner of the other firm was critical of Ted because Ted had only worked for his father? Would that owner think that Ted couldn't make it on his own? And even if he got the job, could he do it? He began to feel unsure; his confidence waned. Ted became stuck on these fears and worried that he had been too dependent on his father, too much under his protection. Did he really have what it takes to be successful on his own? The two weeks leading up to the job interview threatened to be miserable. Ted couldn't shake these thoughts. He was stuck on them. His sleep was poor, he lost his appetite, and he was nervous and edgy.

Mindfulness Approach to Stuckness

Mentally separate yourself from the stuckness. Tell yourself, "I am not my brain. This is my brain's mistake-detection system working too hard. This is not me." This approach to help stuck individuals get unstuck is based on general mindfulness principles, CBT, and the work of Jeffrey Schwartz, M.D., a psychiatrist at UCLA.

Ted used the approach of telling himself, "My stuck thoughts are because of my brain's mistake-detection system going haywire." He found it moderately helpful.

Pencil In a Stuck Appointment

Set aside a specific time to ruminate or obsess. Outside those times, work your best to stay away from the stuckness. When stuck thoughts creep up, tell yourself that you'll indulge in them at the scheduled time.

Ted scheduled "stuck appointments" at eight a.m. and three p.m. each day. He allowed himself fifteen minutes to dwell on his ruminative fears about the interview: the owner wouldn't take him seriously, he wouldn't be able to succeed without his father's guidance, he'd fall flat on his face. On and on he went, but only for fifteen minutes during the stuck appointments. Outside those times, Ted diverted his attention from his stuckness, telling himself that he would indulge in his ruminations during the appointed times.

Diversion

Work on your hobby, exercise, watch a movie, do a crossword puzzle. Do anything within reason to get your mind off your ruminations and stuckness and distract yourself in a healthy way. Do something productive or fun for fifteen minutes to let the pressure of stuckness die down. You are diverting your attention from your ruminations, focusing your attention on alternate behaviors, which helps overcome the stuckness stalemate.

Ted really liked crossword puzzles and used them to escape his rumination about his upcoming interview. Each day, he cut out the New York Times *crossword puzzle, kept it nearby, and used it as a positive distraction when his ruminations flared up.*

Laugh at Your Stuckness

Laughter makes situations more tolerable and moves you away from the negative thoughts and feelings you are ruminating about. Make fun of the rumination and stuckness. Recognize the absurdity of your stuckness and laugh at it.

Ted had a natural sense of humor. He got himself to laugh at his ruminations, seeing them as not so important, by focusing on the fact that in several billion years the sun will burn out and the earth will become a cold, lifeless rock; long before then, whether he did well in the interview and succeeded in the new firm would not be important at all in the grand scheme of things.

These simple techniques gave Ted the relief he needed from his stuckness. Ted was moderately nervous on the day of his job interview, but the two weeks leading up to the interview did not turn out to be miserable, as he anticipated, because he was able to use these techniques to gain mastery over his stuckness. Ted did get the new job, and he has since been successful. Whenever ruminations flare up, he goes back to the techniques he used prior to his interview.

Let's now turn to Barb, who managed a successful nonprofit medical clinic that provided healthcare to people with low incomes. Barb dreaded her monthly meetings with the board of directors, all prominent members of the community, including church leaders, the mayor, and well-off individuals whose financial support made possible the services that the clinic provided. Barb couldn't shake the thought that the board might think she was doing a bad job; if they held a negative view about her work, she worried, they could withdraw financial support or even shut down the clinic. Consequently, each week leading up to the monthly board meetings was miserable for her; she felt nauseated, couldn't sleep, and on occasion had panic attacks.

"Stop" Technique

Mentally, yell "Stop" as loud as you can in your mind. Do this as many times a day as you like.

Barb yelled "Stop" in her mind when she tended to become stuck and ruminate on her fears about the board meetings. She initially thought this would be silly, but she tried it and it helped. Yelling "Stop" gave vent to some of the tension she experienced with her stuckness.

Rubber Band Technique

Wear a rubber band on your wrist and snap it every time you become stuck. You could do this all day, if you find it helpful, as many do. Using the rubber band technique, many people notice that their stuck thoughts decrease rapidly.

Barb tried this technique, found it helpful, and took pleasure in finding the widest, most colorful rubber bands she could get her hands on. Snapping the rubber bands reduced her stuckness.

Head Shake

Shake your head as if you were shaking the stuck thoughts out of your head.

Barb often used shaking her head side to side, as if she were shaking out all her stuck thoughts, with benefit. This was an easy technique for Barb, who suspected that it was so helpful because it served as a diversion from her ruminations.

These techniques helped Barb a great deal. Her stuckness on potentially catastrophic outcomes of her monthly board meetings declined about 80 percent over a few months. And she appreciated that these tools were things she could do on her own, whenever she needed them. She was able to reconfigure her brain's antivirus program and get it to work normally.

OCD and the Price of Fertility

The preceding techniques work for those of us who ruminate or experience occasional stuckness. Formal OCD can be a harder case. Sue's example is an instructive one. Sue, thirty-four, was smart, really smart. She came from a hardworking family in which education was paramount. Fortunately for Sue, education came easy. She attended a prestigious private high school and then studied engineering at an Ivy League school.

When she came to see me, Sue had married Lee, an engineer at the firm she joined following college graduation. During her first few years of marriage, Sue tried to get pregnant, with no success. After a year of trying and consultation with fertility specialists, Sue and Lee tried in vitro fertilization (IVF).

Even with IVF, Sue could not conceive. Unfortunately, the different hormones and other medications Sue took during her fertility treatments caused acne outbreaks on her face. Always perfectionistic,

Sue became obsessed with her facial acne. Dermatological treatment, including medication, chemical peels, and laser treatments, had greatly reduced the acne in my opinion; I couldn't see any blemishes. Yet Sue was stuck on her perceived skin blemishes. She wore hats with broad brims and scarves whenever she went out. And she rarely went out. Sue took a leave of absence from work and stopped seeing her friends. At home, she mostly shut herself off from her husband, isolating herself in their bedroom. All because of blemishes that she could hide with makeup.

Recall that we discussed how stuckness can result from the brain's error- and danger-detection circuits run amok? And recall that we talked about how the potential threats we face in modern society have more to do with our relationships than being attacked by a lion on the savannah? Sue is a prime example. She feared that her blemishes would make her unacceptable to others, perhaps unlovable. You and I might conclude, correctly, that Sue overdid her fears of rejection, but that is precisely the point. Her error-detection circuits made her focus excessively on actual, yet—in the grand scheme of things—rather minor blemishes that could be concealed effectively with makeup. Sue became paralyzed.

I suggested that Sue try some of the mindfulness and other approaches that Ted and Barb used with great benefit—the rubber band technique, yelling "Stop," laughing at her stuckness, trying to divert herself—to distract herself from her stuckness on her blemishes. These approaches did little; in fact, she was so stuck that she was even reluctant to try them. Sue was too stuck. She had formal OCD.

Although reluctant to try more medication, given her reaction to the fertility hormones, Sue agreed to use an SSRI, Zoloft, which at high doses is often effective for stuckness and OCD issues. We gradually worked our way up to a dose of 300 mg/day; this is a dose higher than we typically use for depression, but OCD issues typically require higher doses. At 300 mg of Zoloft Sue reported significant benefit. Her OCD issues were reduced about 70 percent. Sue soon returned to work and started again to socialize with her friends. When she returned to being more social, Sue often noticed that she was preoccupied with her skin rather than being attentive to her friends and coworkers. Here, mindfulness and the other approaches mentioned earlier could help. She committed herself to using the Stop technique, diversion, and the rubber band technique. Now these techniques worked.

To underscore an important point, it was only after medication calmed her overactive error-detection circuit that Sue could then use the self-help approaches we discussed to deal with her obsessions with her skin and to improve her presence with friends and coworkers. After two years of treatment with Zoloft, we were able to taper and discontinue it, and Sue continued to do well off the medication. Whenever she has a flare-up, a moment of increased worry about her skin, Sue effectively uses the mindfulness and other approaches we've discussed to make sure that her momentary flare-up of her error-detection circuit—her skin obsession—does not derail her.

Fortunately for Sue and her husband, Lee, her overactive error-detection circuits did not have a profoundly negative effect on their marriage. We now turn to Betty and Peter, whose marriage was profoundly affected by overactive error-detection circuitry. It's a story with an interesting twist. Peter sought help first, but it was in helping Betty with her issues that we found the key to saving their marriage.

Error Detection in a Marriage

In his late forties, married with two children, Peter was an orthopedic surgeon. He also had ADHD, which is why he came for help. Peter was not good with details when situations were not exciting. The adrenaline rush of a complicated surgical trauma case actually calmed Peter, boosting his underaroused PFC (a bit like the wing walker I mentioned earlier), and Peter was well-known for keeping a cool head during surgical disasters. Yet outside the OR, Peter was less effective with small things. Medication for ADHD helped some, but there were limits to how much benefit Peter obtained from stimulant medication.

Life at home was the real problem. Well-meaning, Peter did his best to be a loving father and devoted husband. I learned that a major problem was that Peter's distractibility, a common ADHD symptom, often caused him to forget to do small things around the house. He'd open the blinds but forget to close them at night. He'd forget to put the mayonnaise jar back in the fridge after making a sandwich. Small things, I thought. But not to Betty, Peter's wife.

It turned out that Peter's forgetting to close the blinds, put back the mayo, and other seemingly small things tormented Betty. She was constantly criticizing him for these oversights. He did what he could to try to improve, but his brain just didn't attend to the small stuff when somebody's health and life were not in jeopardy. His underaroused busy brain was all over the place when he wasn't in the OR; the small stuff—like putting the mayo jar back in the fridge—just didn't get him sufficiently aroused.

I concluded that Peter didn't even see the proverbial mayonnaise jar, but Betty accused him of all sorts of relationship crimes, such as that he was intentionally neglecting these things in order to torment her. As best as I could tell, there was no truth in this accusation.

For years Peter had accepted his wife's accusations and attacks, believing that she was justified in labeling him lazy, passive aggressive, and—at times—a horrible husband. Her attacks were an emotional storm that blew Peter off course. He experienced nervousness around his wife because he was waiting for the next attack. Peter was often discouraged, to the point of being depressed.

Peter benefited significantly from a meditation class. As a result, he was less likely to be blown about by his wife's emotional storms. He could more calmly weather her tirades because he was less reactive emotionally. He didn't fight back, as fighting back was not in his nature. Rather, Peter reached a point at which he was able to keep a calm equanimity when she attacked him. Internally, he responded to Betty's attacks with an attitude of "Is that so?" He neither accepted her accusations nor rebutted them. He realized that defense only exacerbated Betty's attacks.

Peter's calmness with Betty made things worse for a time. She upped the ante, attacking him more vehemently. But he was able to hold his own, not accepting her provocative attacks.

On the brink of a separation, Peter suggested that they first see a marital therapist to discuss their problems. Betty reluctantly agreed for the sake of the children.

The Price of Control

What became clearer during several marital counseling sessions was a surprise to everyone involved. Betty's need to keep control over every little thing in her life stemmed from her own feelings of being completely out of control. Betty often felt on a knife's edge due to a childhood assault that she had never disclosed to Peter. Her extreme focus on these small things was her attempt to ward off future disaster. She experienced Peter's distracted oversights almost as if she were again being violated. Her traumatic past was affecting her present.

Betty had been stuck on these small things—the mayo jar, the blinds—so stuck that it is interesting to consider her motivation. The dynamics of the situation were as follows: Betty tried to control every minute detail in her life, from the dust on the counter to the absolute perfection of the floral arrangement on the dining room table to the symmetrical arrangement of the salt and pepper shakers on the pantry shelf. Her error-detection system went into overdrive whenever her absolute attempt to manage any and every little detail was foiled. She unconsciously believed that controlling the minutest thing would ensure that her world would never again become so out of control that she would risk another assault or violation. For Betty, it all was an impossible life-and-death struggle. For Peter, it was just a mayo jar, and not even that, because he hardly thought about it.

Their marital therapist helped Betty share her trauma with Peter and gradually helped the two of them understand Betty's unconscious motivations that drove her overactive error- and danger-detection apparatus. This was a new opening. No longer was there talk of separation and divorce. Instead, Betty continued seeing the marital therapist individually, with Peter joining at times as appropriate. Betty was able to become more mindful about what was going on inside when she noticed herself becoming instantly enraged at Peter's oversights. She eventually learned to catch herself, stop, and breathe, reminding herself that now was not then, that it was simply a mayo jar on the counter, not a repetition of past trauma. Betty also embraced some of the techniques to combat her stuckness, such as diversion, the Stop technique, and penciling in a daily stuck appointment.

Peter and Betty remained together. Peter's mindful stance helped him understand himself better, not accept Betty's negative attributions, and withstand her attacks. He was able to be more empathic with Betty, seeing her attacks as reflecting her emotional wounds. But his mindful approach also destabilized the marital equilibrium. Eventually, the destabilization helped both of them move ahead, to strengthen their marriage. And both parties grew as individuals.

How to Control the Impulse to Control

We all desire to exert some control over our own lives. The freedom to chart our own course is likely the most cherished value in the United States, a bedrock founding principle. But as with Betty, the desire for too much control can destabilize us—and our relationships. What are some steps you can take to relinquish control and/or to stop being controlled by others?

➤ **Control Assessment:** Assess your life honestly. Are you the author of your life? Nobody can be 100 percent in control, but are you in the driver's seat as much as is realistic? Not enough? Or are you trying to control too much?

➤ **Values:** What is most important in your life? For most of us, it's family, health, friends, productive work, perhaps helping others or a relationship with the divine. Correlate your values with your control: Are you trying your best to control your life in the areas that reflect your basic values? Family, friends, health, and other important values are worth a mighty struggle. Are you fighting to control what is most important to you? Maybe you are, maybe you aren't. Are you fighting to control things that aren't import-ant values? Putting back the mayo jar? Closing blinds? Work on those. They are draining valuable energy from your life.

➤ **Strategies to Reduce Excessive Control Tendencies**
  • **Hand over the reins.** Even if for only a day, let someone else do the planning. It's amazing what you learn about yourself—and about others' capabilities—when you let them take charge.
  • **Let go of perfection.** Remember that "better" is the enemy of "good." Take satisfaction in accomplishing tasks, not in perfecting them.
  • **Talk it through.** Find someone to talk to about your priorities. Sometimes just hearing someone echo back to you what you've outlined shows how far out of whack your priorities have become.
  • **Embrace the chaos.** Do something unplanned. Take up a new activity.
  • **Try a twelve-step motto:** *"Let go, let God."* Of course, *God* could mean the world or the universe, reflecting a broader understanding that nobody can control everything and it's silly to try.

Oppositional Defiant Disorder

Trying to exert excessive control like Betty is one form of stuckness. For Betty, it was as if the sought-after perfection of her home would give her magical protection from far more serious traumas like she had experienced in the past. An even simpler form of stuckness—and control—is to automatically veto whatever others suggest. Tyler was a nine-year-old boy I saw a few years ago who often became stuck. His parents had told Tyler and his brothers that they would go to Six Flags Great Adventure, a large amusement park in New Jersey, that coming Saturday. However, in the meantime, Tyler's parents learned that Tyler's uncle Jeff, whom they love and rarely see, would be visiting from out of town that day. Accordingly, Tyler's parents said that the trip to Great Adventure would have to be postponed one week. "But you said that we were going on Saturday," said Tyler. "Yes, we did," said his father, "but we want to spend time with Uncle Jeff on Saturday. We'll go to Great Adventure the following Saturday." That didn't satisfy Tyler. On and on and on he repeated the same refrain: "But you said we were going this Saturday." Tyler was stuck. Nothing could satisfy him. Not even the thought of seeing Uncle Jeff, whom he loved, could placate him. All of this played out in my office, right in front of me.

Tyler had what we call oppositional defiant disorder, or ODD, a condition seen often in stubborn, oppositional children and teens, and sometimes in adults. Their cingulate activity is strong, and they automatically reject anything someone else says. They act as if they are protecting their integrity by being oppositional, by refusing to shift or change plans. Tyler's stuckness on going to Great Adventure was just one instance of his overall pattern.

ODD can be treated with medication, but I decided to treat Tyler with nutritional supplements to boost his serotonin. His parents started by giving Tyler 5-HTP, which was moderately useful in that Tyler seemed a little less stuck. Then they added inositol, which really reduced Tyler's stuckness. Finally, they added GABA, which doesn't increase serotonin but has a generally calming effect on excessive brain activity. With Tyler's 5-HTP, inositol, and GABA, he became much less stuck and much more reasonable. Family life definitely became easier. About eighteen months after Tyler started these supplements, he was weaned off and continued to do well, without an increase in his stuckness.

You may wonder whether Tyler's parents tried the approaches that Ted and Barb used to try to reduce Tyler's stuckness. They didn't, and the reason is that Tyler couldn't buy into his brain being the problem. He was too young to step away from his behavior to see that it was a problem that needed to be addressed. We say that Tyler's stuckness was *ego-syntonic*, that is, it felt like a part of him. With many adults, their stuckness feels *ego-dystonic*, that is, not a part of them but foreign. This makes it easier to mount an offensive against the foreign troops occupying our minds. Not so in a child, whose brain and psyche are immature.

Suggesting to a child that his stuckness results from his error- and danger-detection circuits run amok will either irritate him even more or fall on deaf ears. Nonetheless, it is likely that overactive error- and danger-detection is at the heart of ODD as it is with other varieties of stuckness. However, I think the motivation is different. Anyone who has had children will vividly remember the "terrible twos," during which the growing child learns to exert her negativity. One of the first words the child learns is "no," and she soon uses it with abandon. Why is this? The reason is that "no" defines the child as a separate individual, one who doesn't agree with parents. Always agreeing would seem to mean that she hardly exists psychologically. Thus, no-ness and oppositional behavior like Tyler's is an attempt at psychic survival. Tyler and others like him act like they are in a fight for their lives, as if it is a matter of basic integrity, a core value, if a young child were able to speak in those terms. ODD, then, can be understood as a mechanism, over-done to be sure, at defending and even saving the emerging self.

There are useful strategies in dealing with individuals prone to stuckness, whether child or adult. One is to offer them choices, assuming that's a viable option. Another approach to dealing with stuck individuals is to use "reverse psychology." If you are planning to go to the mall and you'd like your stuck child to go along, you could say, "I'm going to the mall. You really don't want to come along, do you?" Presenting this in the negative may make their oppositional tendencies flare up. "Yes, I really do want to go. Why do you think I don't?" they might say.

Nutritional Supplement Options for Stuckness

Useful nutritional supplements for stuckness work by increasing serotonin and/or calming the brain to reduce stuckness. Some to consider are 5-HTP, St. John's wort, GABA, L-theanine, glycine, inositol, and NAC.

➤ **5-HTP:** Start with 50 mg twice a day; increase the dose after several days to 100 mg twice daily, and then if needed increase again to 150 mg twice daily. This supplement begins to work quite quickly, in most cases within several days, by increasing serotonin levels.

➤ **St. John's wort:** This is a potent supplement for increasing brain serotonin. The starting dosage is 300 mg daily for children, 300 mg twice daily for teens, and 600 mg in the morning and 300 mg at night for adults. Sometimes the dose in adults is increased slowly to 1,800 mg daily.

➤ **GABA:** GABA has a calming effect on the brain, reducing limbic activity. GABA does not seem helpful for every patient, possibly because it is not always well absorbed and has difficulty crossing the blood-brain barrier. Side effects are few, it is safe, and doses can range from 100 to 5,000 mg/day, divided into two or three daily doses. The large dose range is likely due to variable absorption from one person to another.

➤ **L-theanine:** This amino acid calms, reportedly by increasing alpha waves in the brain. The usual dose of L-theanine is 200 mg three or four times per day. You can take higher doses if you find it useful.

➤ **Glycine:** Take 500 to 3,000 mg/day in divided doses to calm brain activity, including in the anterior cingulate and caudate regions.

➤ **Inositol:** Use up to 18,000 mg/day to boost serotonin.

➤ **NAC (N-acetylcysteine):** Use doses of 600 to 1,200 mg twice daily.

Medication Options for Stuckness

Medications that reduce stuckness include the SSRIs (serotonin blockers), which often cause sexual side effects such as lowered sex drive, difficulty with sexual arousal, and difficulty achieving orgasm. Anafranil, which is often used for stuckness, can cause sexual side effects as well as sedation and weight gain. In severe cases we add atypical antipsychotic medications such as Risperdal and Zyprexa, which are more powerful than SSRIs and work more quickly. But the side effects of Risperdal and Zyprexa can be troublesome (weight gain, increased blood sugar, and increased cholesterol and triglycerides). Medication, when used for several months and at an adequate dosage, can often result in as much as a 50 percent reduction in symptoms.

➤ **Lexapro:** 10 to 50 mg/day

➤ **Zoloft:** 100 to 350 mg/day

➤ **Prozac:** 40 to 120 mg/day

➤ **Anafranil:** as much as 250 mg/day

➤ Risperdal: 1 to 8 mg/day

➤ Zyprexa: 5 to 10 mg/day, or more

ACTION PLAN

➤ **Techniques**
  - **Mindfulness Approach to Stuckness:** It takes time, often days, for this method to become effective, so try it and get started. It works best when combined with distraction.
  - **Diversion:** Some people do this five to ten times each day in the beginning and then decrease gradually.
  - **Pencil In a Stuck Appointment:** Do this twice daily.
  - **Laugh at Your Stuckness:** Do this at least five times each day.
  - **"Stop" Technique:** Do this at least ten times a day for the first week.
  - **Rubber Band Technique:** Do this twenty times or more each day for the first week.
  - **Head Shake:** You can do this whenever you want, although doing it in public could result in some staring.

➤ **Supplements:** Try 5-HTP, NAC, or some of the other supplements.

➤ **CBT:** When these steps do not provide enough relief, consult a professional with experience using CBT for stuckness problems.

➤ **Medications:** When the individual techniques, supplements, and CBT are not effective, medication can give good relief of stuckness. For severe cases, a combination of approaches works best.

→ 10 ←

Branded in the Brain: Emotional Trauma and PTSD

I magine that you are in your car, waiting for the traffic signal to change. Suddenly, a car comes out of nowhere and smashes into a car crossing the intersection, and the driver of one of the cars is decapitated. You see his severed head rolling down the street. How would you react? Most likely you would be shocked by this horrific event, traumatized emotionally. I selected this example because of its shock value, but it is a true story, one that actually happened to Miles, one of my patients.

After the experience, Miles developed post-traumatic stress disorder (PTSD). PTSD is a condition that develops in some individuals who are exposed to or involved in an extremely traumatic event that involves actual or threatened death or serious injury. The individual's response to the traumatic event involves intense fear, helplessness, or horror. They continue to reexperience the event long afterward and avoid stimuli associated with the traumatic event. Emotional overarousal is common, unbalancing the PFC–limbic system relationship and giving rise to a busy brain.

In such instances, the individual's capacity to cope with the traumatic event is absolutely overwhelmed. That's what happened to Miles, and what would happen to many of us if we witnessed such a horrible accident. We all need to feel safe. When we experience traumas, we lose that background feeling of safety. Like Miles, we may have difficulty processing the memories and emotional impact. No wonder. The shock and trauma of such an event is thankfully outside the realm of normal experience, at least for most of us. People like Miles who have PTSD continually reexperience the trauma, as if the past were still alive in the present. Miles had nightmares about the accident every night. During the day, Miles was triggered to reexperience the accident whenever he saw a car similar to the one that caused the horrible accident.

By now you've heard a lot about the fight-or-flight response, activated by protective circuitry that strives to keep us safe. Miles's danger detector, his stress response alarm system, was on constant fight-or-flight high alert. Remember that in danger situations the thinking brain can be turned off while the primitive limbic areas take over. Like Miles, most traumatized individuals have fight-or-flight reactions that continue long after the danger has passed. It is as if the traumatic past is acutely alive in the present. Their feeling of danger never abates. This is the root of the busy-brain experience in trauma—primitive limbic and fight-or-flight areas remain in overdrive, with the PFC unable to rein them in.

"Big T" versus "Little T"

What Miles experienced was a "Big T" trauma: a sudden, single, horrible event that leaves a lasting imprint. Big T traumas are major events in our lives. Examples include horrible events such as rape, kidnapping, war experiences, accidents, and earthquakes. Big T trauma is the kind that most commonly comes to mind when we imagine shattering events. The individual's life often changes forever after a Big T trauma. They struggle to work through the terror, the memories, and even shame. The trauma of the experience is branded in their brains.

"Little t" traumas, in contrast, accumulate over a longer period. They are not as extreme as the horrific experiences associated with Big T traumas, but Little t traumas can have a powerful and detrimental impact nonetheless because they last for a long time. We get our first lessons in self-care from the way others care for us. Little t trauma for a child could be separation from parents, having a depressed mother or father, or growing up in a home in which there is a lack of emotional attunement or in which one is neglected or constantly belittled. Maybe there were not enough nurturing, sustaining, and healing encounters with early caretakers. Perhaps no one ever looked at the child with loving eyes or smiled at the toddler's first achievements of standing unaided. Maybe a mother experienced postpartum depression and was not available to adequately nurture her infant. Or maybe one's parents were struggling with their own unresolved trauma issues themselves and could not be available for their child, attuned to his or her needs.

Other examples of Little t traumas include bullying; substance-abusing family members; unstable families with job loss, financial ruin, violence in the home, or parental incarceration; and physical and emotional abuse in a marriage. We wonder why someone would stay with an abusive spouse. Well, we seek refuge in what is familiar. The known, even if hurtful, seems safer than the unknown.

Why is the Big T/Little t distinction important? Because they are so far out of the realm of normal life, Big T traumas are impossible to miss. The impact on the traumatized individual is devastating, and the individual's psyche may be shattered, but it is difficult to overlook a Big T trauma.

In contrast, Little t traumas can fly under the radar, their traumatic effects going unnoticed for what they are. Emotional traumas are much more common than we would like to admit. Many individuals are traumatized and do not have full-blown PTSD. And too many of these traumas are inflicted on us by the people who are supposed to love and care for us, making it all the more confusing to sort out when someone whom we love and who should love us becomes a traumatizer. When does a depressed and hopeless mother's comments to her son of "You'll end up just like your father, no good" become a Little t trauma? When does a husband's critical nature become for his wife emotionally abusive and a Little t trauma? When does the bullying received by an eighth grader become traumatic? There are no clear-cut rules to help us decide. How traumatic these situations are depends on factors such as the genetic endowment and emotional resilience of the individual, the availability and support of caring, loving figures, and the individual's prior experiences of trauma. We've all been there, we've all been hurt, we've all been traumatized to some degree. But depending on how young or fragile an individual is and the precarious situation they are in, the emotionally traumatized person may not recognize that they are caught in a destructive, traumatic force field.

Early instances of developmental trauma have lifelong effects. In general, the earlier and the more severe and more prolonged the trauma, the more negative and far-reaching its effects. Children cannot select their parents. And children lack the capacity to understand their parents' motivations. They don't comprehend why Mom is depressed, or why Dad directs his anger toward them. Children view the world as being all about them. They assume that their parents' behavior toward them reflects something about their own goodness or badness. They interpret everything about the world from their own vantage point. Plus, they may have nobody else to whom they can turn. Their survival literally depends on their early caretakers. If we are loved and cherished when young, we carry that sense with us through life. If we are abused or neglected during childhood, we carry a sense of defectiveness and humiliation. No wonder some of us go through relationship after relationship as adults in which we are taken advantage of, victimized. We may not protest if mistreated; we feel deep down that we deserve it. It's all we've known, what we believe. And we may not even be fully aware of what we know, what we believe.

In an earlier chapter, we discussed the negative default position of the human psyche. Along with that, I have observed in many individuals a kind of negative egocentricity. I don't mean selfishness, per se. Rather, what I mean is that too many of us reflexively assume that negative interpersonal events reflect negatively on us or are our fault. Remarkably, so many of us assume blame when there is none to be had, at least on our part. A case in point is the young child who assumes that her parents are divorcing because she was a bad girl. This is all too commonplace.

Where it gets confusing is that not all individuals react the same way to similar events. The reflexive assumption of blame for one's parents' divorce can aggravate the Little t trauma of the experience for one child. Another child with a genetic endowment that makes him less reactive to stress—say, not having the short version of the serotonin transporter gene—and more loving support may, however, come through a similar event with fewer lasting wounds.

In part, because emotional traumas are so common and affect different individuals differently, individuals—and those who treat them—aren't always aware that their condition is related to a Little t trauma. I remember a patient from when I first started doing brain SPECT imaging. I evaluated Robin, a twenty-four-year-old woman who complained of anxiety and depression. I questioned Robin, as I do with all my patients, about physical, sexual, and emotional abuse. Robin said that none of those had happened to her. But her brain SPECT scan showed what we call a "diamond plus pattern" (excessive activity in the anterior cingulate, basal ganglia, thalamus, and right temporal lobe areas).

As I showed her the brain SPECT pictures, I said to Robin: "We often see this pattern in people who have been abused or traumatized. Are you sure that nothing like that has happened to you?" Robin thought for a moment. She replied: "Well, when I was four years old, my older brother Hank used to hang me outside his second-floor bedroom window by my ankles and threaten to drop me. Was that abuse?" "How'd you feel when he did that?" I asked Robin. "I was terrified and I thought I was going to die," she said.

I learned that Hank, who later ended up in jail for robbery, had done this dozens of times to Robin. He seemed to love the terror her helplessness created in her. I told Robin that Hank's behavior was more than enough to emotionally traumatize her.

Jill: Blocking It Out

Jill, seeing me for depression, anxiety, and panic attacks, reported a dream in which a baby was being flushed down the toilet. Jill told me this dream on the two-year anniversary of terminating her one and only pregnancy; I would learn later that her pregnancy termination was extremely traumatic for Jill. She had never before told me about that abortion. In fact, she had not thought of the event, which was tremendously troubling at the time, in nearly two years. It was as if she had blocked it from her conscious awareness.

Following her abortion, Jill didn't have anyone with whom she could process what occurred. She had no one with whom she felt safe. Jill's dream did open the door to our exploring the lack of safety and security she experienced early in life. In essence, she had a Big T trauma—the pregnancy termination—but also Little t traumas related to family chaos and lack of parental availability when she was young that seemed to lay the foundation for her trauma of her pregnancy termination.

Blocking it out or repression of the event is not the only reason many individuals have difficulty surfacing or articulating their trauma. Practically, trauma—whether Big T or Little t—can profoundly affect one's ability to think and use language to understand and to process the traumatic events. Research suggests that neglect and abuse early in life reduce gray matter in the self-control areas of victims' brains. We don't know why the gray matter decreases, but we do know that stress can kill cells in an adult's hippocampus. Perhaps the lack of safety the child experiences increases their stress hormones, thus having a detrimental impact on their gray matter. Regardless, the implications are stark: early abuse and neglect can have a lifelong negative impact on the brain, damaging an individual's capacity to self-regulate for the rest of their lives.

Helping patients become aware of how traumatic past events have been can be half the battle in treating trauma, as it was with Robin and Jill. Patients with trauma may even be misdiagnosed precisely because their traumatic experiences lie buried. I've seen many instances in which trauma and PTSD were misdiagnosed as another condition, such as generalized anxiety disorder, major depression, panic disorder, OCD, and psychosomatic conditions such as migraine headaches or irritable bowel syndrome. The treatment for the other, misdiagnosed condition is often effective for a time, but then the treatment effectiveness falls off. When a patient comes for evaluation with a history of several psychosomatic problems, multiple different psychiatric diagnoses, and multiple failed treatments, I always wonder if trauma has been missed. Patients who were previously given a diagnosis of borderline personality disorder are often found to have trauma issues when evaluated carefully.

In part, trauma and PTSD tend to be misdiagnosed because the affected individuals' ability to emotionally process their traumatic experiences has been impaired by the trauma. During episodes of severe trauma, higher cortical centers become shut down. There is active inhibition of language centers. And memory integration is disrupted by a shutdown of the pathways from the frontal cortex to the memory centers in the hippocampus. We often say something like, "There are no words to describe how I feel." In trauma situations, this can be literally true because of the shutdown of the brain's language and memory centers that I've just described. Someone has been so severely wounded that they may not or cannot generate an integrated story of what happened. The event becomes stored in the brain raw, as you experienced it, in its original, unprocessed form, not integrated into the more general memory networks. The memory is still there, but you cannot convey it or remember it in the usual sense.

I have emphasized narratives and storytelling in this book, but with trauma the cognition, emotion, sensations, and memories necessary to integrate an event into a narrative can be dissociated or walled off. They are blocked off and are not consciously accessible. There is nothing consciously there to reflect on. The individual's capacity for self-reflection is thus markedly impaired. Affected individuals simply cannot develop a coherent story of what is happening to them. They cannot explain what they do not know.

And, of course, if the story cannot be told in the first place, it's impossible to rewrite it and heal. It's a situation in which time doesn't heal all wounds. One may still experience pain, sorrow, depression, anxiety, and other emotions about events from years ago.

Lacking adequate capacity to think about and process our traumatic experiences, the traumas become split off and stored in the body. Never being able to integrate the event becomes a key element in the continuation of the trauma. The traumatic past continues to be alive in the present. The body remembers what the mind cannot. We may become like traumatized animals, relying on our primitive fight-or-flight systems. Because of this, being attentive to our bodies and the way they harbor trauma can help us find a path to what's unconsciously stored.

Monty Roberts, Safety, and Emotional Resonance

Let me describe for you a remarkable event I was privileged to witness in person. The event has to do with body memory of trauma. Monty Roberts is the original "horse whisperer." Because of his own experiences with his father, who "broke" horses harshly, using pain and abuse, Monty dedicated his life to finding a different way to "join up" with horses, meaning a way to develop a safe and trusting relationship with a frightened and often traumatized horse. Monty goes around the country demonstrating his techniques. Local individuals bring to the demonstrations horses that have never accepted a saddle, bridle, or rider. Many of these horses were physically abused in the past; as I learned, abuse is quite common in the horse racing industry.

Monty takes these recalcitrant, mistreated horses and enters a ring with them. He is a keen student of the body language of horses.

He also understands that horses want to join up—that is, connect—with a human, but that at the same time the horses need to feel safe and be able to run away if they feel endangered. Using a round pen and his exquisite sense of what is going on inside that emotionally traumatized horse, by forming a safe and secure relationship with the horse, Monty is able to connect with the horse and get it to accept a bridle, saddle, and rider in twenty to thirty minutes. Monty respects and understands horses and their fears, which is key. It's absolutely remarkable to watch the join-up process. What is even more remarkable is that during these demonstrations with horses that were abused, women in the audience who were themselves abused and traumatized often faint! They lose consciousness. Why is that? Because the body speaks louder than words. Our emotions live in our bodies.

Abused women in the audience pick up on the body language of these mistreated and petrified horses; the women somehow sense, unconsciously, that these horses fear humans because of the abuse they have suffered. It's a remarkable demonstration of how unintegrated emotions and trauma are expressed in the body.

Horses have only body language with which to communicate. We humans have our body language and more. It's an extraordinary experience to witness the connection between these women and horses with so much in common yet no real way other than body language to express it. Some individuals at Monty Roberts's demonstrations who don't faint, including men, are overcome with intense emotion and have spontaneous outbursts of laughter. The emotional impact is so powerful that many don't have the words to express what is going on inside; they laugh—seemingly inappropriately, giving vent to the powerful emotions for which they have no words.

Resilience

It is important to underscore that not everyone who experiences a trauma will develop a Big T or a Little t trauma. Some concentration camp survivors emerged from the camps with reasonably good mental health. Other individuals have risen from the ranks of abject poverty and family chaos to become well-adjusted individuals. Studies of *resilience* have addressed this. We're not all cut from the same cloth; genetic differences, such as with the serotonin transporter gene, help explain why some individuals are more resilient than others. Other genes related to resilience or the lack of it are currently being studied. Those with backgrounds of neglect and abuse are more prone to have traumatic reactions. And being surrounded by caring, supportive individuals offers some protection against developing a traumatic reaction following a traumatic incident. The reality is that most war veterans who serve in Iraq and Afghanistan and return with psychiatric problems don't have PTSD; less than half have PTSD, while the rest have other problems, such as mood and anxiety disorders.

For those of us who aren't naturally resilient, there are strategies we can use to address our traumas. Darryl's success story illustrates one effective strategy.

Darryl's EFT

Darryl was five years old when the 9/11 terrorist attacks occurred. His family lived outside New York City and knew four people who lost their lives in the attack on the World Trade Center, one of whom was Darryl's uncle. The television was on constantly in Darryl's home in the aftermath of the attacks, broadcasting the carnage relentlessly, as was the case in many American homes. When Darryl was nine, he was brought to me for evaluation of his depression and school struggles. He also experienced constant anxiety, nightmares, headaches, gastrointestinal complaints, and other physical symptoms that had waxed and waned since 9/11. Remember that the body speaks what the mind cannot remember.

It is by recognizing, bearing, and putting into perspective traumatic life experiences that we begin to heal. A traumatized young person lacks the life experiences, maturity, and cognitive capacity to understand and put into perspective what happened. If an attuned parent or other caring adult is not available for the young person, the traumatic event remains split off from the rest of psychic life and may still reside otherwise in the body.

Parental availability following a trauma is thus crucial to help a child work through his feelings about what happened. Parents who are sensitive, receptive, and available to discuss the trauma with the child can help the child process the event. If they are concerned about their child's emotional state, they will attempt to create a sense of safety for the child and encourage the child to discuss his thoughts, feelings, and reactions to the trauma.

Because Darryl's parents, too, had been traumatized and were grieving the loss of Darryl's uncle and friends, they had not been emotionally available immediately after the attacks to help him work through his feelings about the attacks. In this case, the entire family experienced trauma issues. Four years after the event, they all were still suffering.

Darryl and his parents wanted to avoid medication. I taught them Emotional Freedom Techniques (EFT) so that they all could more effectively deal with post-9/11 trauma. EFT and art therapy helped Darryl recover. He was able to retell his story through his artwork with a top-notch art therapist.

This is just one example of the myriad uses of EFT to calm busy brains and resolve symptoms. EFT does not erase memories. Rather, like eye movement desensitization and reprocessing (EMDR), EFT changes the way painful memories are stored, so that when we think about them we no longer experience such powerful negative emotions or problematic physical sensations. Any disturbing episode that causes emotional and physiological problems can be addressed with EFT. Problems that can be addressed include anxiety, panic attacks, depression, anger, sleep problems including nightmares, fears and phobias, the impact of bullying, and even life-threatening situations such as rape or experiences during wartime. EFT jumpstarts the brain's emotion-processing systems. I like to say that EFT helps integrate the "unthought known."

Emotional Freedom Techniques (EFT)

Emotional Freedom Techniques, also known as *tapping*, are often called "do-it-yourself EMDR," a technique described shortly. Given my skeptical nature, when I first heard about EFT, my initial response was that it was flaky and unlikely to be legitimate. I had my doubts. You may have your own doubts as I describe EFT. Despite my initial skepticism, I was open to learning more about EFT, and I've found it helpful personally. And my patients have found it helpful too. I hope you can keep an open mind and consider EFT.

You probably know about acupuncture, in which needles are inserted into "meridian points" in the body. Acupuncture is effective for a variety of conditions, as research and clinical experience show. EFT was developed as a variant of acupuncture. Instead of using needles, you tap on certain meridian points. It's simple. Here's what you do:

1. **The Issue:** Identify the issue you want to work on, what bothers you right now. Examples could be work, your boss, the fight with your spouse, your aching back, that embarrassing episode in elementary school. Try to be as specific as you can be. Target only one issue at a time.

2. **Testing the Initial Intensity:** To test the initial intensity of your issue, rate the distress you experience with your issue on a scale of 0 to 10, with 10 being the worst possible.

3. **The Setup:** Make a setup statement in the form of "Even though I [fill in the blank with your issue], I deeply and completely accept myself." For example, "Even though I have this aching back, I deeply and completely accept myself." Or, "Even though I was humiliated by the teacher in sixth grade, I deeply and completely accept myself." Tap on your karate chop point (the fleshy part of your hand that you would use to break a board if you

were doing karate) with the fingers of your other hand three times while repeating the setup statement.

4. **The Tapping Sequence:** Tap with your fingertips through the eight points in the EFT sequence that follows while you say a reminder phrase out loud. Tap five to seven times at each point. When there are two possible body points to tap on, just pick right or left. It doesn't really matter which side you pick. The reminder phrase is short— just a couple of words to remind you of your issue. Say this phrase out loud at each of the eight points in the EFT sequence. For example, if your issue has to do with the anger you feel toward a friend who betrayed you, you might tap through each point in the sequence saying, "This anger . . . this anger . . . this anger . . ." Or you might have a reminder phrase such as "the pain in my back" or "my panic attacks." These little reminder phrases are present simply to remind you of the issue you have chosen to tap on. Here are the eight points you tap on, in the sequence given:

Top of the Head (TOH)

Beginning of the Eyebrow (EB), just above the nose

Side of the Eye (SE)

Under the Eye (UE)

Under the Nose (UN)

Chin Point (CH)

Beginning of the Collarbone (CB), either side

Under the Arm (UA), several inches below the armpit

5. **Retesting:** When you have finished tapping, take a deep breath and then test the intensity of your issue again using the 0-to-10 scale to check your progress. Compare this number with what you had before tapping. Your number should be lower,

indicating progress. Sometimes it takes a few rounds to get your number down, so don't get discouraged.

You can repeat this sequence as often as necessary to get the relief you desire. As you tap on particular issues, you will likely notice other, related issues coming to mind. Tap on them too, to maximize your relief. Evidence suggests that EFT reduces an overactive fight-or-flight system related to trauma issues, thus calming a busy brain. Exactly how and why it works is not clear. Proponents of EFT state that EFT addresses disruptions in the body's energy transmission systems—in the Chinese energy meridians—thereby improving energy flow that was blocked by emotional traumas.

Eye Movement Desensitization and Reprocessing (EMDR)

EMDR is a technique developed to activate the brain's emotional processing centers, permitting warded-off, unprocessed, and dissociated emotional traumas to be processed and integrated. EMDR treatment is usually done by a therapist trained in the approach, although some versions of EMDR do not require a trained therapist; you can do them yourself. EMDR does not erase memories. Rather, EMDR changes the way painful memories are stored, so that when we think about them we no longer experience negative emotions or problematic physical sensations.

Any disturbing memory that causes emotional and physiological problems can be addressed with EMDR. Problems that can be addressed by EMDR are the same as those I mentioned for EFT, including Big T or Little t traumas, nightmares, phobias, anxiety, and depression. EMDR treatment usually requires six to twelve sessions. The therapist employs various techniques to activate the emotional processing centers of the brain (which come "online" every night during REM sleep) while the individual puts themselves mentally back into the traumatic experience. These techniques include moving your eyes back and forth, alternate tapping on thighs, and listening to sounds in headphones that travel back and forth from one ear to another. When I first heard about EMDR years ago, I was skeptical about it, just as I was with EFT. But I kept an open mind and learned more about it, and I've found it to be quite helpful to many patients with trauma issues. Remarkably, traumatized people can heal using EMDR even if they don't talk about the traumas with the EMDR therapist. For example, Jill, who was enormously pained about her pregnancy termination, was able to obtain significant help from the EMDR expert to whom I referred her. Jill especially appreciated that she was able to significantly reduce her emotional pain without having to talk about the details of her abortion with her EMDR therapist.

Kristen was a social worker who was assigned to the child abuse team at the mental health center where she worked. Unfortunately, Kristen herself had been sexually abused during childhood by her grandfather. Her exposure during work to case after case of child abuse, difficult enough for anyone, brought Kristen to the point of emotional collapse. The cases resonated too closely with her own abuse issues, and Kristen presented to me with many symptoms of PTSD. Medication helped Kristen sleep and reduced the nightmares that began when she joined the child abuse team. EMDR reduced her constant fight-or-flight symptoms. Ultimately, Kristen concluded that given her personal abuse history, she could not continue to work on child abuse cases, and she transferred to the geriatric psychiatry team, where she did well.

Healing Relationships

Darryl and his family are, unfortunately, not an unusual case. In general, trauma is devastating for relationships, whether parent-child, husband-wife, or even previously close friendships. Hyper-arousal makes the traumatized individual's world feel dangerous and hostile. At the same time, their agitation and wariness make those who are traumatized less desirable companions and reduce their social support. The tendency to avoid, common in people who are traumatized, reduces social connections. Fundamental relationship issues for those who are traumatized are safety and vulnerability; traumatized people often have difficulty trusting.

Yet connecting with others is a human imperative. Though trauma often makes that connection difficult, relationships can be healed, and relationships can be healing. What is necessary is safety, openness, and lack of judgment. Traumatic experiences are, at their core, experiences of lack of safety. Someone in a relationship with a traumatized, wounded soul needs to work hard to enable a sense of safety and security in the relationship. This takes time, whether in the psychotherapist's office or in real life.

A deep, loving relationship can transform traumatized individuals. Even having children can teach traumatized individuals how to love. A calm, devoted, loving partner or spouse who is able to withstand the emotional swings in the relationship with the traumatized person can have a remarkably positive impact. Love goes a long way toward healing. The loving care of others can help us develop positive expectations of other people as we develop a capacity to care for ourselves that is based on the care and love others give to us.

Loving a traumatized individual is not always easy. The promise of closeness generates a danger for traumatized individuals. They fear getting hurt, betrayed, or abandoned again. Their sense of defectiveness plays a part in this fear: "You'll reject me if you find out how disgusting I really am." Some traumatized individuals may try to hurt the other person or break off the relationship as an unconscious way to avoid the greater hurt of being rejected or abandoned by the other person.

A person who is involved with a traumatized individual needs to be especially sensitive and self-aware. In a word, they need to be mindful. They need to be aware of what is happening within themselves, process it, and use it to generate a loving response to the hurts and retreats that their traumatized partner brings to the relationship. They need to be empathic and to know where the other person is coming from. This is no easy task. The challenge in helping others heal is to be nonintrusively present long enough to allow neuroplasticity to take over, so that new brain patterns can develop. The traumatized individual—whose life experiences have taught them that they themselves are helpless and that others may be threats—needs new, positive experiences with others to counteract the old, destructive ones, so that the brain can change.

Being able to be emotionally present and feel safe with another is a goal for emotionally traumatized people. Disaster response studies around the world have demonstrated that social support protects against being overwhelmed by stress and trauma. Social support means being heard and understood by those around us, that they care, that they think of us. Deep friendship and love buffer us against the wounds that life inflicts. Safety is incompatible with terror. A reassuring voice or a warm embrace calms a frightened adult just as it does a terrified child. Recovering from trauma must involve reconnecting with our fellow human beings.

Animal Therapy

Involvement with animals can be helpful in healing. Connection with dogs and horses, both of which are especially sensitive to human emotions, has proven helpful in alleviating trauma reactions and seems to increase oxytocin, which calms. Pets for Vets (www.pets-for-vets.com) is an organization that pairs veterans with shelter dogs that mesh well with their personalities. Other varieties of canine assistance include service dogs and emotional support dogs. Involvement with and caring for animals can help traumatized individuals feel safe enough to begin to relate to humans.

Barry, wounded by a roadside bomb in Iraq, got a service dog following medical discharge from the army with PTSD. He benefited enormously from his emotional support dog, Fletcher, whom Barry obtained from a program called Paws for Purple Hearts. Working with a dog trainer, Barry was able to get Fletcher to obey a myriad of voice commands. Doing this meant that Barry's demeanor had to be confident, even strong, yet calm and focused. Training Fletcher helped Barry step outside himself by focusing on Fletcher.

An emotional assistance dog may also be helpful in regulating their human. Fletcher spent all day with Barry, slept in bed with him, and accompanied him to work when he was able to resume working. His presence likely raised Barry's oxytocin levels, which helped calm him. More important than that, however, is that the relationship between Barry and Fletcher was primarily one limbic system relating to another. I'm speculating here, but I suspect that Barry was able in some way to borrow or absorb the calmness in Fletcher's limbic system. Dog training with his service dog also helped Barry calm down his out-of-control limbic system; in becoming master of Fletcher, Barry developed greater mastery of himself.

Movement Therapies

Trauma literally alters an individual's nervous system. As we've been emphasizing, traumas may reside as much in the body as in the brain. Approaches to address the body are necessary, because so much of the traumatic experience is experienced not in memories but in the body's physical reactions.

Movement therapies can help one become more centered in the present, rather than anchored in past traumatic situations in which they don't feel safe. Approaches to the body give the individual a greater sense of body mastery and self-control. Access to split off memories and feelings is typically increased. Yoga, tai chi, Feldenkrais, Pilates, and martial arts are examples of approaches that can reduce internal numbness and help traumatized individuals get back in touch with their bodies to regain a sense of who they really are.

Similarly, dance and music have been used since time immemorial by individuals and groups and can help traumatized individuals get back in touch with their bodies. Jill, who had blocked out the trauma of her pregnancy termination, had always wanted to study dance. She joined a weekly dance class at a local studio. Dancing helped Jill overcome the body numbness that we eventually realized she had experienced since the termination.

Support Groups

Finding a safe place to share the hurt and terror with others can help a traumatized person begin to feel connected again to the human race. For example, Barry, who witnessed horrible events in Iraq, including roadside bombings, was able to be more open with his family and girlfriend once he shared his emotional pain and gained perspective in a veteran support group.

Writing and Journaling

Writing and journaling can help traumatized individuals connect with their inner feelings. These writings can be private, which reduces inhibitions and allows a safer expression of the traumatized inner world. The traumatized writer doesn't need to worry about how what he or she has to say will be received. On the other hand, some traumatized individuals share their writings with their therapists. Some of my own patients, for example, find it safer to hand me what they've written than to tell me out loud.

When Do You Need a Therapist?

As I've pointed out, healing from trauma is aided by a relationship with a trusted individual with whom the traumatized person feels safe. Sometimes the trusted individual may be a friend, family member, partner, or spouse. But some traumatized individuals have hurts that are so deep that professional assistance is needed—a therapist.

The professional designations and qualifications of a therapist can be important. But what is most important is to find someone who can accompany you on your journey of healing. You need a guide who can listen to the painful messages from deep inside you without overreacting. Your therapist needs to be a mature individual with life experience, including his or her own hurts, who knows how to create a safe place for you. And your therapist needs to be able to tolerate and understand your tendency to run away from treatment because you're scared. Can you resonate with such a person? And can you discuss impasses in treatment? Such impasses are often productive moments for growth and healing if they can be explored. Finally, remember that more than one kind of therapy may be useful. Exploratory psychotherapy, EMDR, and other approaches all could be useful at different points in your healing.

Neurofeedback and Cranial Electrotherapy Stimulation (CES)

Neurofeedback is helpful in reducing the excessive brain arousal that we find in a busy, emotionally traumatized brain. One of my colleagues has studied the use of neurofeedback for soldiers with PTSD returning from Iraq and Afghanistan and has demonstrated its benefit. Neurofeedback likely alters the circuitry that sustains the fear, shame, and rage related to trauma, reducing automatic stress reactions and the hyperaroused brain states we find in people who have experienced trauma.

Cranial electrotherapy stimulation (CES; www.alpha-stim.com and other companies) reduces excessive arousal and improves anxiety, depression, sleep, and stress and can be helpful for traumatized individuals.

Nutritional Supplements

Nutritional supplements can help heal those with emotional traumas by reducing the trauma-based overarousal that leads to a busy brain. One should not expect marked results, but nutritional supplements can help. For example, Barry, the Iraq War vet, used GABA to calm down his overactive brain.

Here are some nutritional supplements that can be beneficial:

➤ **GABA:** GABA is usually taken in doses ranging from 250 to 1,500 mg daily for adults. For best effect, the daily dose of GABA should be divided among two or three daily doses. Start at 750 mg once or twice a day and increase as needed.

➤ **5-HTP:** Start with 50 mg twice a day; increase the dose after several days to 100 mg twice daily, and then if needed increase again to 150 mg twice daily.

➤ **L-theanine:** The usual dose is 200 mg three or four times per day. You can take higher doses if you find it useful. There are no known adverse reactions. Keep some at your bedside to use in the early morning if you wake up too early.

Medications

Medications can offer significant help, especially for sleep and nightmares. Keep in mind that medications do not cure trauma; rather, medications dampen the expressions of physiological dysregulation— the overarousal of a busy brain—caused by the emotional trauma.

➤ **SSRIs:** Examples include Lexapro, Zoloft, and Prozac. SSRIs are useful for anxiety, panic attacks, depression, and stuckness. Doses that are too high can inappropriately deaden feelings, interfering with the work of healing from trauma.

➤ **Benzodiazepines:** Examples include Ativan, Klonopin, and Xanax. They are useful for short-term anxiety but carry addictive potential. They also deaden feelings, which can work against healing.

➤ **Blood Pressure Medications:** These reduce arousal. Clonidine and prazosin have been helpful for sleep and reducing nightmares.

➤ **Anticonvulsant Medications:** Lamictal, Depakote, Trileptal, Neurontin, and Topamax can be useful by reducing arousal.

➤ **Atypical Antipsychotic Medications:** Examples are Risperdal and Seroquel. They can cause significant side effects, but low doses can be useful when a traumatized individual has out-of-control emotions and behaviors.

→ ACTION PLAN ←

➤ **Nutritional Supplements:** Try GABA, 5-HTP, or L-theanine. You can use them together, but start them one at a time.

➤ **EFT:** Learn how to do EFT. It is easy to learn and quick to do. Find a calm, quiet place and spend fifteen minutes twice daily doing EFT on your most pressing issues. You can also do EFT anytime you want during the day when you experience an upsurge of strong emotions related to your traumas.

➤ **Movement Therapy:** Try yoga, tai chi, or other body and movement therapies. Take at least one class or lesson weekly, and practice for fifteen minutes each day you don't have a class or lesson.

➤ **Professional Assistance:** If the emotional difficulties related to your traumas do not resolve sufficiently with nutritional supplements, EFT, and the other approaches I've outlined, consult a mental health professional trained in EMDR. Also consider medication, especially for severe cases of insomnia, nightmares, anxiety, and depression.

$$\longrightarrow 11 \longleftarrow$$

Balance Your Brain, Boost Your Willpower: Addiction

Jerrie started smoking marijuana in her teens. It calmed down her busy brain. Whenever life began to feel overwhelming, she found a certain solace and relaxation in smoking pot. Soon, she felt that she couldn't live without it. Now thirty-nine years old, she smoked multiple times each day. Then she lost her security clearance when an unexpected urine drug test came up positive. Shortly thereafter she made an appointment to see me.

Jerrie had a strong family history of depression. And after I took a thorough history of Jerrie's life before she started using marijuana, it was apparent that she also had started experiencing depression. Putting together the pieces of the puzzle, we understood that Jerrie was using marijuana to self-medicate. In small doses marijuana can calm an overactive limbic system, almost like Prozac and other SSRIs. Unfortunately, in larger doses it can actually increase depression. Marijuana use also negatively impacted Jerrie's cognitive functions. Her memory was worse and her motivation was low because of her smoking.

Despite an addictive substance's negative effects, the idea that it also makes us "feel better" is one that many people with addiction relate to. Why? Because addiction frequently begins as an attempt to self-medicate a real problem. Addiction, in fact, is *often masking an underlying brain imbalance.* And if an addicted person's underlying—and often undiagnosed—condition is an imbalance in the brain, it is no surprise that the addictive substance, often a stimulant to a low-functioning PFC or a calming substance for an overactive brain area, will provide relief.

Boosting Underactive Brains, Calming Overactive Brains

Remember that a busy brain results from brain imbalance between the PFC and the limbic system. We commonly find this same imbalance among the addictions. Take the PFC. Individuals with underactive brains—for example, those with lower PFC function due to ADHD or physical brain injury to the front of the brain—are more likely to experience substance abuse and addictions for two key reasons. The first is that lower PFC activity correlates with impulsivity and poor judgment. The second reason is that these individuals are drawn to abuse substances—such as cocaine, meth, and prescription stimulants—as self-medication to boost the front of the brain.

Aside from the PFC, the other key affected area we find with an unbalanced busy brain is the limbic system, where there is overactivity. We commonly find this as well in individuals who wrestle with addictions. Those who wrestle with the stuckness of an overactive anterior cingulate, or the worry and anxiety of overactive basal ganglia, or mood issues related to excessive thalamic activity, may discover great relief from substances that calm down these overactive areas. Just like Jerrie, they partake excessively of alcohol, marijuana, narcotics, and/or other calming substances precisely because these substances provide substantial relief from their painful feelings.

It is also possible—even common—for individuals with addictions to have both an underactive PFC and overactive limbic areas, compounding the difficulty in helping them overcome their addictions. Like Jordan Belfort and his friends in *The Wolf of Wall Street*, these individuals may snort coke, perhaps to stimulate an underactive PFC, and then drink heavily, perhaps to calm an overactive thalamus. Alternating stimulants and depressants only deepens the existing brain imbalance and increases the difficulty in getting off the addiction merry-go-round.

Once we understood Jerrie's underlying brain imbalance, we were able to help address her depression with CBT and Zoloft. After she received adequate treatment for her depression, she was able to wean herself off marijuana and remain off. Eventually, with my help, she was able to regain her security clearance. Moreover, she appreciated that her memory and motivation were much improved once she stopped using marijuana. Jerrie's case illustrates that once an underlying brain imbalance is addressed, individuals typically experience an improvement in their willpower and can more successfully deal with substance issues that were masking fundamental problems of brain balance.

The Brain and Willpower: Genetic Factors Explain Why "Just Say No" Doesn't Always Work

The correlation between an imbalanced brain and addiction also helps us understand why regulating our addictive behavior through willpower alone can be especially difficult. Dr. Nora Volkow, a research psychiatrist and scientist and director of the U.S. National Institute on Drug Abuse, has performed important research that revealed inherited brain abnormalities involving the PFC that make individuals more vulnerable to addiction. In other words, she looked at genetic factors that weaken willpower. Her work shows that willpower is not just culturally or socially based. There can be genetic and biological components to lack of willpower.

Crucially, Dr. Volkow found that people who are addicted to cocaine, alcohol, or methamphetamine have fewer D2 receptors in their brains, a whopping 30 percent fewer. This is due to their fundamental, inherited biological makeup and not a result of their substance abuse. Why do fewer receptors matter so much? Because D2 receptors determine how sensitive people are to dopamine, a key neurotransmitter for the prefrontal cortex and the limbic system. If you have fewer D2 receptors, you are less sensitive to dopamine. And because dopamine is associated with feelings of reward and pleasure, lower sensitivity to dopamine means you are less sensitive to things that give others pleasure, like money, food, drink, or sex. Individuals with fewer D2 receptors simply do not receive the same rewards others receive for the same behaviors. They have what's called reward-deficiency syndrome. So they keep going in order to feel the same level of satiety as those with more receptors. In other words, they overindulge. This can play a large role in why they become addicted.

Because drugs and alcohol seem to be among the few things that give affected individuals pleasure, the drive to partake of these particular substances is equally strong if not stronger for a person who is addicted compared to the average individual. But the problem for those who are addicted isn't just decreased sensitivity; lower D2-receptor density negatively affects prefrontal cortex function, which means one has a weaker ability to self-regulate (an ADHD-like pattern). The PFC normally lets you know that you should stop an unhealthy behavior; with fewer D2 receptors, the PFC is too weak to exert self-control. Your pleasure centers override the ability of your weak PFC to inhibit the drive of your pleasure-seeking centers; your pleasure and reward system literally hijacks your brain, and the drugs and alcohol you seek for pleasure further weaken your PFC's ability to self-regulate, creating a vicious cycle of addiction.

In sum, some people with addiction have a genetic double-whammy: lower D2-receptor density means a weakened ability to regulate themselves—an ADHD-like pattern—and fewer D2 receptors means that their brains cannot take pleasure in things that others usually find pleasure in. Given that lower D2-receptor density is genetically determined, it is no wonder that some people become addicted, and no wonder that addictions can be so difficult to overcome.

There is some good news. Just because some individuals are genetically vulnerable doesn't necessarily mean that they will become addicted. Those who learn to regulate themselves may prevent a downward spiral. Also, factors other than D2 receptors are involved in addiction, such as early parental involvement; coexisting psychiatric issues such as anxiety, depression, and ADHD; head injury; developmental and emotional traumas; peers who abuse substances; and use of the substance earlier in life. If your child has strong parenting and healthy peers and stays away from addictive substances, he or she has a much better chance of beating a genetic predisposition to addiction. Moreover, physical exercise may help boost D2 receptors. Exercise has been shown to increase D2 receptors in rats. It's possible that that daily turn you take on the elliptical may be increasing your sensitivity to dopamine and your ability to feel pleasure with one beer rather than six.

Increasing Motivation for Change

The challenges for people with addiction are great. But success in dealing with substance abuse issues and self-regulation is possible. As described earlier with Jerrie, one key is often addressing one's underlying brain imbalances first. If the brain imbalance is addressed, you may actually have *more* ability to change yourself than you think you do.

Recall that lower PFC function weakens your capacity to regulate yourself—because your self-control is worse. Even after the brain imbalance has been treated, a person with addiction often needs to boost motivation to recruit their PFC to strengthen their self-regulation. They need to strengthen their weakened, underfunctioning PFC. A stronger PFC is in a better position to inhibit the more primitive limbic centers that may push them toward addictive behaviors. In lay language, they still need to boost their willpower.

One of the approaches I recommend for boosting motivation and willpower and improving the balance of activity between your PFC and limbic system is based on an approach called *motivational interviewing*. Motivational interviewing helps you think about and set important goals, including your goals to tackle your addiction. Although this approach is not formally backed by research, I have found it useful for individuals who struggle with addictions. The effectiveness of this approach likely results from enhanced self-monitoring. You can't hit a goal you cannot see. This approach shines a spotlight on what you wish to change. Close monitoring of behavior, which this approach enhances, increases the likelihood of change, reducing addictive behavior and improving the PFC–limbic system balance.

Motivational interviewing is usually done with a trained professional. But you can adapt the approach to use on your own. Here are questions to ask yourself to get help kicking your addiction. Record your answers on paper or on your computer. As an example, I've included in italics the responses of Bart, a forty-year-old roofer I treated who had lost $100,000 gambling on horse races, football games, and online poker, really anything he could find to wager on. Not surprisingly, Bart had excessive anterior cingulate activity and low PFC activity consistent with ADHD and poor ability to self-regulate. Even after we treated Bart's brain imbalances, we needed to deal with his addiction to gambling and boost his ability to self-regulate. Bart needed to learn to exercise more willpower. Focusing directly on his motivation helped Bart change his behavior.

Assess Your Motivation to Change

To start out, rate on a scale from 1 to 10 the importance for you of making a healthy change at this time.

➤ Look at the advantages of making a change. How will things be different in X number of years if you . . . ? How would you like things to be different? If you decided to change, how would that benefit you?

➤ Consider the disadvantages of the status quo: What concerns you most about your health? How much does that concern you? What worries you if you don't make a change? What do you suppose are the worst things that can happen if you keep on this track?

➤ If you feel ambivalent, you may want to chart the decisional balance. Make a list of the good things about what you want to change, including what you'll look forward to if you successfully change; the not-so-good things about it; and the bad things about making changes, including what might be difficult and what you're afraid of.

➤ Once you've considered the advantages and disadvantages of making a change, again rate the importance of making a change on a scale of 1 to 10. You will likely see that your rating is higher, underscoring the importance of making a change.

Bart initially rated his motivation to make a healthy change at 6 on the 1-to-10 scale. He then considered the advantages of a change. He'd feel better about himself. There would be more free time to play golf and engage in other hobbies. He would have more time with his family. Bart then considered the disadvantages of the status quo. He struggled to hide his gambling from his wife and kids. He spent endless hours at the race track and casino, and gambling online. He risked plunging his family into even more severe debt. He was burdened by shame and guilt. After considering the advantages of a change and the disadvantages of the status quo, Bart rated his motivation to change at 7–8 out of 10.

Reinforce Your Beginning Interest in Making Changes

Once you've expressed at least an initial interest in change, you will still need reinforcement and support.

➤ Begin by making a list of the strengths you have that may help you quit or change.

➤ Then confront your possible challenges head on. What ideas do you have about overcoming the challenges? What would you like to try this time to overcome challenges (i.e., that you haven't tried in the past)? What things have been successful for you in the past, either specifically in your health journey or in the other areas of your life that you can use to manage your new goals?

Bart listed his strengths: he actually had demonstrated a good amount of willpower in the past—he'd quit smoking and he lost twenty-five pounds and kept off the weight for two years and counting. He considered the challenges: his coworkers liked to gamble, and discussions about gambling took up a good part of the workday with his peers. He would have to make sure that these discussions didn't serve as traps to lure him back to gambling; he couldn't avoid these discussions, but he decided to plan simple strategies he could use to gently shift the work conversations away from gambling.

Formulate Small Initial Changes

➤ Ask yourself what you will do to start to make small changes in your life.

➤ If you have questions related to making small changes, how can you find help? Are there "up and down" periods affecting your habits? How do these barriers/obstacles affect you? What ideas do you have for overcoming these barriers?

Bart decided to start with the small change of telling his brother-in-law Pete that Bart wasn't going to accompany Pete to the race track every weekend. Pete pressured Bart about that, but Bart was able to stand firm and not be swayed by Pete's pressure. Bart also decided that he would join Gamblers Anonymous, where he could find help as he worked to make the necessary changes in his life.

Set Smarter Life Goals

What are the life goals you want to set for yourself? These can be broad life goals such as being healthier, living longer, or being able to play with your children or grandchildren. How is your health affecting you currently?

To make your goals SMARTER (Specific/Measurable/Achievable/Realistic and Relevant to overall goals/Time-Bound/Evaluated/Rewarded), consider the following:

➤ How will you make your goal Specific? In other words, what exactly are you going to do to achieve this?

➤ How are you planning to Measure this? In other words, how will you know that you attained your goal?

➤ Is it Achievable, or do you need to rework it? (Is this goal dependent on someone else? If so, can you rephrase the goal so it only depends on you and not on others?)

➤ Is the goal Realistic and Relevant? (Is my goal realistic within the resources at hand? Is it relevant to my life purpose? Will achieving this goal lead me to the life I want to have?)

➤ When will you accomplish this goal? We use the term Time-Bound, which means you must give yourself a target date.

➤ How will you know you have succeeded? We use the term Evaluated to reflect assessment of success or lack thereof.

➤ When you succeed, what is your plan to Reward your accomplishment?

Bart had a number of important life goals. He wanted to make sure that he was healthy. Therefore, he committed himself to yearly physical exams by his primary care doctor. Bart wanted to take a more active role in the lives of his children, especially because he would have more free time when he stopped gambling. He committed himself to at least one engagement, outing, or activity each week one-on-one with his son and daughter. Bart also wanted to support his wife. He decided to work toward helping his wife return to school so that she could train to be a dental hygienist. Bart also wanted to improve the family's finances. To increase his income and begin to save for retirement, Bart decided to work overtime one Saturday each month. He would devote 25 percent of the additional income to making needed home repairs; the remaining 75 percent of additional income he would place in a retirement account.

To increase the chances that he would take steps to carry out these goals, Bart printed them out and pasted them on his bathroom mirror, to remind himself of their importance. He also discussed these goals with his wife, who agreed with them. Bart asked her to help him be accountable to these goals, not by nagging him but by lovingly supporting and encouraging him to work on these goals, which were important for Bart and his family. For each goal, Bart wrote down a target date by which time he expected to have met the goal. For example, he anticipated that his wife would begin her dental hygiene training within six months.

Dealing with Setbacks

Everyone encounters setbacks along the way. The important thing is how you deal with them. Here are some things to remember and ask yourself as relapses occur:

➤ **Be kind to yourself:** Setbacks will happen. Accept your slip and remind yourself to move on.

➤ **Take note of the setback:** Think about the experience. When did it occur? Who were you with? What environment were you in? What were the circumstances surrounding the setback?

➤ **Learn from the experience:** How will you change the situation in the future, so you are less likely to have a setback?

➤ **Go back to your plan as soon as possible:** A temporary slip should not derail everything you have worked so hard for; that's why it is called a "slip."

➤ **Make a plan for the future:** How will you handle things the next time this situation presents itself? What strategies can you use to help you be successful in the future?

Like everyone, Bart experienced slipups in his efforts to abstain from gambling. For example, he slipped up and joined his brother-in-law for a day at the track gambling on horse races. Rather than beat himself up, Bart reminded himself that they don't keep using that phrase "one day at a time" for no reason. He thought about why he slipped, and he concluded that too much work and lack of sleep weakened his willpower. Bart affirmed to himself the need to avoid the exhaustion that comes from over-working and to make sure that he had enough sleep.

Change is not easy—deciding to move forward can be as difficult as actually doing it. And different people are ready at different times for different kinds of change. Addressing motivation this way helps you address your ambivalence, strengthens your movement to your goal, and helps you find within yourself the necessary resources to succeed with your plan.

Support Groups

Support groups, although not everyone's cup of tea, are resources that help many improve their motivation and strengthen their willpower. Alcoholics Anonymous and other twelve-step traditions tackle addiction by helping individuals improve their self-control. Their goals are clear: one day at a time—do not gamble, do not use drugs, do not drink, do not look at pornography. Addictive behaviors are monitored by reporting in at meetings and receiving chips that recognize and celebrate periods of abstinence. These programs serve as substitutes for addictive behaviors—go to a meeting rather than go out drinking or gambling. Participants see models of hope and success—they can learn from others in the program who have wrestled with and managed similar problems. Accountability is emphasized and life goals are more likely to be met when commitment to change addictive behavior is made out loud to others. Personal and twenty-four-hour assistance is available in the form of sponsors. Finally, there is lack of criticism in the programs—one is not criticized for lapses in sobriety; rather, one is assisted in getting back on the path to abstinence.

Bart joined a twelve-step fellowship, Gamblers Anonymous, and received help there.

Let's look at the story of another person who benefited from a twelve-step program. Forty-four-year-old Martin, a successful architect who was married with four children, came for treatment after he was arrested for driving under the influence (DUI). Martin drove while drunk, ran his car into a telephone pole, and narrowly missed hitting a bus filled with passengers. He was fortunate not to have been severely injured and even more fortunate that he didn't maim or kill anyone else.

Ever since puberty, Martin had unstable moods, with frequent high and low fluctuations. During the high periods, he felt confident, creative, nearly invincible, and able to manipulate any situation to his advantage. When low, Martin wanted to sleep, couldn't concentrate, had low energy, and was overwhelmed easily.

It was not difficult to diagnose Martin with a bipolar disorder and to understand that Martin had self-medicated for his unstable moods. I would learn later that Martin's father had a similar mood disorder and also self-medicated with alcohol. Both Martin and his father had tried to stop drinking over the years; neither was successful in becoming sober.

A small dose of lithium was quite effective for stabilizing Martin's moods. But he needed more than that. Although we eliminated the original impetus for his alcohol abuse—self-medication of his mood disorder—Martin's alcohol abuse was long-standing and had taken on a life of its own. He needed help for his alcohol addiction. But he wasn't ready.

Because Martin's motivation to give up alcohol was weak, I worked with him over several months using the approaches to increase his motivation that we've discussed in detail with Bart. Eventually, Martin's motivation increased and he could no longer deny that he needed to stop drinking. I then referred him to a structured outpatient treatment program, which he attended three times a week for a month, with fewer weekly meetings afterward. At the program's and my urging, Martin started attending AA meetings, doing "90 in 90." He found a sponsor and has been able to stay sober, although he realizes that they don't talk about "one day at a time" for no reason.

Martin's story is one of many similar success stories I could recount. What is important to understand is that many individuals use alcohol and drugs to try to self-medicate for underlying brain problems, such as mood disorders like Martin's, anxiety, ADHD, emotional trauma, OCD, traumatic brain injury, and chronic pain. Even after the underlying brain problem has been treated, whipping one's addiction still takes willpower and motivation. For those who have spent most of their lives self-medicating, taking follow-up steps to treat the addiction is absolutely crucial. If I may add a happy note, Martin told me that being arrested for DUI was one of the best things that ever happened to him.

Motivating Change: Spiritual Factors

If we pause for a moment, the steps just outlined to increase motivation are likely more helpful to boost an underactive PFC than they are to help manage an overactive limbic system. The structure of twelve-step programs clearly assists individuals in self-regulation; the regular meetings, the steps, and the program enhance the efforts of the PFC to implement appropriate self-regulation.

But twelve-step programs assist people with addiction in another way, helping individuals dampen excessive limbic system activity through an emphasis on spirituality. Twelve-step programs' emphasis on spirituality—not religion—helps individuals find meaning amid the pain and occasional darkness of their lives, helps them find lived acceptance of their own and others' imperfections, and provides a way for them to help heal other people with addictions while they seek healing for themselves. Seeking and finding meaning outside ourselves is an effective way for us to manage the excessive limbic system that tends to accompany the pain of a hurting soul's existence.

Nutritional Supplements to Increase Your Self-Control

Many individuals use alcohol, drugs, food, sex, gambling, and other addictive behaviors to try to self-medicate for their imbalanced brains. When some brain areas are underactive, individuals may turn to addictive stimulating behaviors and substances—such as caffeine, cocaine, and prescription stimulants—and stimulating behaviors to rev up their brain. This was the case for Bart, whose gambling boosted his dopamine. Other individuals with overactive brain areas, especially in the limbic system, use addictive downers—such as alcohol, marijuana, sedatives, painkillers, and high-carb foods that increase serotonin—to calm the brain.

Nutritional supplements can help balance the brain so cravings are lower, there is less need to self-medicate, and self-control is improved. Nutritional supplements alone are rarely sufficient to balance the brain of somebody struggling with addiction, but the supplements do provide some benefit. A nutritional supplement for ADHD helped Bart. He needed less of a dopamine rush once he started using the supplement L-tyrosine, which improved his PFC function, increasing his impulse control and self-regulation. A supplement to increase serotonin, 5-HTP, reduced his tendency to get stuck on gambling. Here are more commonly used supplements that help rebalance underactive and overactive brain areas, followed by medications that are commonly used for the same reasons. Just so we keep things clear here, think of underactive brains (e.g., underactive PFC) as those with ADHD features—problems with focus, attention, concentration, easy distractibility, impulsivity, poor judgment, and boredom. Think of overactive brains (e.g., overactive limbic system) as those wrestling with anxiety, depression, and stuckness.

Supplements to Boost Underactive Brains (Problems with ADHD, Focus, Attention, Concentration, and Impulsivity)

➤ **L-tyrosine:** This amino acid helps with focus, energy, and motivation. For the first three days, take 500 mg before breakfast, midmorning, and then midafternoon. After three days increase to 1,000 mg before breakfast, midmorning, and midafternoon. Take on an empty stomach.

➤ **SAMe:** This supplement works best when taken at least twenty to thirty minutes before breakfast and lunch on an empty stomach. If taken later in the day it may interfere with sleep. In higher doses it can cause insomnia and restlessness. Start at 200 or 400 mg/day and then increase the daily dose gradually, if tolerated, by approximately 200 mg per week. A person may start seeing some benefit at 200 to 400 mg but may require 1,600 mg or more per day. Individuals with features of bipolar disorder should use SAMe with caution. It can cause mood swings or mania.

➤ **Ginkgo Biloba:** This supplement helps with mental sharpness. The dose is 60 to 120 mg twice daily. It boosts blood flow and improves function in the front of the brain.

Supplements to Calm Overactive Brains (Anxious, Depressed, or Stuck Brains)

➤ **5-HTP:** We generally start 5-HTP at 50 mg twice a day, increase the dose after several days to 100 mg twice daily, and then if needed, increase again to 150 mg twice daily. This supplement begins to work quite quickly, in most cases within several days. Sometimes we add 500 to 1,000 mg of L-tryptophan for additional boosting of serotonin, especially for insomnia.

➤ **GABA:** We use GABA to calm the brain, aid sleep, calm mood swings, decrease irritability, temper, and anxiety, and to stabilize the temporal lobes. GABA is usually taken in doses ranging from 250 to 1,500 mg daily for adults. For best effect, the daily dose of GABA should be divided among two or three daily doses. Start at 750 mg once or twice a day and increase as needed. On occasion, we have used daily doses as high as 5,000 or 6,000 mg.

➤ **L-theanine:** L-theanine is an amino acid that promotes relaxation and sleep. The usual dose of L-theanine is 200 mg three or four times per day. You can take higher doses if you find it useful. There are no known adverse reactions. Keep some at your bedside to use in the early morning if you wake up too early. Pregnant women and nursing mothers should avoid L-theanine supplements. Children over age six can use theanine, but start with 100 mg twice daily.

➤ **Glutamine:** A dose of 500 mg twice daily is recommended for reduction of cravings. Twinlab brand seems to be preferred.

Medications to Boost Underactive Brains (Problems with ADHD, Focus, Attention, Concentration, and Impulsivity)

➤ **Stimulant Medication:** Vyvanse, Adderall and Adderall XR, Concerta, Focalin

➤ **Other Medications with Stimulating Effects:** Provigil and Nuvigil, Wellbutrin XL

Medications to Calm Overactive Brains (Anxious, Depressed, or Stuck Brains)

➤ **SSRIs:** Lexapro, Zoloft, Prozac, and others

➤ **SNRIs:** Effexor XR and Cymbalta

➤ **Anticonvulsant Medications:** Neurontin, Lamictal, Depakote, Trileptal

➤ **Antipsychotic Medications:** Risperdal or Zyprexa, if all else fails; powerful and effective, but with many side effects

ACTION PLAN

Keep in mind the acronym HALT. It stands for Hungry, Angry, Lonely, and Tired. These are situations in which individuals are more prone to engage in addictive behaviors. These steps will help you boost self-control and combat addictions.

➤ **Hungry (Diet):** Our willpower is weaker when we are hungry. Low blood sugar is a problem because it decreases brain activity and effectively lowers your ability to say no to unhealthy substances and behaviors. Consume a higher-protein diet, with several daily snacks that include protein and minimize refined carbohydrates. This helps keep your blood glucose levels steady.

➤ **Anger:** Anger is unavoidable in life. Keep in mind what triggers you to anger and take steps in advance to reduce the possibility of your being triggered to anger. When you are angry, the limbic system becomes too powerful and may override the self-regulating capacity of the PFC.

➤ **Lonely:** Humans are social animals, as we've pointed out. Connecting with supportive others helps strengthen our motivation and willpower. Those prone to addictive behaviors need to take steps to minimize lonely times.

➤ **Tired:** Americans work longer hours than most other countries. Exhaustion is a common problem: We spend too much time at work, then go home fatigued, depleted, and exhausted. At home we then reward ourselves with that extra helping of ice cream, or worse, sometimes far worse. . . . I cannot offer specific hourly limits for you; this varies from one person to another and with the specific nature of the work activities. It is clear, however, that all of us have the potential to become depleted by our work, which weakens our willpower, increasing the risk of addictive behavior. Determine your personal limits for work and try to stick with them.

➤ **Sleep:** Sleep at least eight hours each night. Most of us get less sleep than we need, and the quality of our sleep is often less than ideal. Poor sleep = suboptimal brain function; in particular, lowered PFC activity = impaired willpower.

➤ **Exercise:** The benefits of exercise are well-known. They include improvement in cardiovascular status, reduction of anxiety and depression, and possible increase of D2 receptors, as mentioned earlier. Exercise also improves sleep quality—but don't exercise too late in the day. Try exercising for forty-five minutes four or five days each week. Work up a sweat, walk briskly as if you're in a hurry; do something to increase your heart rate and get your blood flowing.

➤ **Caffeine:** Excessive caffeine use creates a roller-coaster effect of swings and crashes of mood and energy, which weakens self-control. To avoid these swings, limit yourself to two cups of coffee or less per day, or the equivalent. Some individuals should not consume caffeine after early morning because it interferes with quality sleep.

➤ **Alcohol:** For those who do not have a problem with drinking, do not consume more than four alcoholic drinks per week. If you have an alcohol problem, abstinence is the best route. Alcohol lowers self-control by lowering blood glucose and by reducing self-awareness. In medical school, they taught us a pithy phrase: "The prefrontal cortex is the portion of the brain that dissolves in alcohol," meaning that alcohol makes the PFC—the governor of the brain—less effective.

➤ **Friends:** Choose your friends wisely. If you are looking to increase self-discipline, delay gratification, and set high goals and standards for yourself, you need to surround yourself with others who do the same. We become most like the people we associate with, so choose your friends well.

➤ **Twelve-Step Programs:** Seriously consider participation in a twelve-step program if you struggle with addictions. If your sobriety is new, do "90 in 90"—attend ninety meetings in the first ninety days, and find a reliable sponsor as soon as you can.

$$\longrightarrow 12 \longleftarrow$$

Healing the Hurting Brain and Body: Brain Injury and Medical Problems

T hanks to the press, the public is more aware than ever of traumatic brain injury (TBI) and its effects. You may have heard that individuals with TBI often seem to have personality problems, bad attitudes, anger dysregulation, or substance abuse problems. These are symptoms, all pointing to the underlying problem of brain injury. I've witnessed the impact firsthand. I've treated soldiers who served in Afghanistan and Iraq who were injured by rocket attacks and blasts from roadside bombs. Beyond wartime brain injury, there have also been many reports about the effects of repeated blows to the head that retired NFL players received over the course of their football careers. I've evaluated and treated some of these players, superb athletes who are often reduced by their brain injuries to shells of their former selves. In fact, Amen

Clinics has done the largest study of these former football players. The brain injury that many football players sustain is profound. But the good news is that many improve significantly with approaches to heal their injured brains.

Moreover, TBIs aren't something we see solely in vets and NFL players. As with Bill, from Chapter 1, we are witnessing a silent epidemic in this country of TBIs in young people. You don't have to be knocked unconscious to experience brain trauma, and it's not just NFL players and boxers who get injured brains. We are seeing traumatic brain injury in pee-wee league players, cheerleaders, soccer players, hockey players, skiers, and skateboarders.

Maybe you've never done any of these activities. But we even see TBI in people who don't recall a significant head injury—sometimes it's just a minor fall, or a two-year-old running into the coffee table. Even those who don't recall a significant blow to the head can have a TBI. And we often have to ask people five or six times whether they had a head injury—often they will recall one after repeated questioning. Maybe it was that fall off the ladder. Or the fall you took when you tripped over the dog's toy. Maybe a mother dropped her six-month-old infant—and never before told anybody because of her extreme guilt. Or maybe you just slipped, fell down, and whacked your head. That's happened to us all.

Unfortunately, we are seeing many people with TBI only years after the traumatic events. Once the damage has been done, it may reveal itself in a number of apparent psychiatric disorders, including ADHD, anxiety, and depression. Misdiagnosis and missed diagnosis of TBI, which is rampant, can result in great suffering, violence, and even suicide. It seems that hardly a month goes by without the tragic news of yet another suicide by an individual who sustained a sport-related head injury and could not cope or function afterward.

Further, it's not just TBI that's a problem. Physical brain injuries are just the tip of the iceberg. Brain imaging reveals a whole host of ways in which our brains and bodies can be damaged that rarely show up as the culprit in psychiatrists'—or physicians'—offices. Lyme disease, cysts, toxic substances, and other factors can injure the brain in ways that we may never have suspected. We see the symptoms in the psychiatric disorders, the suffering, and the functional impairment, but the symptoms may be misleading. To really help these individuals, we need first to address the root cause of their difficulties.

As I've underscored earlier, most readers will not need SPECT scans to benefit from the approaches in *Reclaim Your Brain*. However, I would be remiss if I didn't talk about what SPECT can offer in select cases. Therefore, let me take this opportunity to explain how SPECT works. Following that, we'll look at different types of brain injury that most people are not aware of.

Brain SPECT Imaging

Single-photon emission computed tomography (SPECT) measures blood flow to the brain. To initiate a SPECT study, a small amount of radioactive tracer is injected into a vein in the arm. Within a few minutes that tracer goes to the brain and becomes fixed in the different brain areas. Areas of the brain that are more active receive greater blood flow and thus more radioactive tracer. We're technically measuring blood flow to various areas of the brain. But because blood flow correlates so closely with brain activity, we're also measuring brain activity.

A few minutes after receiving the tracer injection, the individual reclines for fifteen to twenty minutes in the scanner. Using the photons emitted from the radioactive tracer in the brain, computer software constructs a 3-D image of brain function, permitting us to make pictures of what the brain activity looks like. The pictures show us areas of the brain that are too active, areas that are not active enough, and areas that have activity that is where it should be. SPECT does not give us a diagnosis; rather, SPECT helps us ask better questions so we can arrive at more informed ideas about why the brain is not functioning optimally. These questions are prompted by areas of the brain that do not have the degree of activity that we would expect.

We typically do two scans—one with the brain at rest (the person is sitting calmly and quietly), and one with the brain at work (the person is engaged in a simple computer test of attention and concentration). We compare the two scans. Differences between the resting and concentration scans provide us with important information about areas of the brain that are not functioning properly. For example, with many forms of ADHD there is lower activity in the front of the brain during the concentration scans as compared with the resting scans. With mood disorders, we often see greater activity throughout the brain—especially in the limbic system—in the concentration scans as compared with the resting scans.

SPECT imaging has shown us that physical brain injury is much more common than we would have realized. It also often shows us brain problems that we could never have known about any other way. For example, injuries to the temporal lobe, the part of the brain behind the temple and above the ear where memories and feelings reside, can be detected by SPECT. Temporal lobe problems, which are otherwise difficult to detect, can contribute to mood and anxiety problems, learning problems, hallucinations, irritability, and rage problems. Temporal lobe damage, when missed, often results in an individual being misdiagnosed and not receiving the correct treatment. Recall that in my work with Bill, described in Chapter 1, SPECT showed us previously undetected temporal lobe damage. Brain SPECT is not magic, but it often points to brain (and body) problems that we would not have otherwise discovered.

The stories that follow illustrate some of the unusual suspects, or the more surprising types of damage that we've discovered—in some cases using SPECT, and in other cases using different means. This is the realm of the more seriously hurting and even damaged brains, including those with physical trauma, metabolic imbalances, inflammation, infections, and heavy metal toxicity. At this level, something is often seriously disordered in the way the brain functions. Understanding the nature of this brain dysfunction allows us to understand these serious problems and then better target treatment. Various rehabilitation and healing strategies can often restore hurting and broken brains like these, sometimes remarkably so. To reiterate, most readers will not have brain injury as serious as most of these cases. On the other hand, my intention is to illustrate various brain problems that readers—or their caregivers—might not have considered, especially when they don't respond as expected to reasonable approaches and interventions.

PTSD and Brain Injury

Not surprisingly, a number of individuals with PTSD have also experienced brain trauma during the experience that caused the PTSD. To heal the PTSD, one must also heal brain injury when it is present. An injured brain is more easily overwhelmed by the traumatic experience, making it more likely that PTSD will develop. This situation is common in soldiers who were injured by roadside bomb blasts in Iraq. Another common scenario is that of a woman who was in a horrible auto accident in which she hit her head against the windshield, injuring her brain. She developed PTSD from witnessing her fellow passengers get killed. And her brain injury makes it that much more difficult to process the emotional trauma. Brain areas commonly injured in a wartime bomb explosion or a horrible auto accident include the prefrontal cortex and the temporal lobes. These brain areas, because they are more vulnerable, are the ones most likely injured in more common traumatic experiences such as auto accidents.

Harold: Undetected Brain Cyst

Harold was a boy for whom having a brain SPECT scan showed me a problem that other doctors were not able to detect. Fourteen years old, small but stocky, Harold had been a relatively sweet-natured boy for his first twelve years. Around his twelfth birthday, his family began to notice Harold's moodiness and irritability, which they had not seen before. Harold developed a simmering negativity that was always there, just beneath the surface. His irritability progressed, and soon Harold was having several episodes each week during which he broke a lamp, punched a wall, or kicked a hole in a door. Therapy with a caring counselor did no good; the counselor told the family that Harold was having "normal teenage issues." Family therapy was problematic in that the family therapist blamed Harold's parents for not setting good limits; in fact, firmer limits only worsened Harold's rages. Psychiatrists prescribed several different classes of medication, with few benefits and significant side effects. His family brought Harold to see me when Harold tried to stab his father with a kitchen knife in a fit of rage.

Given his failure to respond to previous treatments, I recommended brain SPECT, and the family agreed. We were surprised to find on SPECT that Harold had a large cyst, a fluid-filled sac, pressing on his left temporal lobe. Cysts like this in the area of the left temporal lobe can give rise to problems just like Harold had— moodiness, irritability, rage.

I suggested to his family that Harold consult a neurosurgeon about having the cyst removed. The first surgeon they consulted declined to operate, saying that he would operate only if and when the cyst caused "real" problems—as if intermittent rages, destruction, and attempting to stab your father were not real issues. Not giving up, I steered the family to another neurosurgeon, one more sympathetic to the neuropsychiatric effects of temporal lobe cysts. This surgeon agreed to operate, and Harold had surgery a few weeks later. Following removal of the cyst, Harold's moodiness, irritability, and rages disappeared completely—well, almost completely. He still was, after all, having "normal teenage issues."

Counseling, family therapy, and medications have limited or no impact on problems caused by a cyst or a brain tumor. Harold and his family could have had years of psychotherapy without any benefit. Harold's serious brain problem had to be addressed first. Only then could effective psychotherapy and other approaches take over.

Mercury, Carbon Monoxide, and Other Toxins

Thirty-nine-year-old Clark had seemed to be an up-and-comer. He had breezed through medical school, completed a dermatology residency at a prestigious university, and started his own medical practice, which was booming. But things started not going well. Clark could no longer remember simple treatments and differential diagnoses. Unusual for him, he began forgetting the names of longtime patients. And his staff told him that he had become irritable and curt with them. At that point, Clark came to see me.

Clark wanted to have his brain scanned. He was visually oriented, and for Clark a picture was worth a thousand words. I was surprised to find that Clark's brain scans looked horrible, like somebody who had used hard-core drugs for a long time—we call this SPECT pattern a toxic, scalloped appearance. I carefully questioned Clark about his use of street drugs or alcohol or abuse of prescription drugs. I also asked him about his possible exposure to furniture refinishing, unusual pesticides, or other toxins. Clark's answer was "no" to all of these questions. Racking my brain, I asked Clark what he ate. Clark surprised me when he told me that he loved sushi and had literally eaten sushi three times a day for years!

Sushi set off a lightbulb for me. I knew that sushi can contain mercury, and I tested Clark's mercury levels; they were sky-high. Mercury is highly toxic. We had our answer. I referred Clark to a specialist in toxic metals, who helped Clark eliminate his mercury through chelation therapy, a treatment that removes heavy metals from the body, and infrared sauna treatment, which also removes toxins. Gradually at first, and then a bit more quickly, Clark's cognitive functions returned to his previous high level and he became less irritable and abrupt with his staff.

Clark's case wasn't the first time I'd encountered a problem with mercury exposure. Years ago, I found that another of my patients had high mercury levels because he spent hours hunting and fishing in swampy, marshy waters downstream from a paper-processing plant. Investigating the problem, I learned that paper plants use lots of mercury and discharge the toxic, mercury-laden pollutants into the surrounding water. This patient, an avid hunter and fisherman, had experienced significant cognitive impairment because of his toxic level of mercury.

Mercury and lead are among the most toxic substances for humans and are often not considered in patients with cognitive impairment whose brains are obviously not working well. Aluminum is another one. A simple blood lead, mercury, or aluminum level is not adequate. A "provocation" test that measures the amount of heavy metals in the urine is the most useful test to check for heavy metal toxicity.

Carbon monoxide is another toxin that I've found to have a devastating impact on brain function. One patient, who lived in New England, had had a new oil-burning furnace installed, but the technician did not properly vent the furnace to the outside. Incredibly, over a period of two years, my patient was constantly exposed to carbon monoxide exhaust from her furnace. Her brain SPECT had a toxic scalloped pattern and her cognitive function had deteriorated dramatically. Hyperbaric oxygen treatment (HBOT) saved her. HBOT is an important brain-healing treatment that involves resting in a sealed chamber while oxygen is pumped in under higher than atmospheric pressure (see www.ihausa.org for a list of centers). Another of my patients had similar problems from carbon monoxide because the exhaust system in the used car he purchased vented carbon monoxide—which is odorless and colorless—into the passenger compartment of the car. HBOT also helped him.

Other patients we've seen with "toxic brains" include a man who breathed in toxic fumes from furniture refinishing, landscape workers poisoned by pesticide exposure, and patients with mold and biotoxin exposure. And we also unfortunately see a toxic brain pattern in patients who receive chemotherapy for cancer; these problems are commonly called "chemo brain." Finally, we've all heard about "huffing," in which young people inhale gasoline and other solvents in order to get high. Don't do it! These fat-loving organic solvents lodge themselves in the fatty parts of the brain (yes, we are all "fat-heads," with a lot of fat between the ears). Brain SPECT pictures of huffers look horrible—among the most damaged brains we see.

Toxicities are not just the result of man-made chemicals or elements known to be harmful such as mercury. Some of the most toxic substances for the brain are actually natural ones that many consider harmless. Alcohol is one example. Marijuana is another.

Marijuana Mike

More times than I can count, a teenager or young adult patient comes to me extolling the virtues of smoking marijuana. Mike was one of these. In his early twenties, Mike reported lifelong anxiety and attention and focus problems that he said were made better by smoking marijuana. Treatment with previous psychiatrists had been relatively unsuccessful; they had given Mike various medications to try to calm his busy brain and improve focus. Mike said that these medications didn't help much and caused all manner of side effects. Mike said that marijuana was the only thing that helped.

Evolving laws legalizing marijuana may give marijuana users the mistaken impression that marijuana is certified effective and totally safe. The reality is that for some individuals, marijuana seems to have an ideal calming effect. For others, certain strains of marijuana reportedly improve attention and concentration, seemingly improving symptoms of ADHD.

Yet when we do brain SPECT imaging on these individuals, we typically see lower activity in the prefrontal and temporal cortex areas. So, while they feel better, their brain functions worsen and deteriorate even further over time with chronic marijuana use. Why does this happen? The prefrontal cortex and temporal lobe areas seem especially sensitive to injury by toxins and other means. I suspect it is because of the different cell types that the brain uses in those areas. These cells are evolutionarily newer and thus more easily damaged.

Mike and others often want to argue with me, saying that it would be better to have the driver in the car behind me be under the influence of marijuana than alcohol. That's probably true, but that doesn't mean that marijuana is totally safe for the brain. When we scanned Mike, we did see significantly lower activity in his temporal lobe areas; his prefrontal cortex had lower activity too. And he had a diffuse scalloped pattern on SPECT, indicative of toxic brain damage. He was not helping his brain by smoking marijuana. Showing these pictures to Mike was sobering for him, literally and figuratively. Health-conscious Mike wanted to live a healthy life, and the evidence from brain SPECT suggested big problems if he kept smoking.

Gradually, I helped wean Mike from marijuana, and he was able to calm and balance his brain using meditation, neurofeedback, and natural supplements. He was able to return to college, graduate, and obtain a good job as a hotel manager. Mike eventually worked his way up the corporate ladder, achieving the position of district manager with a nice salary, all the while staying off marijuana. A repeat SPECT scan one year after stopping marijuana use showed that his brain had healed significantly—the toxic pattern was gone and frontal and temporal lobe activity was increased, which was a good sign.

It should go without saying that other drugs that are commonly abused can have a devastating impact on brain function. These include alcohol; street drugs like cocaine, heroin, and Ecstasy; and prescription narcotics. Alcohol abuse can cause widespread damage to the brain, similar to other drugs of abuse. Even high amounts of caffeine can have a negative impact on the brain—caffeine stimulates the PFC, which many appreciate, but it is a vasoconstrictor, reducing blood flow to the brain, and it is a diuretic, dehydrating the brain.

Individuals often select substances to abuse in order to try to balance an overactive or underactive brain; they experience short-term relief of symptoms, but on the whole, abusing drugs and alcohol to try to balance one's brain is like killing a fly on your dining room table with a sledgehammer. You may kill the fly, but there will be many splinters and other collateral damage on your table.

Robert the Snorer

Sleep apnea is a condition that's received much more publicity in recent years. Nowadays you even see travelers at airports carrying small cases with their continuous positive airway pressure (CPAP) machines. These machines are used to keep increased air pressure pumping into the airways at night in order to keep the airways open and patients breathing. What's less well-known, however, is the impact on the brain when the disorder goes untreated.

Robert, a married father of three, struggled in his work at a marketing firm. He couldn't keep up with the work, seemed "out of it," and was disorganized. Robert's job was on the line. He complained of never feeling refreshed when he woke up. He said he had brain fog. Beth, his wife, worried about him but didn't know what she could do to help.

I met with Robert and Beth to discuss his problems. Robert was down on himself. He berated himself for his job struggles: "I'm stupid, I'll never be able to succeed, I'm no good as a husband and provider." What wasn't clear was why he was failing. Robert had a good education from a leading university and reportedly had a high IQ. He didn't seem to have ADHD. What became clear was that Robert's diet worsened as work stress increased. He ate more and more and gained more and more weight; with increased work demands, he stopped exercising. Now, at age thirty-six, Robert weighed fifty pounds more than he did when he graduated from college.

I inquired about Robert's sleep. Beth told me that he didn't always snore, but now he snored constantly after gaining so much weight. It was so bad that she slept in their guest room. I asked Beth if Robert stopped breathing during sleep. "Oh, yes," she said. He stopped breathing many times each night, often gasping and choking. These were the clues I needed. I strongly suspected sleep apnea, which an overnight sleep study confirmed. Using the CPAP device recommended for his apnea, Robert slept much better and awoke more refreshed, and his brain fog disappeared. Robert's job performance improved, and his job was no longer in jeopardy. Eventually, Robert improved his diet, began to exercise, and lost the fifty pounds he'd gained. He no longer needed his CPAP machine following his weight loss.

Undetected and untreated sleep apnea has a devastating impact on the brain. Sleep apnea should always be considered in patients like Robert who have gained weight, have large necks, snore loudly, or stop breathing during sleep. Individuals with apnea simply do not get enough oxygen at night—a definite no-no for the brain.

Elizabeth in the Lyme Light

An often overlooked condition that can have a markedly negative effect on brain function is Lyme disease and its co-infections. Lyme disease has received more press in recent years, but there is still much ignorance, even among medical professionals, regarding the damage Lyme can do. I know from personal experience.

My daughter, Elizabeth, now twenty-eight, had a severe case of mono at age twelve or thirteen. It was so severe that her pediatrician wanted to hospitalize her. Eventually, Elizabeth recovered from the mono, sort of. What followed the mono is clearer now in retrospect. But suffice it to say that for many years she struggled, and for many years my wife and I felt totally lost as we tried to help Elizabeth.

Following her mono, Elizabeth became much more moody and irritable. Typical teen stuff, some thought, including respected counselors, therapists, and psychiatrists and other physicians whom we consulted. She complained of difficulty sleeping and wouldn't get up for school; much later we realized that the "wouldn't" was really "couldn't." Elizabeth complained of severe daily migraine-type headaches and exquisite light sensitivity. I remember sitting in a dimly lit restaurant with Elizabeth, who was wearing a pair of dark sunglasses; she reminded me of some paranoid patients who don't want you to see their eyes. Elizabeth wasn't paranoid, however.

Off we went in search of headache relief. Neurologists, headache doctors, pediatric ophthalmologists, and sleep specialists were consulted, with minimal benefit. The psychiatrists we consulted weighed in that Elizabeth seemed depressed; maybe she was bipolar, they said. Here I was, myself a physician and a psychiatrist, and my wife an experienced nurse, and we couldn't help my daughter.

Elizabeth continued to be moody and irritable. She often seemed pressured and spoke about all the jumbled thoughts in her head. Elizabeth was also weak and fatigued, had severe difficulty sleeping, and could not concentrate at school. Medical consultations continued. To no avail.

By the time Elizabeth reached her early twenties, I began to notice that a number of patients in my practice had Lyme disease. This was unfortunate for my patients, but fortunate for us in that I began to notice similarities between their complaints and the problems Elizabeth had. Moreover, her dog and horse had had Lyme. On a hunch, I called up a local Lyme expert, who said that he'd be willing to evaluate Elizabeth. The result was that Elizabeth did have Lyme and likely had had it for years. And she also had a number of the so-called co-infections in addition to Lyme. Looking back, I believe that Elizabeth's mono at age twelve or thirteen weakened her immune system so much that it made her susceptible to Lyme and co-infections.

Following her diagnosis we finally had answers and had something to treat. Her treatment was and continues to be complicated. She received IV and oral antibiotics, supplements to boost her immune system and kill the Lyme and other organisms, hyperbaric oxygen treatment, and IV infusions of glutathione, Myers' Cocktails, and high-dose vitamin C. Elizabeth's treatment has not been quick or easy, but she is improving. I kick myself for not recognizing Lyme sooner, but many physicians know little about Lyme; as best as I recall, it was never mentioned when I attended medical school.

Elizabeth has undergone multiple SPECT scans at my clinic, which have helped us monitor her treatment. Her SPECT images show incredible overactivity in her limbic system, which correlates with her moodiness and irritability. I believe that the overactivity is caused by her infections and treatments. Seeing these images enabled us all to understand Elizabeth's behavior as well as show the need for continued treatment. As Elizabeth's treatment progressed, we did follow-up SPECT scans that showed slow but steady improvement in her scans; her limbic overactivity was reduced.

Lyme disease and co-infections (*Babesia*, *Bartonella*, Rocky Mountain spotted fever, anaplasmosis, and others) can mimic or cause any medical, neurological, or psychiatric issues. For these reasons, we call Lyme "the great imitator." I have seen Lyme present with issues that seem like ADHD, depression, bipolar disorder, anxiety, OCD, and psychosis. But if Lyme and co-infections are present, these issues often go away when the infections are treated.

Individuals with Lyme are often exquisitely sensitive to the environment; they feel constantly assaulted by light, sounds/noise, and fragrances. Their brain is overwhelmed and cannot process and manage the stimuli. Often they complain of noise in the brain. Many individuals with Lyme are disabled, not being able to work or attend school. They often are bereft of energy, don't sleep well, and complain of brain fog.

One woman with Lyme was so impaired that she struggled to say more than one or two words; she had been a research scientist prior to getting sick. Another patient, a boy of eleven, developed severe OCD symptoms of excessive hand washing and fears of contamination within a week or two of getting infected with Lyme following a tick bite.

Blood tests for Lyme are unreliable. We often use the IGeneX lab in Palo Alto, California, for testing. IGeneX does much better testing for Lyme and co-infections than labs that do not specialize in Lyme—which have high rates of false-negative results. Without intending to do so, I have become one of the leading experts in the use of brain SPECT imaging to diagnose and treat Lyme disease, having presented this information at a number of professional conferences.

There is much controversy in the medical field about whether chronic Lyme disease is a legitimate condition. I believe that it is legitimate. Lyme absolutely must be considered in the differential diagnosis of most psychiatric issues. Unfortunately, the diagnosis is often missed, with tragic consequences. Importantly, it is likely that many individuals with the common diagnoses of chronic fatigue syndrome (CFS) and fibromyalgia have tick-borne infections like Lyme and its co-infections. Psychiatric experts of the future will need expertise in diseases that infect and affect the brain, like Lyme and its co-infections.

Another condition that I see often in Lyme patients is Irlen syndrome, which my daughter Elizabeth has as a result of her Lyme. It is to Irlen syndrome that we now turn.

Julie: Severe Headaches and Light Sensitivity

Julie, age twenty-four, single, and working as a receptionist in a dental practice, came to see me because of headaches. She had daily, severe, pounding migraines. She also felt constantly overwhelmed, as if the environment were assaulting her. Over the years, she consulted her internist, a neurologist, and two headache specialists. Medications for headaches helped the pain, but nothing seemed to prevent them. As is often typical when physicians struggle to find the answer to a patient's problems, her last doctor told Julie that he thought that she needed to see a psychiatrist.

When I first met Julie, she was sitting alone in our waiting room wearing sunglasses. This was a little unusual, but she was not the only person to have done that. Julie told me all about her saga of searching for help. Medications, injections in her scalp, biofeedback, psychotherapy, and diet changes had done little. She was still having daily, excruciating headaches. And she struggled with extreme light sensitivity, especially in the dental office, which had overhead fluorescent lights.

Julie found it depressing to have these headaches, but she was not depressed. Nor did she struggle with anxiety, ADHD, OCD, or other common psychiatric issues. Julie had good fortune in coming to me, because I know about Irlen syndrome. Irlen is a common visual-processing disorder. We see it in many people with traumatic brain injury, autism, Lyme disease, and ADHD. And we can also find Irlen in people without any of those conditions. A tendency for Irlen syndrome can be inherited. Irlen has four key features: light sensitivity, especially to fluorescent lights; severe headaches; reading difficulties; and depth perception issues.

I explained Irlen syndrome to Julie and referred her to an Irlen specialist for additional evaluation and treatment. Julie's Irlen specialist confirmed that Julie does have Irlen syndrome. Julie received the typical treatment for Irlen syndrome, which consists of "filters," special color coatings on her eyeglass lenses. Coated contact lenses are also available. Immediately, when Julie received and started wearing her Irlen lenses, her headaches were reduced 99.9 percent and her light sensitivity went away. She also found that she could read better and that words no longer ran together on the page as they had done before her Irlen lenses.

Experience using brain SPECT shows remarkable overactivity in the limbic systems of those who have Irlen syndrome. This overactivity is eliminated when these individuals wear their Irlen lenses. It's a remarkable change. Irlen is controversial; not everybody "believes" in it, just like not everybody "believes" in Lyme disease. Some medical professionals, including optometrists and ophthalmologists, deny that Irlen syndrome is a valid condition. But I've seen positive changes with treatment in many patients with Irlen syndrome. Anyone suspecting Irlen syndrome should look at the Irlen website (www.irlen.com), where helpful information and self-tests are available.

Cynthia: Impact of Low Thyroid Function

Sometimes the problem isn't that our *brain* has been literally damaged by a temporal lobe injury, toxicities, or other brain injuries. Sometimes, it is dysfunctions in other parts of our *bodies* that are causing a problem for our brain. For example, thyroid disorders are extremely common yet often go undetected. Similarly, the connection between thyroid problems and busy brains is often missed. The result is frustrated patients trying to solve their problems through therapy who actually need to first heal their bodies, in this case their thyroids. Cynthia's case is a good illustration.

Cynthia, twenty-eight, was bubbly and smart. She had a passion to help the poor and started law school in order to devote herself to the legal needs of underprivileged children. But when Cynthia came to see me, she told me that she had flunked out of law school. She couldn't concentrate and had failed most of her exams; the law school suggested an indefinite leave of absence.

Like Sam, discussed later, Cynthia reported scattered and jumbled thinking patterns; at first, she, too, seemed to have ADHD. Her busy brain attacked Cynthia for her failure at school with a constant stream of negative thoughts—"I'm a failure." "I can't do anything right." I taught Cynthia techniques to deal with her negative thoughts, but they did little good. I would eventually learn why these approaches failed. As I came to know Cynthia, she also reported chronic depression, low energy, memory difficulties, dry skin, brittle hair, cold hands and feet, and constipation—common symptoms of low thyroid function. I asked Cynthia to have screening bloodwork to check her thyroid and other issues. Her test results showed that Cynthia had low thyroid function and low iodine levels (which make it more difficult for the body to make thyroid hormones).

To deal with her thyroid issues, I asked Cynthia to optimize her diet, including eliminating gluten, which is often associated with thyroid problems. I prescribed thyroid hormones and iodine supplementation. Over six months, we optimized the doses of her hormones and iodine. Gradually, Cynthia's mood, energy, and memory improved. Her other symptoms of low thyroid function—constipation, cold extremities, dry skin, and brittle hair—also improved. With improved thyroid function, the techniques for rewriting her negative thoughts and stories finally worked.

How does thyroid function affect our thoughts? To grasp the body-to-brain connection here, it's important to understand that the thyroid has a profound impact on all areas of the body, including the brain. Every cell in the nervous system has receptors for thyroid hormones. Thyroid hormones control a cell's metabolism. And if thyroid hormones are lower, the metabolic rate goes down. In other words, lower thyroid hormones lower your metabolic rate, which is like lowering the idle rate of the brain. The engine will run, but not at 100 percent. When the thyroid doesn't work well, the brain doesn't work well. People with thyroid issues commonly report brain problems such as focus, attention, concentration, and memory issues.

I wrote a letter to Cynthia's law school, explaining that we now knew why Cynthia had had difficulty doing her coursework; it was because of thyroid problems. Her law school agreed to give her another try, and she reenrolled the following semester. Cynthia was able to complete her law school studies, graduate, and set up her own law practice helping immigrants with their legal needs. I was pleased to play a part in her success. Cynthia's case shows that thyroid issues should be considered whenever patients complain of mood, energy, memory, constipation, cold extremities, and other symptoms of low metabolism. If the thyroid doesn't work right, the brain doesn't work right.

While Cynthia had low thyroid function due to an underactive thyroid gland, Edward, another patient who had difficulties responding to regular treatment, turned out to have an overactive thyroid. Both kinds of thyroid trouble can negatively affect brain function.

Edward: Overactive Thyroid

Edward's parents brought him to see me. They were desperate. Edward had periodic flare-ups of irritability, anger, and violence. He was anxious, constantly agitated, and panicky and always seemed overwhelmed. There were more than a few holes in the wall. Nearly two years in a residential treatment program had failed to put a dent in his problems. Home life was miserable; Edward's parents and sister walked on eggshells around him. Edward's school performance was abysmal. He wasn't interested, didn't or couldn't pay attention, and was in danger of failing tenth grade. Importantly, Edward spoke about never feeling at peace. His mind raced constantly, but he didn't seem to have bipolar mania, and there was no family history of bipolar disorders. For months I asked, prodded, cajoled, and begged Edward to do some blood tests. I especially wanted to check his thyroid function, because there was a strong family history of thyroid issues. But Edward refused; he seemed to be afraid of needles but wouldn't admit it. Finally, after nearly a year of unsuccessful medication trials to calm his busy brain—unsuccessful because he always had major side effects—Edward agreed to do the blood tests I requested.

The blood test results confirmed my suspicions. Edward had thyroid problems—but his thyroid was overactive, too much activity. This was why his thoughts raced, he couldn't concentrate, and he was so irritable. I referred Edward to an endocrinologist; there was no quick fix, but addressing Edward's thyroid problems eventually calmed his brain. Anger and rages decreased, family life improved, and Edward did passably well at school. Edward's overactive thyroid had the impact of pouring gasoline on a fire. We needed to take away the fuel for Edward's fire.

Other hormone issues also need to be considered in situations of obvious brain dysfunction. For example, falling estrogen levels in menopause increases the risk of depression. Lower progesterone levels contribute to increased anxiety and sleep difficulty. And low testosterone levels in middle age and beyond, especially in men, contribute to depression, low energy, and loss of vitality, not to mention sexual drive and stamina, in this age group.

Sam: More than ADHD—Vitamins, Nutrients, Hormones, and Diet

In his midforties, Sam, married with two young sons, came to me for help with ADHD. He'd had a successful career in the biotech field. Sam made a killing when his company went public; he'd sold his stock and was able to retire early. Lucky guy. Despite his good fortune, Sam struggled with what seemed to be typical ADHD issues: focus, attention, concentration, organization, and easy boredom. Motivation was a problem; Sam could never get himself to complete the tasks he set out for himself. These even included artistic goals he sought, such as learning to play the piano and developing his earlier passion for oil painting. Sam also struggled with scattered thoughts that seemed to race at times in his mind, especially when he tried to sleep; Sam had a busy brain. He attacked himself with a constant stream of negative thoughts along the lines of "What is wrong with me that I can't do what I want and need to?" and "I can't believe what a failure I am."

Initially, Sam and I discussed lifestyle changes, such as steps to improve his sleep and the need to exercise. He knew that these were important but couldn't get himself to do what we both knew that he needed to do. We decided to try medication for ADHD. Adderall XR and Vyvanse provided some help, but still not enough.

I began to hear Sam talk about low energy. At this point, I

carefully explored with Sam what he ate. I was surprised to learn that he was a vegan—no meat or any animal products whatsoever. Sam had been a vegetarian since his teens but had adopted a more rigorous vegan lifestyle six months earlier when one of his sons did the same. Knowing that vegetarians and vegans can have difficulty obtaining all the nutrients they need, I had Sam do a full blood-work panel to check for vitamin and mineral deficiencies. What I found was that Sam had low levels of vitamins B12 and D, low testosterone, and low thyroid function. I had Sam take supplements to boost vitamins B12 and D, arranged for him to have testosterone supplementation via weekly injections, and gave him a prescription for Armour thyroid medication to boost his thyroid function. Low levels of B12, testosterone, and thyroid had negatively affected his energy and motivation because of their impact on the brain.

After Sam had been on this new regimen for several months, his energy and motivation increased significantly. I also suggested that he change back to a vegetarian diet, which he did, thus improving his intake of essential nutrients. I then suggested that Sam avoid gluten, which is often associated with thyroid problems. After making the diet changes and being on the supplemental vitamins and hormones for four months, Sam was able to attain the response we wanted from his ADHD medication. Now the Vyvanse had its intended effect—significantly improved attention, focus, concentration, motivation, and the like. Sam could then actively pursue his piano studies and painting, and he could accomplish the repair jobs around the home that had heretofore stymied him. And, importantly, Sam's busy brain was calmed.

Sam's story shows that there is often more than meets the eye. What at first seemed to be a simple case of ADHD was much more than that. Sam didn't respond to typical treatment because his body physiology was way out of balance. Hormones, minerals, and diet can significantly affect body—and brain—function, and need to be attended to if we aim to heal hurting individuals.

My aim in *Reclaim Your Brain* is to help you calm your thoughts, heal your mind, and bring your life back under control. The primary emphasis has been on what you can do yourself, without professional assistance, to bring about these positive changes. Then why have I devoted so much space to addressing hurting brains and bodies? The reason is that many people—and their doctors—are not aware of the impact of physical brain injury, brain infections, toxicity, hormonal problems, and the other factors I've highlighted in this chapter. If you don't improve by using the strategies and Action Plans I've laid out for you, seek professional help and consider whether one of the problems illustrated in this chapter is interfering with your healing.

I repeat what I've said several times, that not everyone needs a brain scan. But I also want to underscore that brain scans and other appropriate medical studies can help you and your health professional "think outside the box," to identify reasons why you may not have found healing thus far for your brain and your health.

Conclusion:
Beyond Mind and Brain

W hat do you think of Western civilization?" someone supposedly asked Gandhi. "I think it would be a good idea," he replied.

Eating, sleeping, reproducing, defending our territory, even conquering, we share these fundamental behaviors with our primate ancestors, our animal cousins. But is there more to human beings, more to life? There should be more. Indeed, civilization becomes possible only when we attain some mastery of our primitive natures. It is our mind (PFC) that tames the primitive (limbic system), unleashing the flowering of human achievement: music, art, literature, science, philosophy, beauty, and spirituality.

Yet despite the grand achievements of civilization, despite all that our mind is able to master and accomplish, most of us hurt and seek healing. We seek to assuage our pain. And we seek to transcend our own limitations. Some of us find relief in art. Some in science. Some in a richer spiritual life.

Note that I am not referring to the spirituality of traditional religious institutions. Rather, I mean by spirituality that which goes beyond the material, beyond the concrete, really beyond ourselves—a way for each of us to be in harmony within ourselves and others, despite faults, failings, and flaws. More emphasis on who and how we are, less emphasis on what we do. Something greater than ourselves that can anchor us. Without that anchor, we may focus excessively on ourselves, exacerbating our hurts and continuing to rev our busy brains. We seek purpose, to belong to something greater than ourselves. Spirituality can help us find that purpose and go beyond our biological destiny. Beyond mind and brain.

Charles, in his midforties, came to me because of moderate depression. Married, a father of two girls and three boys, Charles had a good job as a senior healthcare recruiter. I had the opportunity to scan Charles using brain SPECT. When I saw Charles's brain SPECT images, I was shocked. His brain looked extremely unhealthy. I discussed with Charles what made his brain look so bad. Multiple head injuries from sports and seven years of heavy drug and alcohol abuse in his late teens and early twenties, he told me. But here was a puzzle: Charles's brain looked like the brain of somebody who would be barely able to function. How was it that, apart from mild to moderate depression, he functioned well at work, as a husband, and as a father? That's what I asked Charles. He told me that when he met his wife, he joined her in her faith tradition of the Society of Friends, the Quakers. It was his dedication to pacifism and the betterment of society, and the structure of regular participation in Quaker activities, that allowed Charles to overcome his poor brain function. External structure and purpose overcame his unhealthy brain. Eventually, I was able to help Charles improve his brain and deal with his depression. But the key point of his story is that the structure, love, and meaning he found in his relationship with his wife, her family, and their religious tradition helped mightily to offset what should have been—and would have been—a debilitated life. Spirituality and purpose may allow us to transcend our brain limitations.

Or consider the story of my French tutor, Madame Renelle Gannon. Born in France during the Nazi occupation to a large, impoverished family, in difficult circumstances, Madame Gannon at a young age dedicated herself to a profound spiritual life, with many hours devoted each day to prayer and meditation. These spiritual practices give her life meaning, and she experiences her life's purpose in helping others find their own spiritual path. The meaning and purpose that she has found have allowed her to escape what likely would have been a life of misery and depression.

My intention in describing Charles and Madame Gannon is not to advocate that readers adopt this or that religious or spiritual tradition but to underscore that finding our own individual meaning and purpose helps us rise above potentially unhealthy brains and difficult life circumstances. And an important lesson seems to be that in helping others heal, we find purpose, go beyond the solipsistic emphasis on self, and heal and grow ourselves. We can all be creators of something good. I think that is our purpose, and that can be our legacy.

Your main job is to figure out the lifestyle—the schedule of daily and weekly practices—that keeps your spiritual well filled up. Consider what activities—whether prayer, meditation, music, contact with like-minded people, spiritually focused readings, or time in nature—keep you emotionally and spiritually centered. What are the activities that reliably produce "spiritual fruits" of joy, gratitude, compassion, and acceptance of yourself and others? What are the choices that anchor you most effectively in your authentic self?

Think about how you orient yourself to the world each day. What is the mind-set, the emotional and spiritual center, out of which you relate and function most effortlessly, meaningfully, joyfully, and fruitfully? This means: How do you want to *be* in the world? Do you want to radiate positivity, support, love, energy, creativity, hope? If so, how can you best do that? It might mean making sure that you have enough quiet time to center yourself through reading, writing, meditation, prayer, or walking in nature.

What are your current priorities—your purposes—going into the next chapter of your life? Stop and form a mental picture of how you want your life to look in the near future. Build on your mind-set and spiritual values to create a plan that will lead you successfully ahead, step by step. You may find that social justice is a passion; dedicating yourself to advocacy for social justice gives you a purpose beyond yourself. Or you might be drawn toward immersing yourself in a field of study, or broadening yourself with music, art, or literature. Perhaps you will seriously consider a career change. In the realm of your relationships, nurturing important friendships, being a more available and loving parent, and being a less critical, more supportive spouse may be important priorities.

Think about who are you now and what's most important in the upcoming phase of your life. To carry out your spiritual priorities, think about whether you will need to make changes in your relationships, work, schooling, finances, and physical and emotional health. What will you need to do to be able to fulfill your mission or calling? What could you do today or this week to begin to embed those spiritual priorities and purposes you've just clarified into your life, so that you experience an ongoing, deep sense of purpose and meaning, rather than having it be a rare or random experience? For example, if your goal is to set aside time for reading and meditation, start with thirty minutes a week. Find the thirty minutes by unplugging from your electronics. Expand beyond thirty minutes as the weeks go by.

"The only thing worse than being blind is having sight but no vision," said Helen Keller. In conducting this spiritual survey of your life, the important thing is that *you* decide what gives your life joy and meaning. What is *your* vision? Reflecting and clarifying for yourself what stance toward your life yields spiritual fruit, joy, and purpose, and participating in something greater than yourself takes time, but the investment will be worth it. You might decide to make a written contract with yourself, using the SMARTER goals approach discussed earlier. And sharing your intentions with those close to you may help you keep on the path toward fulfilling your spiritual goals.

It's so easy to be caught up in the daily to-and-fro of life and to be waylaid by our busy brains. But we can choose to address our negativity, to rewrite our stories, to live mindfully, and to improve our relationships. We can move beyond the mundane and beyond our busy brain. We can reclaim our brains by managing our minds and balancing our brains. We can bring our lives back under control. And through developing our own spiritual meaning and purpose, we can transcend the limitations of our minds and brains.

Nutritional Supplements

Please consult your healthcare professional before starting any supplement.

5-HTP: Use for depression, insomnia, OCD, pain intolerance, migraines, and fibromyalgia pain. Start with 50 mg twice a day; increase the dose after several days to 100 mg twice daily, and then if needed increase again to 150 mg twice daily. This supplement begins to work quite quickly, in most cases within several days. Sometimes we add 500 to 1,000 mg of L-tryptophan for additional boosting of serotonin, especially for insomnia. By boosting serotonin levels in the brain, 5-HTP calms limbic system (including anterior cingulate gyrus) hyperactivity. We often suggest using 50 mg of vitamin B6 daily because this vitamin is essential for converting amino acids into serotonin. The most common side effect of 5-HTP is an upset stomach, although this is usually mild. Stomach upset can be improved by starting 5-HTP slowly and increasing the dose as you get used to the supplement; taking 5-HTP with food also helps minimize stomach upset.

GABA (gamma-aminobutyric acid): Use for calming the brain, anxiety, mood swings, irritability, and temper. GABA is usually taken in doses ranging from 250 to 1,500 mg daily for adults. For best effect, the daily dose of GABA should be divided among two or three daily doses. Start at 750 mg once or twice a day and increase as needed. On occasion, we have used daily doses as high as 5,000 or 6,000 mg. GABA does not seem helpful for every patient, possibly because it is not always well absorbed and has difficulty crossing the blood-brain barrier. There are few side effects, apart from sedation.

Ginkgo Biloba: Use for ADHD, focus, concentration, memory, and mental sharpness. Take 60 to 120 mg twice daily. Ginkgo can thin your blood, which is usually a good thing. Mention that you are using it if you are going to have surgery.

Glutamine: Use to calm the brain and reduce cravings. Take 500 mg twice daily. Twinlab brand seems to be a good one.

Glycine: Use for stuckness/OCD and cravings. Take 500 to 3,000 mg/day in divided doses. We usually recommend taking it with food. At higher doses, you may notice a "dirty sock smell," which comes from the sulfur in glycine.

Inositol: Use for depression and stuckness/OCD. Take up to 12,000 mg/day for depression and up to 18,000 mg/day for stuckness/OCD.

L-theanine: Use for anxiety, insomnia, stress, and focus. The usual dose is 200 mg three or four times per day. You can take higher doses if you find it useful. There are no known adverse reactions. Keep some at your bedside to use in the early morning if you wake up too early. Pregnant women and nursing mothers should avoid L-theanine supplements. Children over age six can use theanine, but start with 100 mg twice daily.

L-tyrosine: Use for ADHD, focus, energy, motivation, and depression. For the first three days, take 500 mg before breakfast, midmorning, and then midafternoon. After three days increase to 1,000 mg before breakfast, midmorning, and midafternoon. Take on an empty stomach.

Lemon Balm: Use for anxiety. The daily dose is 600 mg. Lemon balm is an herb from the mint family. It has no significant side effects.

Magnesium: Use for anxiety, insomnia, and stress. I often recommend Tri-Mag 300 (by DaVinci Labs, with which I have no financial or other relationship). Start with two capsules twice daily and increase the dose every day or two until your stools become loose. Then reduce the dose slightly.

Melatonin: Use for mild to moderate insomnia associated with anxiety and possibly even anxiety and depression apart from insomnia. Doses typically range from 0.5 to 10 mg taken thirty to sixty minutes before bedtime. Melatonin seems more useful for difficulty falling asleep than difficulty staying asleep. Those who have difficulty staying asleep should use a melatonin preparation that is formulated for extended release. Occasionally there can be a "hangover" the next morning; other side effects can include headache or vivid dreams, but these occur rarely.

NAC (N-acetylcysteine): Use for stuckness/OCD. Doses for this widely used antioxidant are 600 to 1,200 mg twice daily.

Omega-3 fatty acids: Use for anxiety, depression, mood stability, and overall brain health. I recommend obtaining a fish oil product that contains both EPA and DHA (look on the label). Aim for a more or less 3:2 ratio of EPA:DHA. Add up how much EPA and DHA is in a capsule or a dose of the liquid concentrate. Take 3,000 mg/day of the total of EPA and DHA. Side effects can include bloating, loose stools, and "fish burp." Individuals taking omega-3 supplements may also experience increased bruising and mildly prolonged bleeding times—it is a blood thinner, which is why cardiologists recommend it. Individuals using blood thinner medication can still take omega-3 supplements, but they should consult their physician prior to starting omega-3 supplements.

Passionflower: Use for anxiety. The dosage is 90 mg/day. Side effects are minimal.

Phosphatidylserine (PS): Use for memory, learning, and ADHD. Take 300 mg/day. Many PS products are derived from soy and can cause reactions in those sensitive to soy.

SAMe: Use for depression, low energy, and ADHD. Start at 200 or 400 mg/day and then increase the daily dose gradually, if tolerated, by approximately 200 mg per week. A person may start seeing some benefit at 200 to 400 mg but may require 1,600 mg or more per day. It works best when taken at least twenty to thirty minutes before breakfast and lunch on an empty stomach. If taken later in the day it may interfere with sleep. In higher doses it can cause insomnia and restlessness. Individuals with features of bipolar disorder should use SAMe with caution, because it can cause mood swings or mania.

St. John's wort: Use for depression and stuckness/OCD. Start at 600 mg in the morning and 300 mg at night. If needed, the dose may be increased slowly to 1,800 mg daily. Wear sunscreen, because St. John's wort increases the risk of sunburn. Other side effects can include nausea and loose stools. St. John's wort can decrease the effectiveness of other medications, including birth control pills and blood thinners. It can bring on mania in individuals who have bipolar disorder.

Vitamin D: Use for depression and mood cycling (bipolar disorder). Aim for a blood level between 60 and 100. I often recommend that people take 5,000 to 10,000 IU/day of over-the-counter vitamin D3. The prescription vitamin D supplements given by physicians seem to work less well.

Medications

Please consult your healthcare professional before starting any medication.

Abilify: Use for depression and psychosis. Abilify is not strictly an antidepressant but is helpful as an add-on to antidepressants in some cases.

Adderall/Adderall XR: Use for ADHD. These stimulant medications increase dopamine and boost function in the prefrontal cortex. They are often quite effective. Some teens and young adults abuse them. There are some side effects (insomnia, appetite suppression). In cases of severe abuse, the individual can become psychotic.

Amantadine: Use for ADHD. Amantadine is less effective than stimulants like Adderall XR.

Anafranil: Use for OCD. Take as much as 250 mg/day. Side effects include lowered sex drive and difficulty attaining sexual arousal and orgasm.

Ativan: Use for anxiety, calming, and sleep. Ideally, Ativan is used only on a short-term basis. Physical dependence can develop when benzodiazepine medications like Ativan are used regularly for a few weeks. Common side effects of the benzodiazepines include sedation and coordination problems. These medications also negatively affect memory. They are useful for short-term anxiety but carry addictive potential. They also deaden feelings, which can work against healing of emotional traumas.

BuSpar: Use for anxiety. BuSpar is useful in cases of mild anxiety when the individual has never used a benzodiazepine medication. Side effects are generally minimal. Unfortunately, the therapeutic benefit for anxiety is also minimal.

Clonidine: Useful for sleep in ADHD busy brains and for overall calming of hyperactive individuals with ADHD. Clonidine is also helpful for treating nightmares in PTSD.

Concerta: Use for ADHD. Concerta is a longer-acting stimulant and is often not quite as effective as Vyvanse or Adderall.

Cymbalta: Use for depression, anxiety, chronic pain, and sometimes OCD. Side effects include lowered sex drive and difficulty attaining sexual arousal and orgasm.

Depakote: Use for bipolar disorder, anxiety, anger/rage, mood stabilization, and temporal lobe problems. The doctor will need to monitor blood tests when using Depakote.

Desipramine: Use for ADHD and depression. This is an older antidepressant with some usefulness for ADHD. Children should have an electrocardiograph (EKG) before use because desipramine can affect heart rhythms, and we need to make sure their heart is healthy enough to tolerate a trial of this medication.

Effexor/Effexor XR: Use for anxiety, depression, and OCD. Common side effects include difficulties with sexual function, as with Cymbalta, and gastrointestinal effects. Effexor can be difficult to stop because of significant withdrawal symptoms that some individuals experience.

Focalin/Focalin XR: Use for ADHD. This drug is similar to Concerta.

Intuniv: Use for ADHD and to reduce brain overactivity. Intuniv helps with calming ADHD. It is not as useful as stimulants. It provides some benefit for sleep in ADHD.

Klonopin: Use for anxiety and sleep. Klonopin is similar to Ativan, but longer-acting and causing more sedation.

Lamictal: Use for bipolar disorder, anxiety, anger/rage, mood stabilization, and temporal lobe problems. Lamictal has few side effects for most patients. I find that the generic version of Lamictal made by Teva often does not work well for my patients.

Lexapro: Use for depression, anxiety, panic attacks, and OCD. Lexapro has the fewest side effects of any SSRI medication. The most common side effects are sexual, including lowered sex drive and difficulty attaining sexual arousal and orgasm. Other side effects include nausea and headaches. Doses that are too high can inappropriately deaden feelings, interfering with the work of healing from trauma.

Lithium: Use for bipolar disorder and as an add-on in the treatment of depression. Lithium is the gold standard treatment for bipolar disorders, likely the most effective medication.

Neurontin: Use for sleep, anxiety, and chronic pain. Neurontin is very sedating at first, so start with 100 mg at bedtime.

Nuvigil: Use for ADHD, narcolepsy, fatigue, and low energy in multiple sclerosis and in depression. Nuvigil is a cousin of Provigil.

Paxil: Use for depression, anxiety, panic attacks, and OCD. Paxil is a "dirty" medication, meaning it has the most side effects of any SSRI, including lots of sedation and sexual side effects. Because of its significant side effects, and because other SSRI medications work as well or better than Paxil works, in my opinion there is no practical reason to use it.

Prazosin: Use for sleep and nightmares, especially with trauma.

Pristiq: Use for depression, anxiety, and OCD. Pristiq is a relative of Effexor but probably easier to discontinue. It has side effects similar to those of Effexor, but they are probably milder.

Propranolol: Use for anxiety, especially public-speaking and performance anxiety. This is a blood pressure medication with few side effects at the low doses we use for anxiety.

Provigil: Similar to Nuvigil.

Prozac: Use for depression, anxiety, panic attacks, and OCD. Prozac was the first SSRI; it is also the longest-acting SSRI and can be used effectively to cross-taper other SSRIs. It has more side effects than Lexapro or Zoloft.

Risperdal: Use for bipolar disorder, mood instability, anger, rage, psychosis, and severe OCD and PTSD. Risperdal often has significant side effects of weight gain and increases in blood lipids and blood glucose.

Seroquel: Use for insomnia, bipolar disorder, mood instability, anger, rage, psychosis, and severe OCD and PTSD. Seroquel often has significant side effects of weight gain and increases in blood lipids and blood glucose. It is used quite often for sleep, too often in my view.

Strattera: Use for ADHD. Strattera has low abuse potential, but it is not very useful in my experience and often has side effects, including urological problems in males and mood instability.

Tenex: See Intuniv. Intuniv is a slightly longer-acting version of Tenex.

Topamax: Use for sleep, nightmares, and binge eating. Topamax is so sedating for some patients that we have a nickname for it—"Dopamax," because it makes individuals feel dopey.

Trileptal: See Depakote and Lamictal, for which Trileptal has similar uses, but Trileptal tends to be less effective. It has few side effects apart from low sodium levels in a small percentage of patients.

Vyvanse: Use for ADHD. Vyvanse is the longest-acting and smoothest stimulant available. Insurance companies are reluctant to cover it because no generic is available and it is more expensive than other stimulants that are available in generic form.

Wellbutrin: Use for depression, ADHD, smoking cessation (available as Zyban), and sometimes anxiety. It has no sexual side effects, in contrast to the SSRI medications.

Xanax: See Klonopin, to which is it similar, but Xanax is shorter-acting and more likely than Klonopin to cause "rebound" anxiety and insomnia when it wears off. Xanax is an effective medication, but patients can easily become dependent on it.

Zoloft: See Lexapro, to which Zoloft is quite similar.

Zyprexa: See Risperdal.

Annotated Bibliography

Here I list authors and books that particularly influenced me, either during the course of my career or more recently during the work of writing *Reclaim Your Brain*. Although this list is not in any way a systematic review, readers interested in learning more about the topics I covered may benefit from investigating the authors and works below.

Chapter 1: Balancing the Brain

Amen, Daniel. *Change Your Brain, Change Your Life: The Breakthrough Program for Conquering Anxiety, Depression, Obsessiveness, Anger, and Impulsiveness*. New York: Three Rivers Press, 1998. This is Daniel Amen's first major publication, one that set the stage for his subsequent work. CYBCYL, as we affectionately call it, will be reissued as a new edition in late 2015. CYBCYL is a groundbreaking work that will show you much about why you need to understand how your brain works and what you can do about it.

Barkley, Russell. *Executive Functions: What They Are, How They Work, and Why They Evolved*. New York: Guilford, 2012. Barkley is a key researcher in the fields of executive function and ADHD. Not recommended for the general public but useful for academics and mental health professionals.

Cozolino, Louis. *The Neuroscience of Psychotherapy: Healing the Social Brain*. New York: Norton, 2012; and *The Neuroscience of Human Relationships: Attachment and the Developing Social Brain*. New York: Norton, 2006. Cozolino is a brilliant writer and clinician. Engaging and readable, his works are to be savored. I've used them in some of the courses I've taught. You will learn much about how the brain is wired to optimize social relations and especially about the importance of early attachment.

Damasio, Antonio. *The Feeling of What Happens: Body and Emotion in the Making of Consciousness*. New York: Harcourt Brace, 1999; and *Self Comes to Mind: Constructing the Conscious Brain*. New York: Pantheon,

2010. Damasio's work is breathtaking in its scope. His writing can be difficult-going and often is best read in the context of a study group, but Damasio's thinking is of the highest level. Read Damasio if you want to be challenged by the thinking of one of the world's best neuroscientists.

Goldberg, Elkhonon. *The New Executive Brain: Frontal Lobes in a Complex World*. New York: Oxford University Press, 2009 (paperback). Goldberg is a witty and thoughtful writer. It is very much worth the time to read him. Goldberg helpfully describes how a well-functioning PFC is the CEO of the brain and what goes wrong when the PFC doesn't work well. He also movingly writes about growing up in the Soviet Union and his apprenticeship with the renowned Russian psychologist Alexander Luria. Goldberg ultimately made the painful decision to defect from the Soviet Union, which required great courage.

LeDoux, Joseph. *The Emotional Brain: The Mysterious Underpinnings of Emotional Life*. New York: Simon & Schuster, 1996; and *Synaptic Self: How Our Brains Become Who We Are*. New York: Viking, 2002. LeDoux is a brilliant researcher who has done fundamental work on primitive memory and anxiety systems. He is quite readable and compellingly writes about the practical and human applications of basic neuroscience research.

Schwartz, Jeffrey, and Sharon Begley. *The Mind and the Brain: Neuroplasticity and the Power of Mental Force*. New York: HarperCollins, 2002 (paperback). Schwartz has written widely and is admired for his research and the scope of his writings.

Siegel, Daniel. *The Developing Mind: How Relationships and the Brain Interact to Shape Who We Are*. New York: Guilford, 1999. This is a classic, a real gem, but more for professionals than the lay audience.

Chapter 2: Conquering Negativity

Beck, Aaron, et al. *Cognitive Therapy of Depression*. New York: Guilford, 1979. Beck is the father of CBT. He has written many books on the subject that clearly present the theory and practical application of his ideas. My ideas about negativity and rewriting stories are related to how one approaches negative thinking in CBT.

Cozolino, Louis. See the Chapter 1 bibliography.

Chapter 3: Rewriting Your Stories

Katie, Byron. *Loving What Is: Four Questions That Can Change Your Life*. New York: Harmony, 2002. This is a key book for my approach to addressing negativity and rewriting stories. I really do think this book can change your life for the better.

Newberg, Andrew, and Mark Robert Waldman. *Words Can Change Your Brain: 12 Conversation Strategies to Build Trust, Resolve Conflict, and Increase Intimacy*. New York: Hudson Street Press, 2012 (Kindle). Newberg is a noted brain researcher, a proponent of structural brain imaging, and a noted writer on religious and spiritual issues as they apply to the brain. His writings are more for professionals than the lay audience, although he is often in the news because of his work on spirituality ("the God Spot"). See the Chapter 4 bibliography for other Newberg titles.

Schafer, Roy. *A New Language for Psychoanalysis*. New Haven, CT: Yale University Press, 1976; and *Retelling a Life: Narration and Dialogue in Psychoanalysis*. New York: Basic, 1992. Schafer is a brilliant psychoanalytic theoretician and teacher. I love this book because he attempts to jettison all of the psychoanalytic jargon that has hindered the development of psychoanalysis. Only for mental health professionals.

Schwartz, Jeffrey, and Rebecca Gladding. *You Are Not Your Brain: The 4-Step Solution for Changing Bad Habits, Ending Unhealthy Thinking, and Taking Control of Your Life*. New York: Avery, 2011. This is an important book for showing how thinking can change the brain. Schwartz's ideas influenced my thinking about how to rewrite stories.

Chapter 4: Becoming Mindful

Andreas, Jamie. *The Principles of Correct Practice for Guitar: The Perfect Start for Beginners, and the Answer to the Problems of Players*. Woodstock, NY: Guitar Principles, 1999; and *The Deeper I Go the Deeper It Gets: Meditations on Life and Guitar*. Woodstock, NY: Jamey World, 2004. Andreas is a gifted guitar teacher, but she also writes movingly about life and mental health. Guitar players, other musicians, and nonmusicians would enjoy the *Meditations* book.

Csikszentmihalyi, Mihaly. *Flow: The Psychology of Optimal Experience*. New York: Harper and Row, 1990; and *Finding Flow: The Psychology of Engagement with Everyday Life*. New York: Basic, 1998. These books are both classics.

Davidson, Richard, and Sharon Begley. *The Emotional Life of Your Brain: How Its Unique Patterns Affect the Way You Think, Feel, and Live—and How You Can Change Them*. New York: Hudson Street Press, 2012 (Kindle). Davidson is an important researcher on the emotions and mindfulness.

Kramer, Garret. *Stillpower: Excellence with Ease in Sports and Life*. New York: Atria/Beyond Words, 2012. I love the idea of stillpower.

Newberg, Andrew, et al. *How God Changes Your Brain: Breakthrough Findings from a Leading Neuroscientist*. New York: Ballantine, 2010 (Kindle); and *Principles of Neurotheology*. Burlington, VT: Ashgate, 2010. Great work, but not easy going, especially the second one. Only for academics or mental health professionals.

Siegel, Daniel. *The Mindful Brain: Reflection and Attunement in the Cultivation of Well-Being.* New York: Norton, 2007; and *The Mindful Therapist: A Clinician's Guide to Mindsight and Neural Integration.* New York: Norton, 2010. Siegel has written widely on mindfulness.

Sterner, Thomas. *The Practicing Mind: Bringing Discipline and Focus into Your Life.* Wilmington, DE: Mountain Sage, 2005. I love this little book. Find it, buy it, read it. It really influenced some of my ideas about mindfulness.

Tolle, Eckhart. *The Power of Now: A Guide to Spiritual Enlightenment.* Vancouver: Namaste, 1997. Many find this book unreadable, but I do think that Tolle is speaking to an unmet longing. Thanks to Oprah, he's become a rock star of spirituality. I included this book because Byron Katie's work, *Loving What Is*, mentioned earlier, is really the "how-to" manual for what Tolle is trying to teach readers in *The Power of Now*.

Chapter 5: Righting Relationships

Artiss, Kenneth. *Therapeutic Studies.* Rockville, MD: Psychiatric, 1986. Artiss developed the little-known vertical and horizontal relationship paradigms that I discussed in this chapter. I think that only mental health professionals would find Artiss's work interesting.

Berne, Eric. *Games People Play.* New York: Grove, 1964. A hit from years ago. A nice review of relationship patterns. 'Nuff said.

Cozolino, Louis. See the Chapter 1 bibliography.

Havens, Leston. *Making Contact: Uses of Language in Psychotherapy.* Cambridge, MA: Harvard University Press, 1986; and *A Safe Place: Laying the Groundwork of Psychotherapy*, Cambridge, MA: Harvard University Press, 1996. *Making Contact* is my favorite book about how to do psychotherapy. Havens had a knack for finding unusual ways to express things that others had seen before but had not grasped well. Although the book is written for mental health professionals, nonprofessionals interested in how minds and relationships work will benefit from Havens's writings.

Ogden, Thomas. *The Matrix of the Mind: Object Relations and the Psychoanalytic Dialogue.* New York: Aronson, 1993; and *Projective Identification and Psychotherapeutic Technique.* New York: Aronson, 1977. These are just two of Ogden's many books. For a psychotherapist or psychoanalyst, his works are top-notch. Others will find them heavy going.

Wallin, David. *Attachment in Psychotherapy.* New York: Guilford, 2007. This is a difficult-to-read but important book about the importance and nuances of attachment. It is intended only for professionals.

Chapter 6: Bored Brains, Excitable Brains: ADHD

Amen, Daniel. *Healing ADD: The Breakthrough Program That Allows You to See and Heal the 7 Types of ADD*. New York: Berkley, 2013. Daniel Amen at his best. This book is great for learning about different ADHD subtypes and why some treatments fail.

Cain, Susan. *Quiet: The Power of Introverts in a World That Can't Stop Talking*. New York: Broadway Paperbacks, 2013. I loved this book. It was very helpful to me in thinking about managing arousal. Most people will find this book interesting.

Palladino, Lucy Jo. *Find Your Focus Zone: An Effective New Plan to Defeat Distraction and Overload*. New York: Free Press, 2007. This book helped me think through my ideas about stimulation and brain arousal patterns.

Chapter 7: Heart Matters: Anxiety

Aron, Elaine N. *The Highly Sensitive Person: How to Thrive When the World Overwhelms You*. New York: Broadway Books, 1996 (paperback). I love this book, probably because it resonates with my own temperament. It helped me think through ideas about stimulation and arousal. Read it if you or a loved one is more sensitive than the average person.

McCraty, Rollin, et al. *The Coherent Heart: Heart-Brain Interactions, Psychophysiological Coherence, and the Emergence of System-Wide Order*. Boulder Creek, CA: HeartMath, 2006.

Paddison, Sara. *The Hidden Power of the Heart: Discovering an Unlimited Source of Intelligence*. Boulder Creek, CA: HeartMath, 1998. There is significant overlap among the various publications I've listed here on HeartMath. Nonetheless, they present interesting information that will be unknown to most readers.

Pearce, Joseph Chilton. *The Heart-Mind Matrix: How the Heart Can Teach the Mind New Ways to Think*. Rochester, VT: Park Street Press, 2012.

Rozman, Deborah, and Doc Childre. *Transforming Anxiety: The HeartMath Solution for Overcoming Fear and Worry and Creating Serenity*. Oakland, CA: New Harbinger, 2006.

Servan-Schreiber, David. *The Instinct to Heal: Curing Depression, Anxiety, and Stress Without Drugs and Without Talk Therapy*. New York: Rodale, 2004 (paperback). This is a nice book that helped me sort out HRV and EMDR issues.

Chapter 8: Mood Matters: Depression

Amen, Daniel, and Lisa Routh. *Healing Anxiety and Depression*. New York: Berkley, 2003. This book is good for subtyping anxiety and depression.

Beck, Aaron, et al. *Cognitive Therapy of Depression*. New York: Guilford, 1979. See the Chapter 2 bibliography.

Burns, David. *Feeling Good: The New Mood Therapy*. New York: Avon, 1980, 1999. This is probably the most-recommended self-help book for patients by mental health clinicians. It is a great "how to" book on do-it-yourself CBT for depression—very easy to read and simple to use.

Frank, Ellen. *Treating Bipolar Disorder: A Clinician's Guide to Interpersonal and Social Rhythm Therapy*. New York: Guilford, 2005. This book presents important research on IPSRT. It is intended mainly for clinicians.

Kramer, Peter. *Listening to Prozac*. New York: Penguin, 1994. This classic book opened the door to thinking about how medication can change temperament and personality.

Jamison, Kay Redfield. *An Unquiet Mind: A Memoir of Moods and Madness*. New York: Vintage, 1995. A poetic and enlightening book about personal struggles with bipolar disorder.

Rosenthal, Norman. *Winter Blues: Everything You Need to Know to Beat Seasonal Affective Disorder* (4th ed.). New York: Guilford, 2004. This book by the father of SAD is a classic.

Styron, William. *Darkness Visible: A Memoir of Madness*. New York: Vintage, 1990. This book is a classic description of his severe depression by the author of *Sophie's Choice*.

Chapter 9: Getting Unstuck: OCD

Ratey, John J., and Catherine Johnson. *Shadow Syndromes: The Mild Forms of Major Mental Disorders That Sabotage Us*. New York: Pantheon, 1997. This good book helped me think about the function of milder stuckness vis-à-vis social functioning.

Schwartz, Jeffrey. *You Are Not Your Brain: The 4-Step Solution for Changing Bad Habits, Ending Unhealthy Thinking, and Taking Control of Your Life*. New York: Avery, 2011 (Kindle). People seem to like this book and benefit by using it on their own to tackle stuckness.

Chapter 10: Branded in the Brain: Emotional Trauma and PTSD

Church, Dawson. *The EFT Manual* (3rd ed.). Fulton, CA: Energy Psychology, 2014 (Kindle). Church is a leading figure in EFT.

Ortner, Nick. *The Tapping Solution: A Revolutionary System for Stress-Free Living*. Carlsbad, CA: Hay House, 2013. A readable and helpful book about EFT.

Roberts, Monty. *Horse Sense for People*. New York: Penguin, 2002 (paperback). Love the book, love the man. If you liked the vignette about Monty, you'll like the book.

Servan-Schreiber, David. See the Chapter 7 bibliography.

Shapiro, Francine. *Getting Past Your Past: Take Control of Your Life with Self-Help Techniques from EMDR Therapy.* New York: Rodale, 2013. A good book from the founder of EMDR.

van der Kolk, Bessel. *The Body Keeps the Score: Brain, Mind, and Body in the Healing of Trauma.* New York: Viking, 2014. This thorough book from a key researcher of emotional trauma is important and useful for lay readers and especially mental health professionals.

Wallin, David. *Attachment in Psychotherapy.* New York: Guilford, 2007. I mentioned this book in the Chapter 5 bibliography. It helps one understand how attachment disruption can result in Little t traumas. It is intended for professionals.

Chapter 11: Balance Your Brain, Boost Your Willpower: Addiction

Amen, Daniel, and David Smith. *Unchain Your Brain: 10 Steps to Breaking the Addictions That Steal Your Life.* Costa Mesa, CA: MindWorks, 2010. This book is a good one and very thorough. It is geared toward the lay public, but professionals will benefit significantly too.

Baumeister, Roy, and John Tierney. *Willpower: Rediscovering the Greatest Human Strength.* New York: Penguin, 2011. This book is an interesting read.

Kurtz, Ernest, and Katherine Ketcham. *The Spirituality of Imperfection: Storytelling and the Search for Meaning.* New York: Bantam, 2009. This book elucidates the importance of spirituality in healing from addictions.

Ratey, John J., and Catherine Johnson. *Shadow Syndromes: The Mild Forms of Major Mental Disorders That Sabotage Us.* New York: Pantheon, 1997. This book helped me think through some ideas about addictions. Also see the Chapter 9 bibliography.

Chapter 12: Healing the Hurting Brain and Body: Brain Injury and Medical Problems

Horowitz, Richard. *Why Can't I Get Better?: Solving the Mystery of Lyme and Chronic Disease.* New York: St. Martin's, 2013 (Kindle). This important book on Lyme disease is for both professionals and nonprofessionals.

Irlen, Helen. *Reading by the Colors: Overcoming Dyslexia and Other Reading Disabilities Through the Irlen Method.* New York: Perigee, 2005; and *The Irlen Revolution: A Guide to Changing Your Perception and Your Life.* Garden City Park, NY: Square One, 2009. These books provide important information by Helen Irlen on the approach she developed to treat Irlen syndrome, which should be much more widely known than it is.

Mettler, Fred, and Milton Guiberteau. *Essentials of Nuclear Medicine Imaging*. Philadelphia: Saunders Elsevier, 2006. This textbook provides information on brain SPECT.

Morton, Kathryn, et al. *Diagnostic Imaging: Nuclear Medicine*. Salt Lake City, UT: Amirsys, 2007. This textbook provides information on brain SPECT.

Spreen, Kathleen. *Compendium of Tick-Borne Disease: A Thousand Pearls*. Pocopson, PA: Pocopson, 2013. This big book, literally and figuratively, is lovingly crafted.

Stone, Rhonda. *The Light Barrier: Understanding the Mystery of Irlen Syndrome and Light-Based Reading Difficulties*. New York: St. Martin's Griffin, 2003. This is another good book on Irlen syndrome.

Conclusion: Beyond Mind and Brain

Barbery, Muriel. *The Elegance of the Hedgehog*. New York: Penguin, 2008. English edition, translated by Alison Anderson. This delightful French novel is about philosophy, wisdom, spirituality, and life.

Kurtz, Ernest, and Katherine Ketcham. *The Spirituality of Imperfection: Storytelling and the Search for Meaning*. New York: Bantam, 2009. Also mentioned in the Chapter 11 bibliography, this book is applicable to much more than addiction. It is a wonderful book about storytelling, especially vis-à-vis wisdom and spirituality.

Index